FOR ORGANS, PIANOS & ELECTRONIC KEYBOARDS

284

THE GREAT
AMERICAN SONGBOOK

THE SINGERS

MUSIC AND LYRICS FOR 100 STANDARDS FROM THE GOLDEN AGE OF AMERICAN SONG

On the cover:
Nat King Cole, Ella Fitzgerald, Mel Tormé,
Louis Armstrong, Judy Garland, Bing Crosby and Peggy Lee.

Photos of Bing Crosby, Judy Garland and Peggy Lee,
courtesy of Photofest.

Photos of Louis Armstrong, Nat "King" Cole, Ella Fitzgerald and Mel Tormé
courtesy of William "PoPsie" Randolph.
www.PoPsiePhotos.com

ISBN: 978-1-5400-3325-3

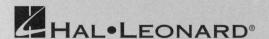

Visit Hal Leonard Online at
www.halleonard.com

Contact Us:
Hal Leonard
7777 West Bluemound Road
Milwaukee, WI 53213
Email: info@halleonard.com

In Europe contact:
Hal Leonard Europe Limited
Distribution Centre, Newmarket Road
Bury St Edmunds, Suffolk, IP33 3YB
Email: info@halleonardeurope.com

In Australia contact:
Hal Leonard Australia Pty. Ltd.
4 Lentara Court
Cheltenham, Victoria, 3192 Australia
Email: info@halleonard.com.au

CONTENTS

Singer Index

All of Me

Registration 4
Rhythm: Fox Trot or Swing

Words and Music by Seymour Simons
and Gerald Marks

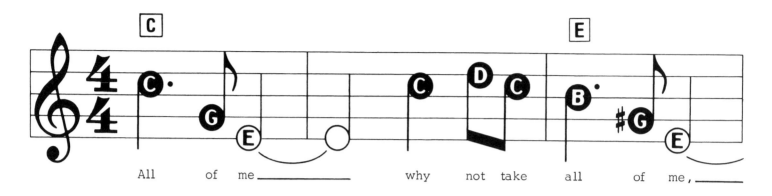

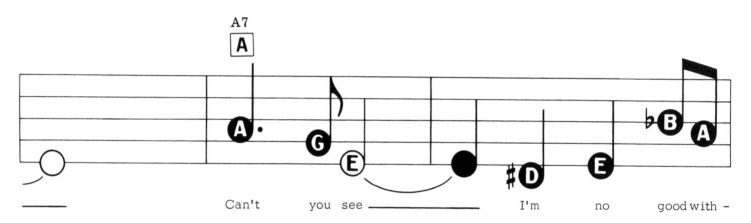

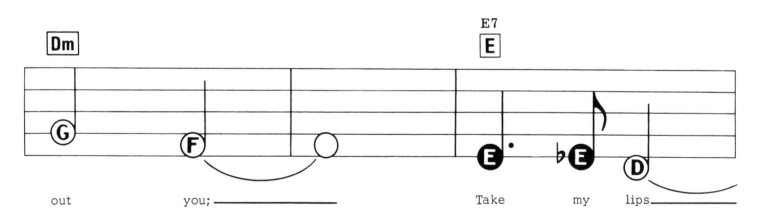

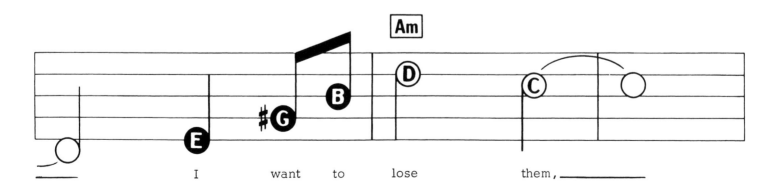

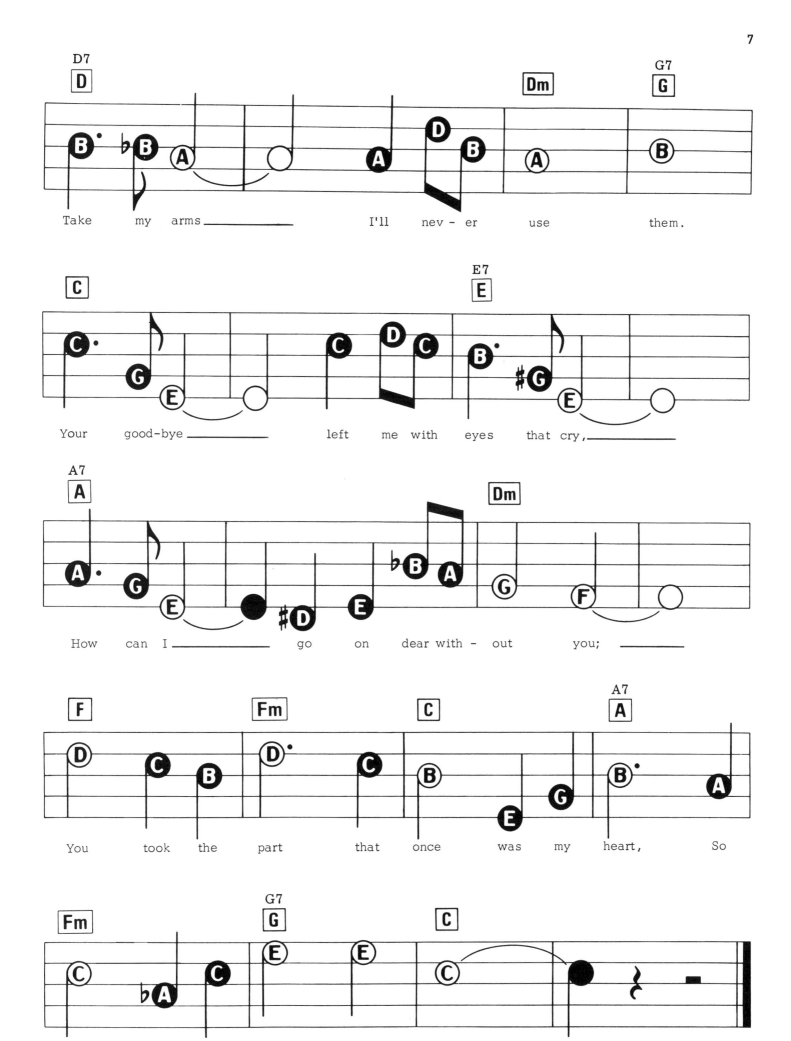

All the Way
from THE JOKER IS WILD

Registration 3
Rhythm: Ballad

Words by Sammy Cahn
Music by James Van Heusen

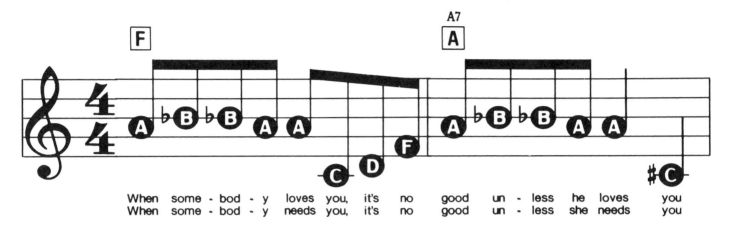

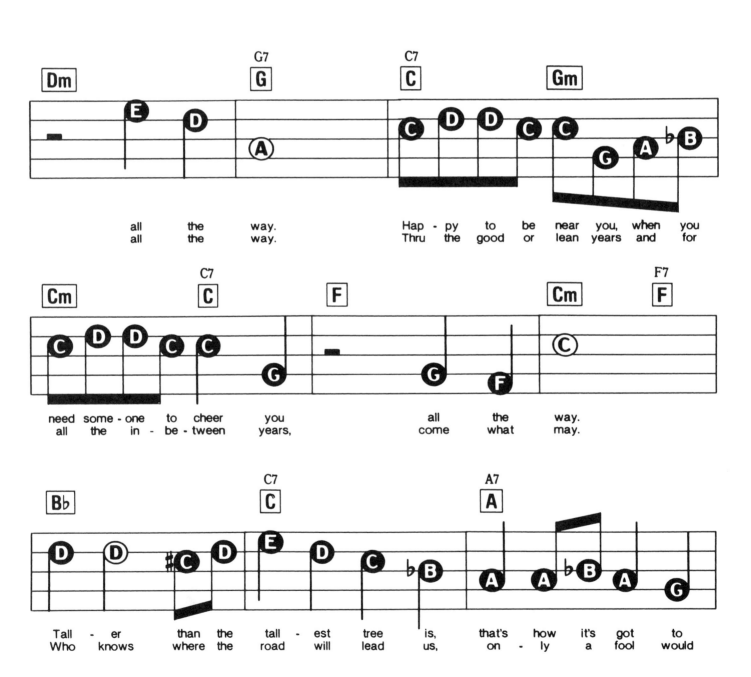

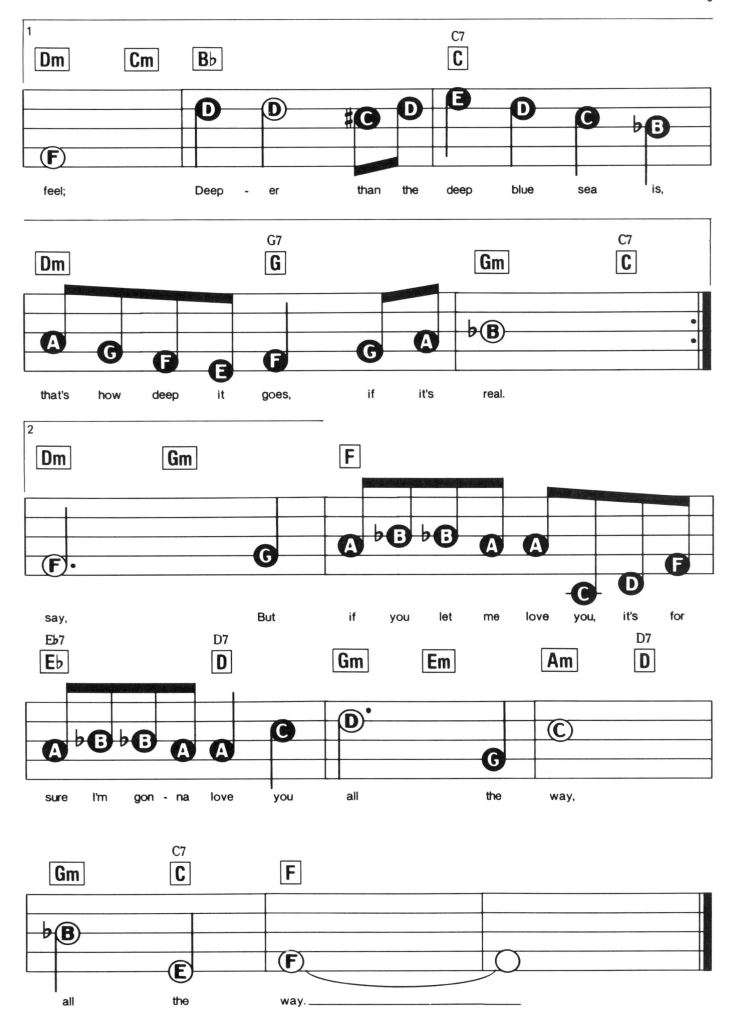

And I Love You So

Registration 3
Rhythm: Pops or 8-Beat

Words and Music by
Don McLean

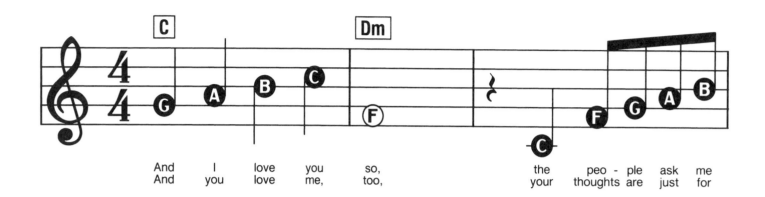

And I love you so, the peo - ple ask me
And you love me, so, too, your thoughts are just for

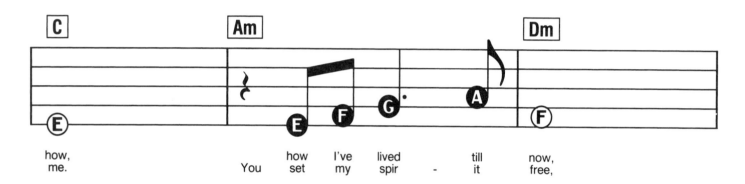

how, You how I've lived till now,
me. You set my spir - it free,

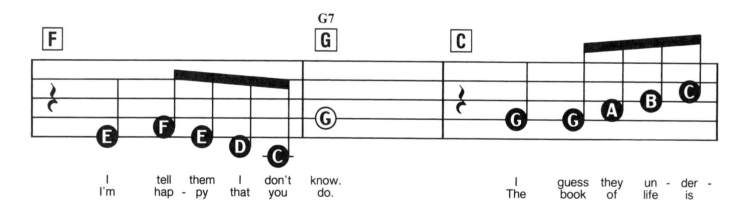

I tell them I don't know. I guess they un - der -
I'm hap - py that you do. The book of life is

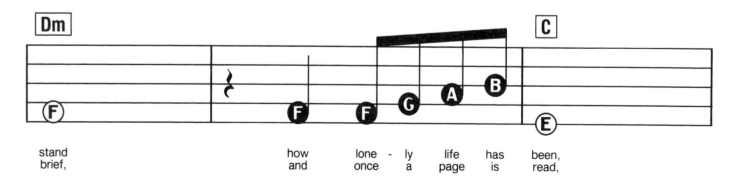

stand how lone - ly life has been,
brief, and once a page is read,

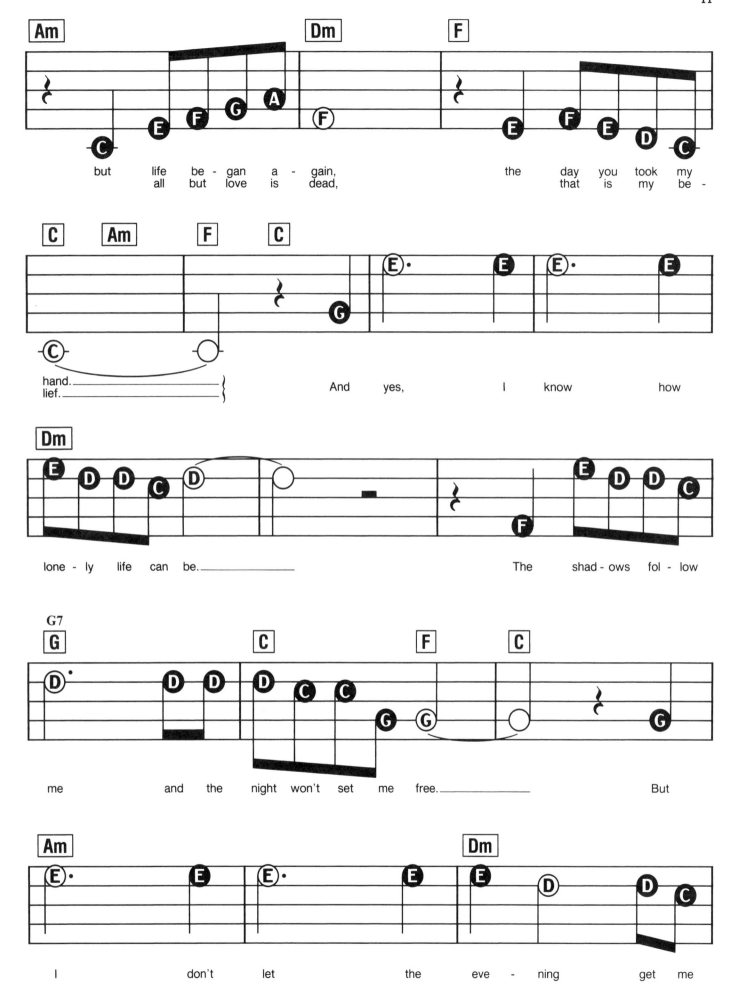

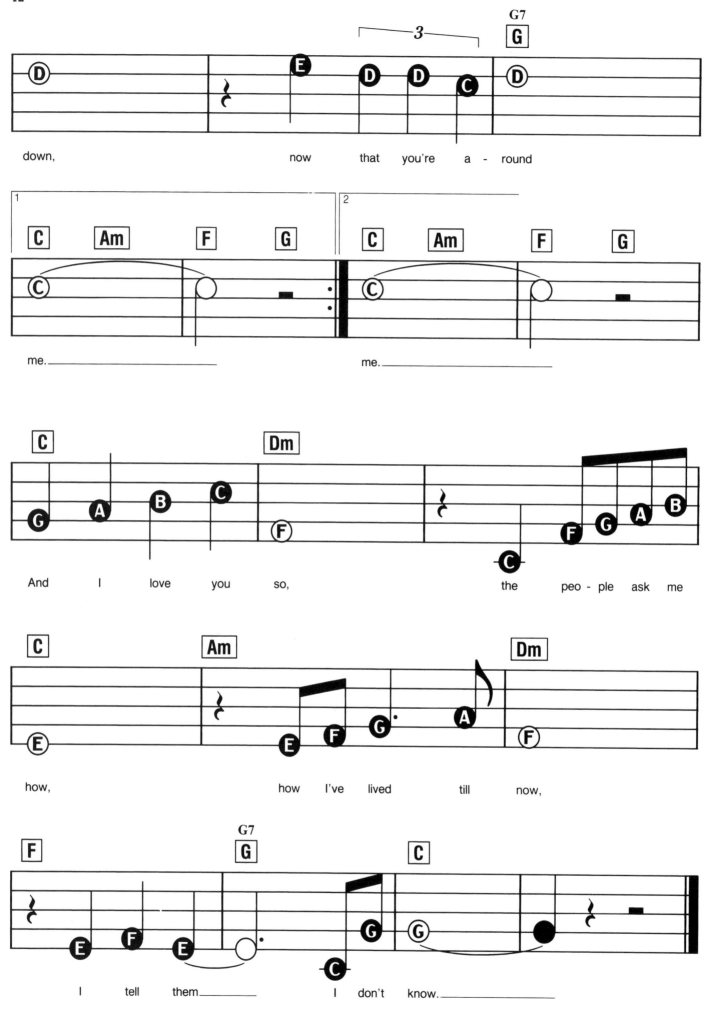

Any Place I Hang My Hat Is Home

from ST. LOUIS WOMAN

Registration 4
Rhythm: Shuffle

Words by Johnny Mercer
Music by Harold Arien

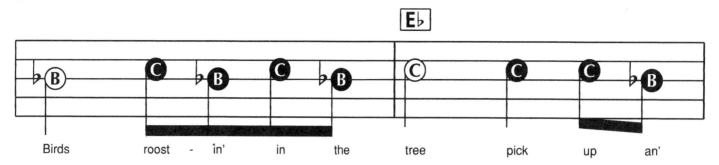

Birds roost - in' in the tree pick up an'

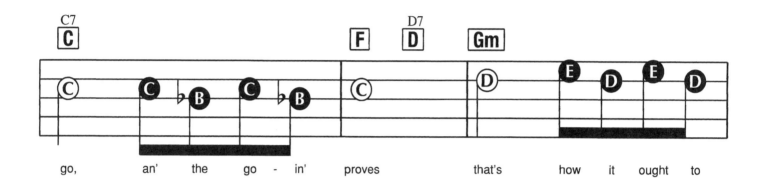

go, an' the go - in' proves that's how it ought to

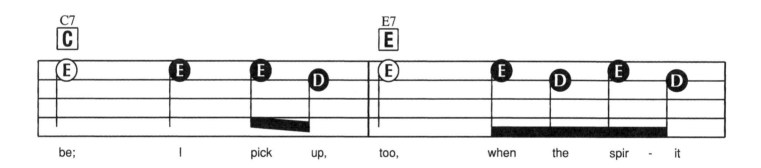

be; I pick up, too, when the spir - it

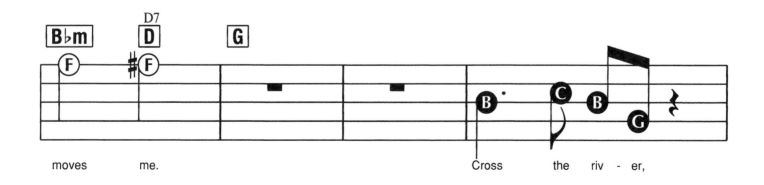

moves me. 'Cross the riv - er,

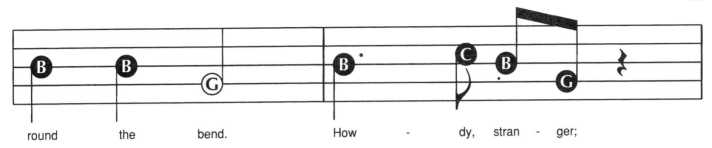

round the bend. How - dy, stran - ger;

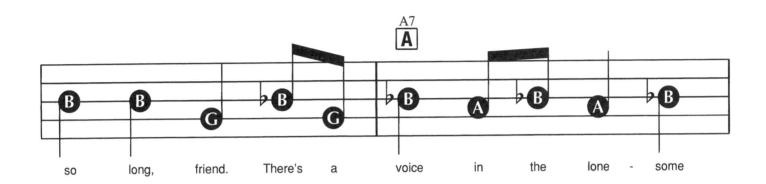

so long, friend. There's a voice in the lone - some

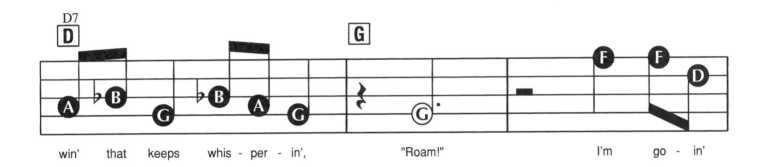

win' that keeps whis - per - in', "Roam!" I'm go - in'

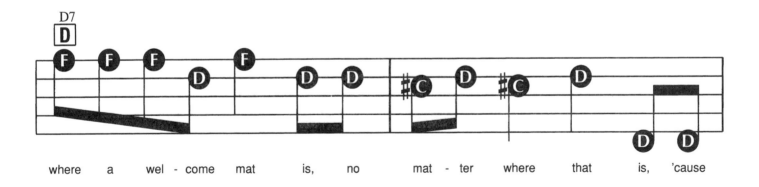

where a wel - come mat is, no mat - ter where that is, 'cause

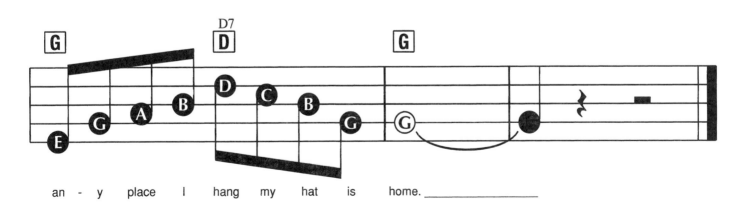

an - y place I hang my hat is home. _____

Autumn Leaves

Registration 2
Rhythm: Fox Trot or Ballad

English lyric by Johnny Mercer
French lyric by Jacques Prevert
Music by Joseph Kosma

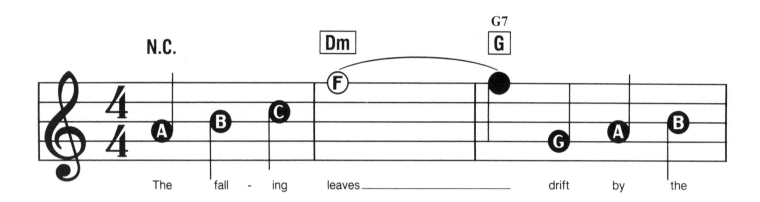

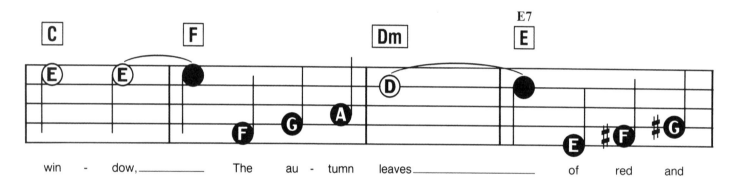

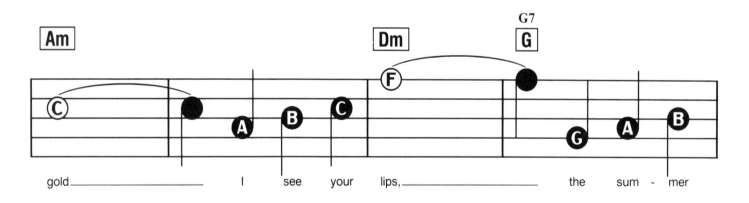

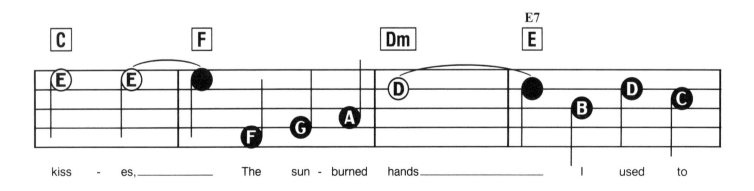

17

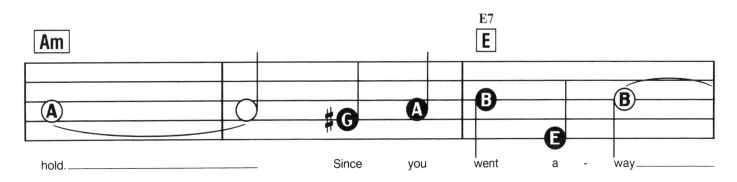

hold._____ Since you went a - way_____

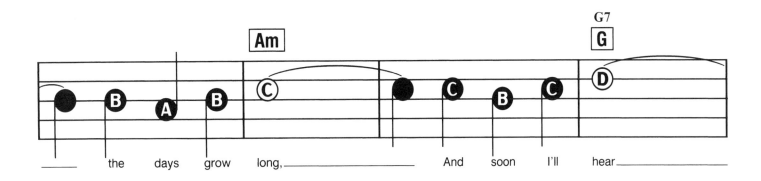

_____ the days grow long,_____ And soon I'll hear_____

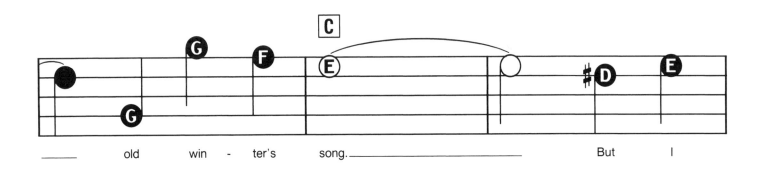

_____ old win - ter's song._____ But I

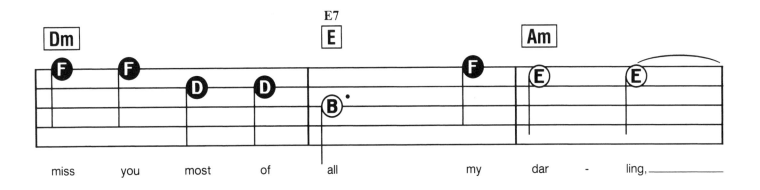

miss you most of all my dar - ling,_____

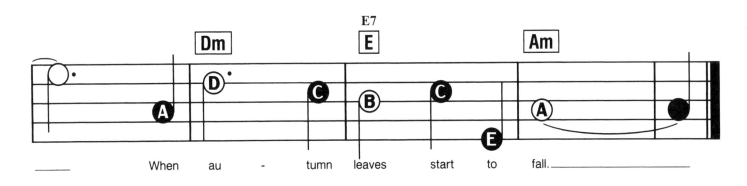

_____ When au - tumn leaves start to fall._____

Baby, It's Cold Outside
from the Motion Picture NEPTUNE'S DAUGHTER

Registration 1
Rhythm: Fox Trot

By Frank Loesser

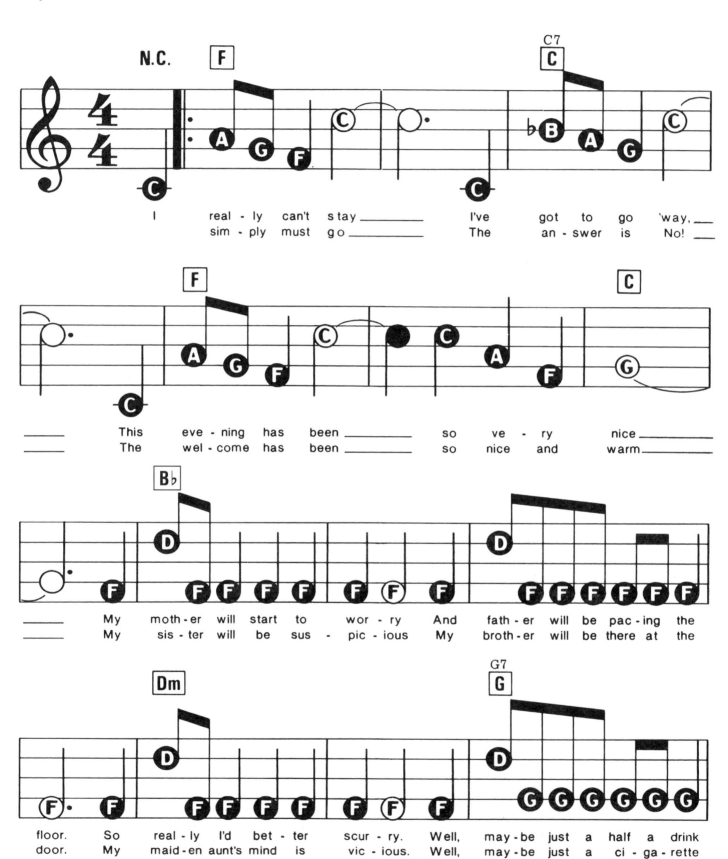

19

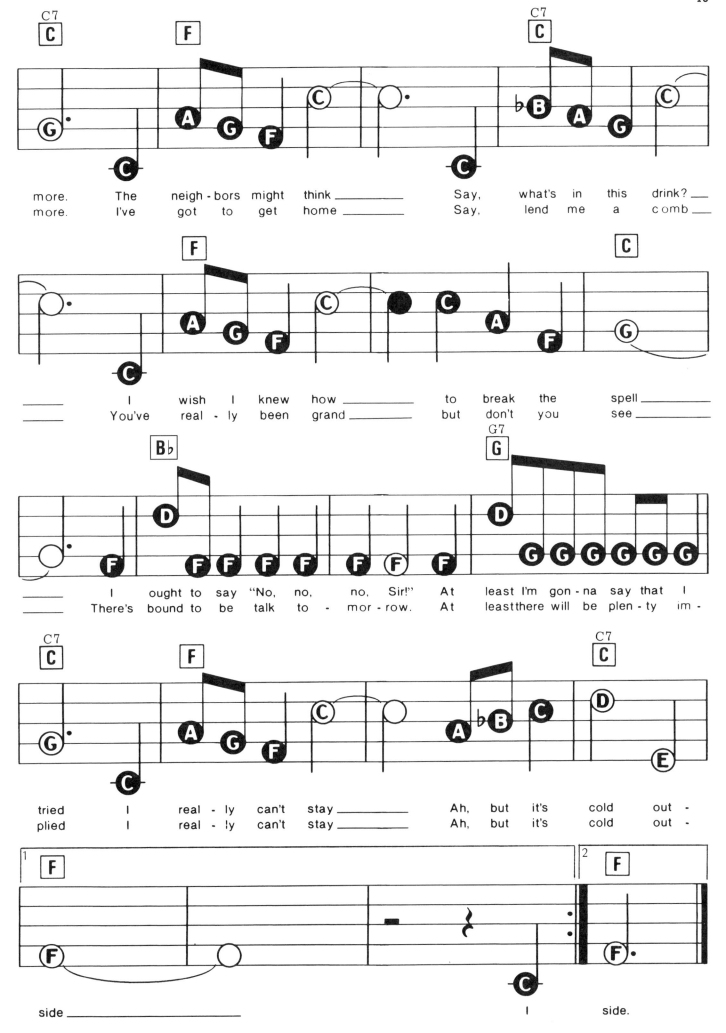

Between the Devil and the Deep Blue Sea
from RHYTHMANIA

Registration 1
Rhythm: Fox Trot or Swing

Lyric by Ted Koehler
Music by Harold Arlen

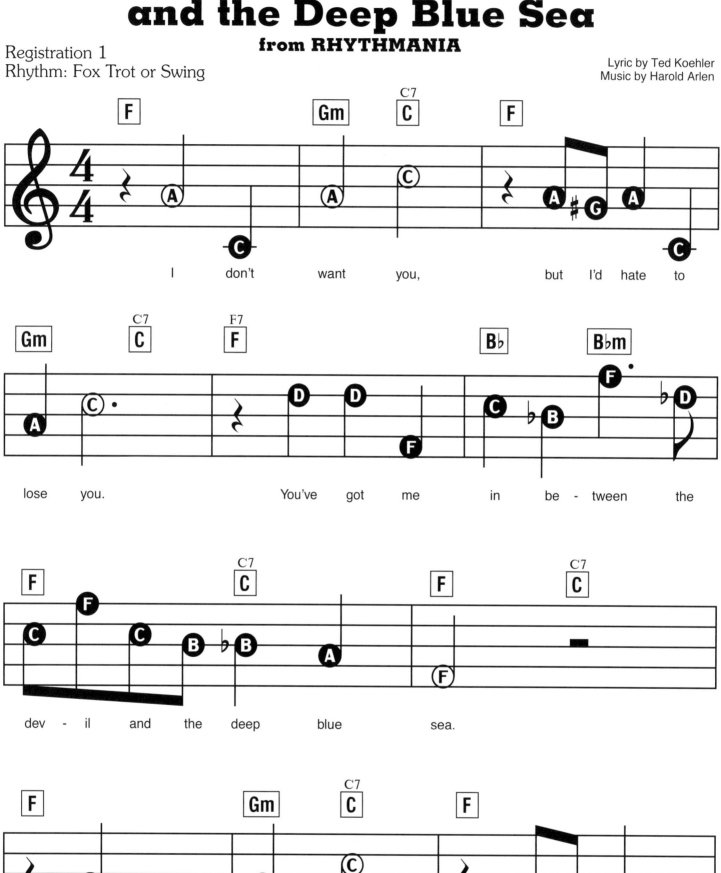

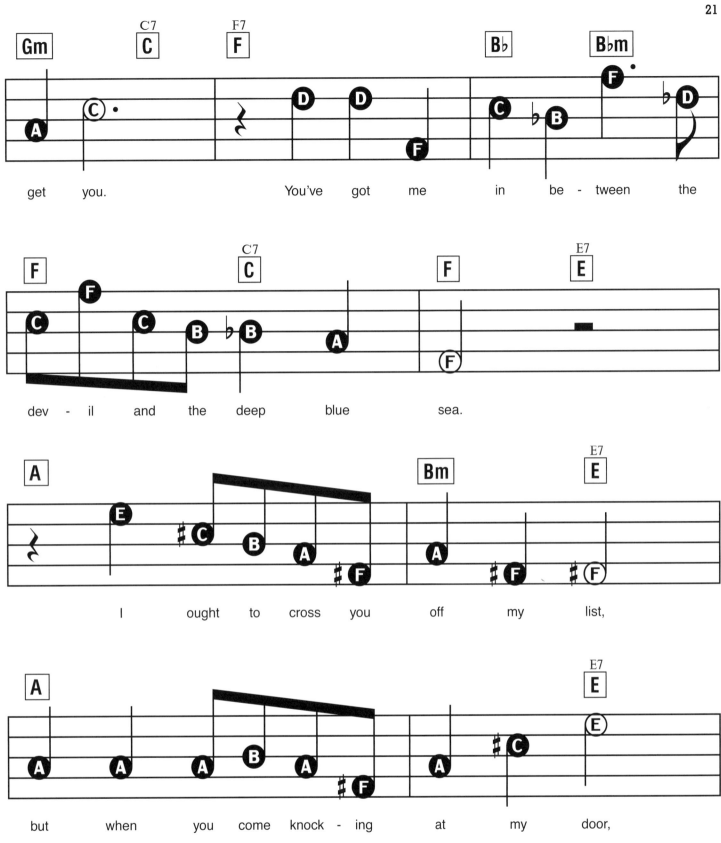

get you. You've got me in be - tween the

dev - il and the deep blue sea.

I ought to cross you off my list,

but when you come knock - ing at my door,

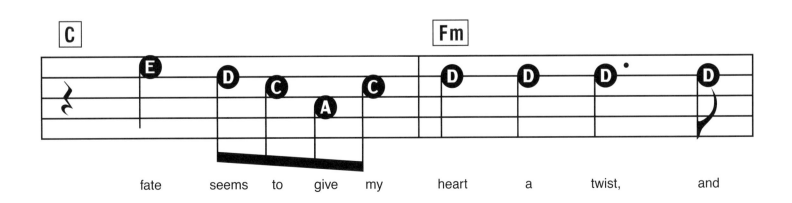

fate seems to give my heart a twist, and

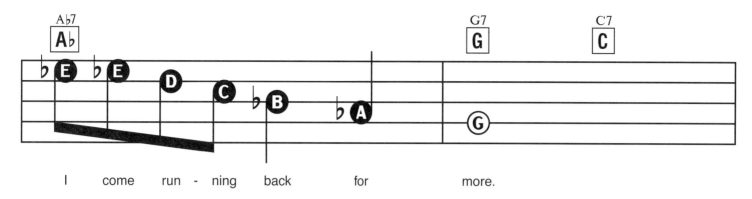

I come run - ning back for more.

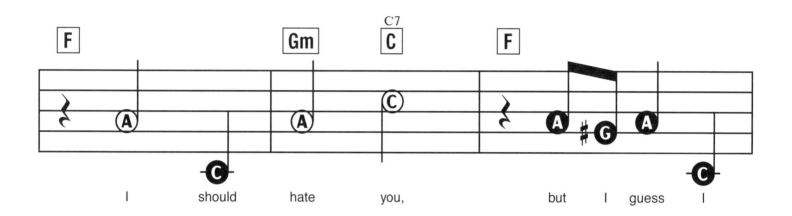

I should hate you, but I guess I

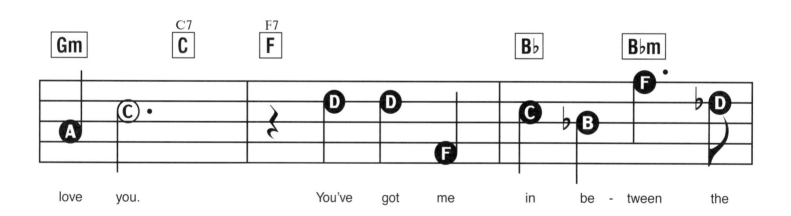

love you. You've got me in be - tween the

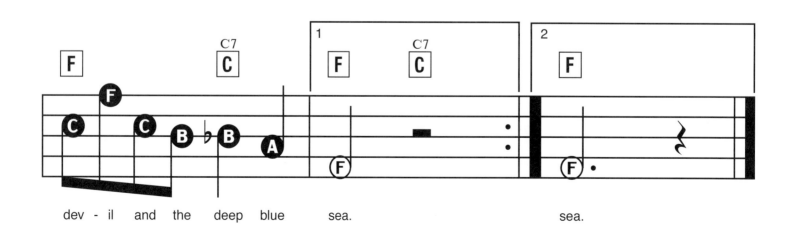

dev - il and the deep blue sea. sea.

Cabaret
from the Musical CABARET

Registration 7
Rhythm: Swing

Words by Fred Ebb
Music by John Kander

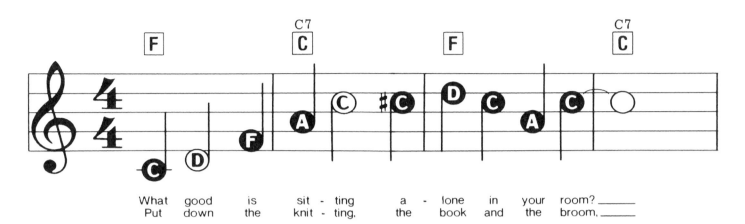

What good is sit - ting a - lone in your room? _____
Put down the knit - ting, the book and the broom, _____

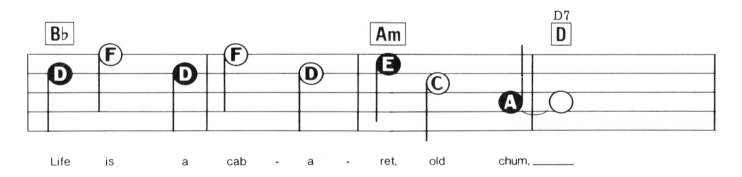

Come hear the mu - sic play; _____
Time for a hol - i - day; _____

Life is a cab - a - ret, old chum, _____

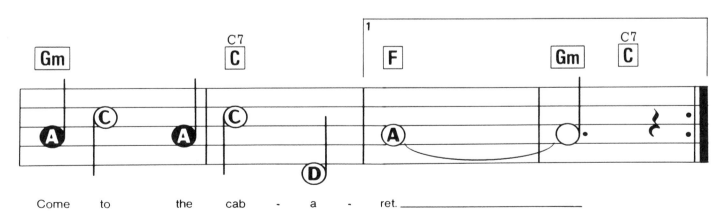

Come to the cab - a - ret. _____

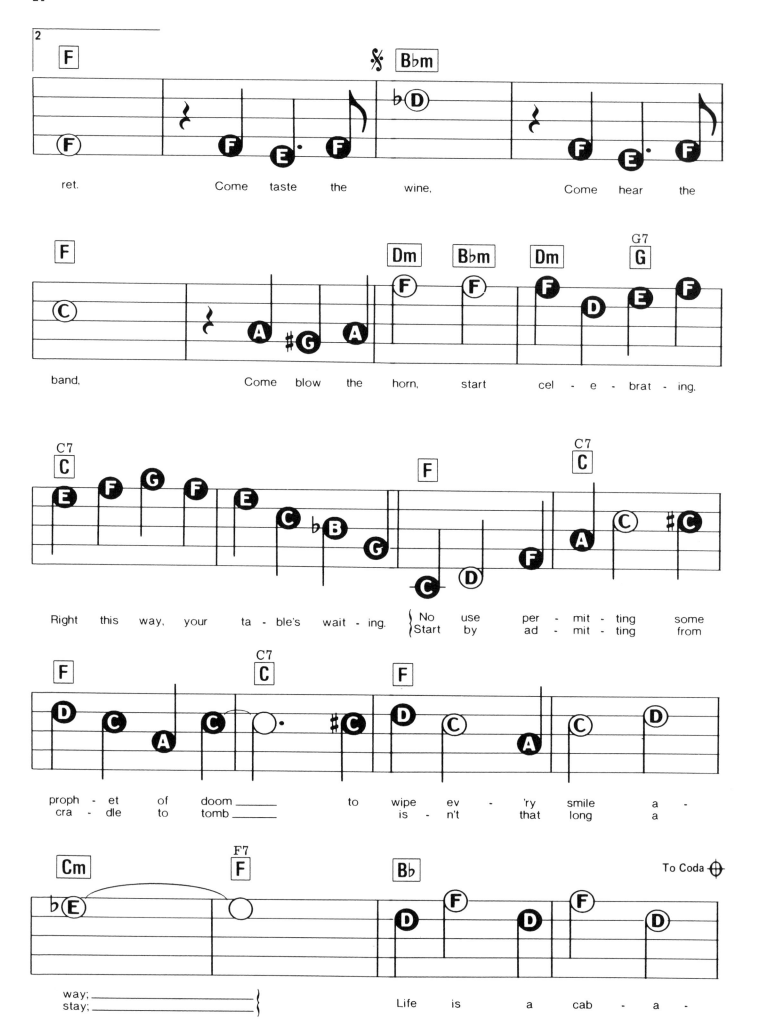

ret. Come taste the wine, Come hear the

band, Come blow the horn, start cel - e - brat - ing.

Right this way, your ta - ble's wait - ing.
No use per - mit - ting some
Start by ad - mit - ting some from

proph - et of doom _____ to wipe ev - 'ry smile a -
cra - dle to tomb _____ is - n't that long a

way; _____
stay; _____
Life is a cab - a -

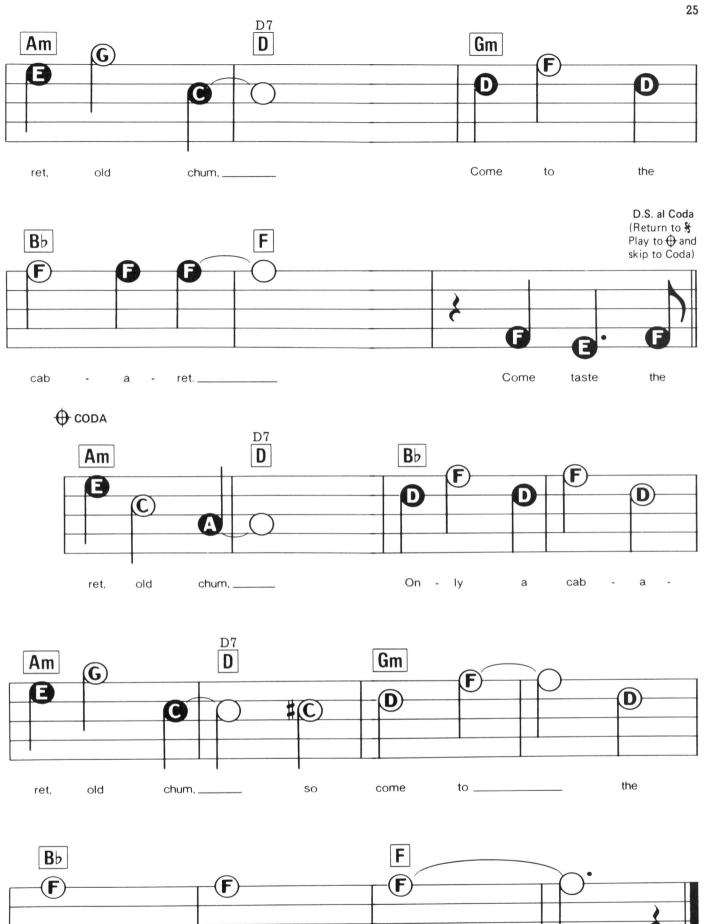

ret, old   chum, _____   Come to   the

D.S. al Coda
(Return to %
Play to ⊕ and
skip to Coda)

cab - a - ret. _____   Come taste the

⊕ CODA

ret, old   chum, _____   On - ly a cab - a -

ret, old   chum, _____   so   come to _____   the

cab   -   a   -   ret. _____

Bewitched
from PAL JOEY

Registration 10
Rhythm: Ballad or Fox Trot

Words by Lorenz Hart
Music by Richard Rodgers

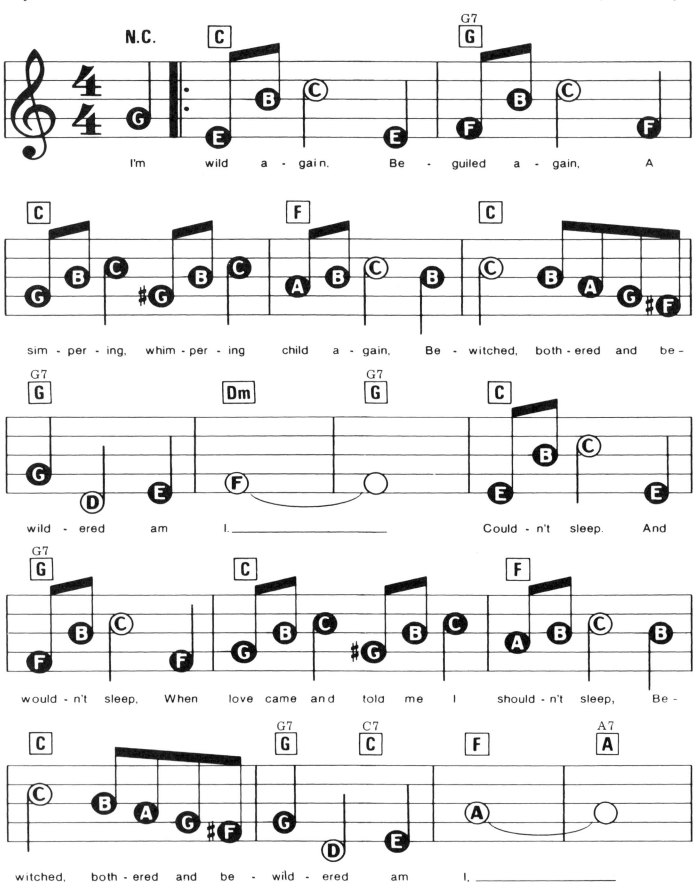

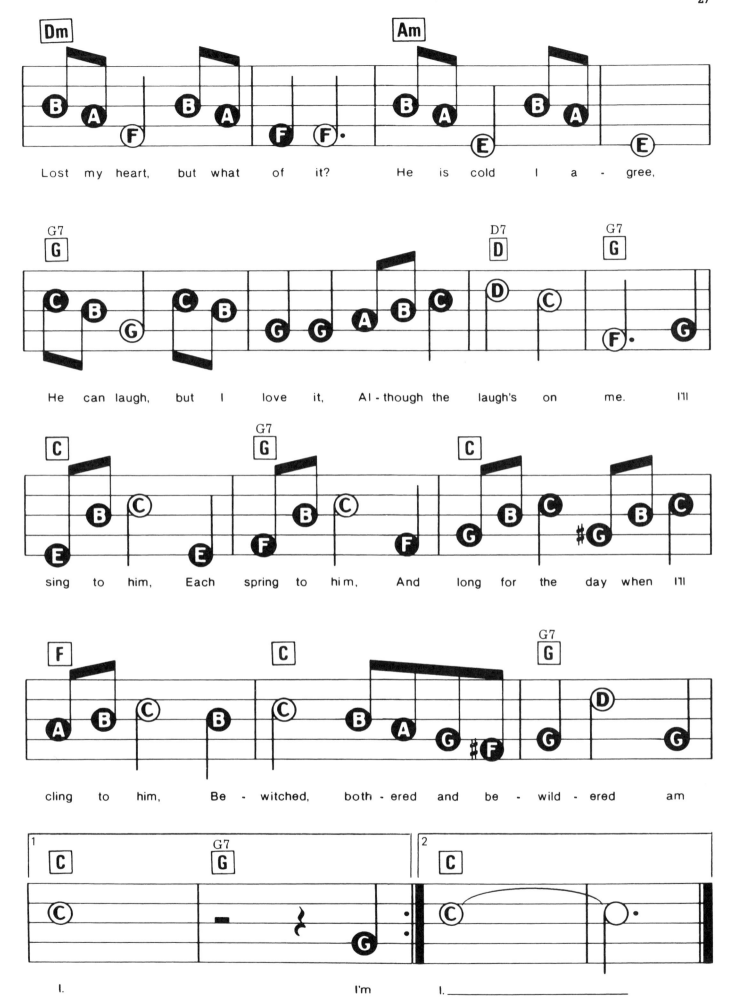

Blame It on My Youth

Registration 10
Rhythm: Pops or Fox Trot

Words by Edward Heyman
Music by Oscar Levant

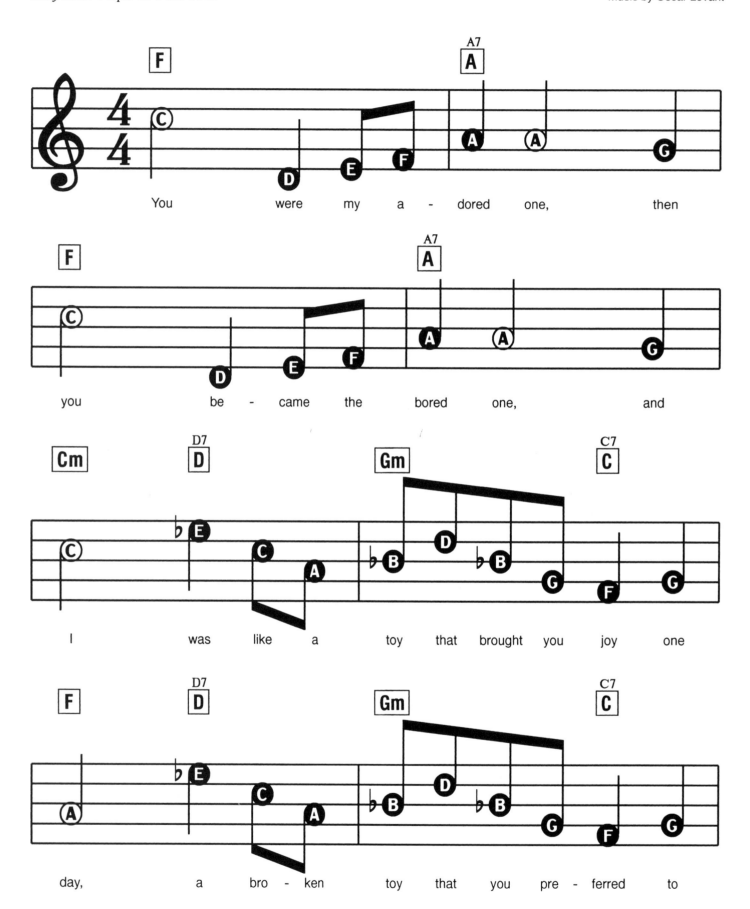

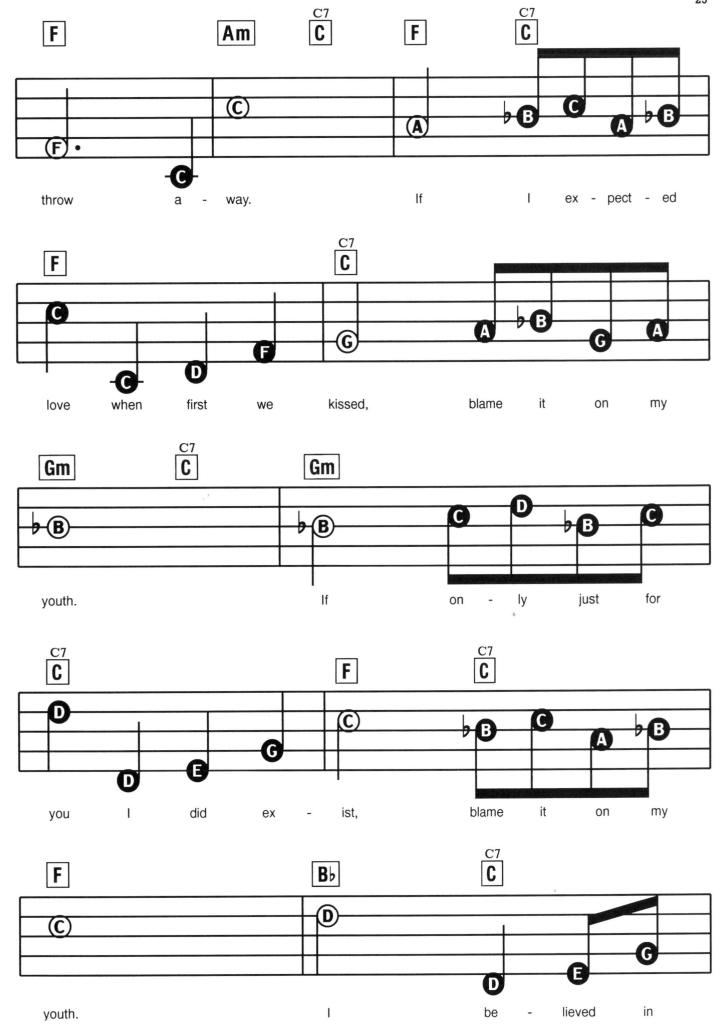

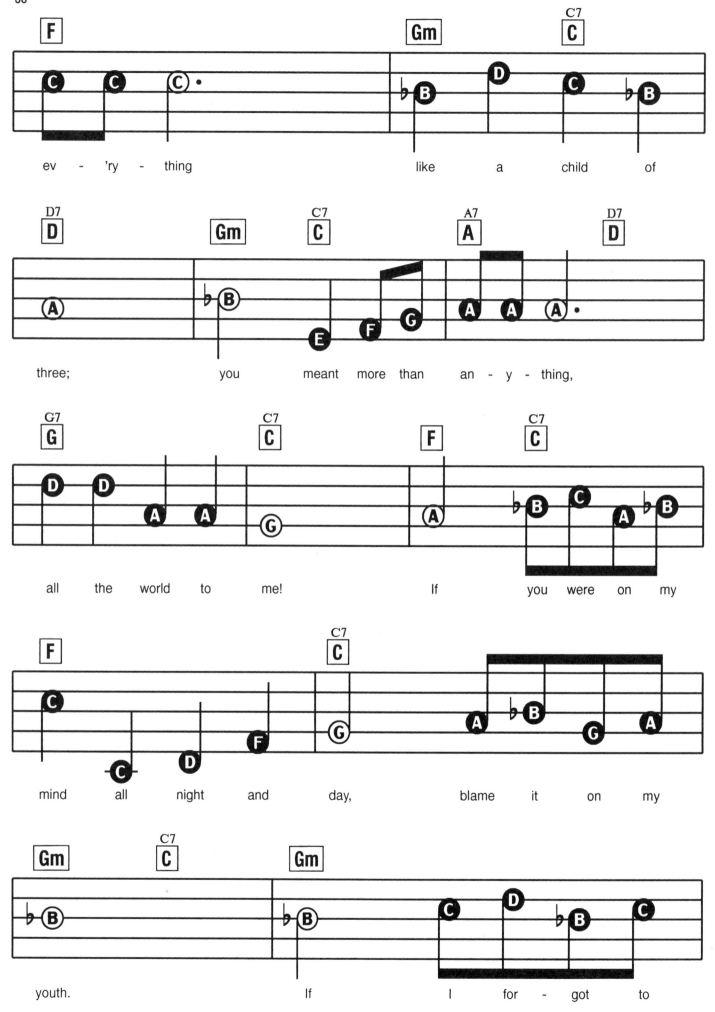

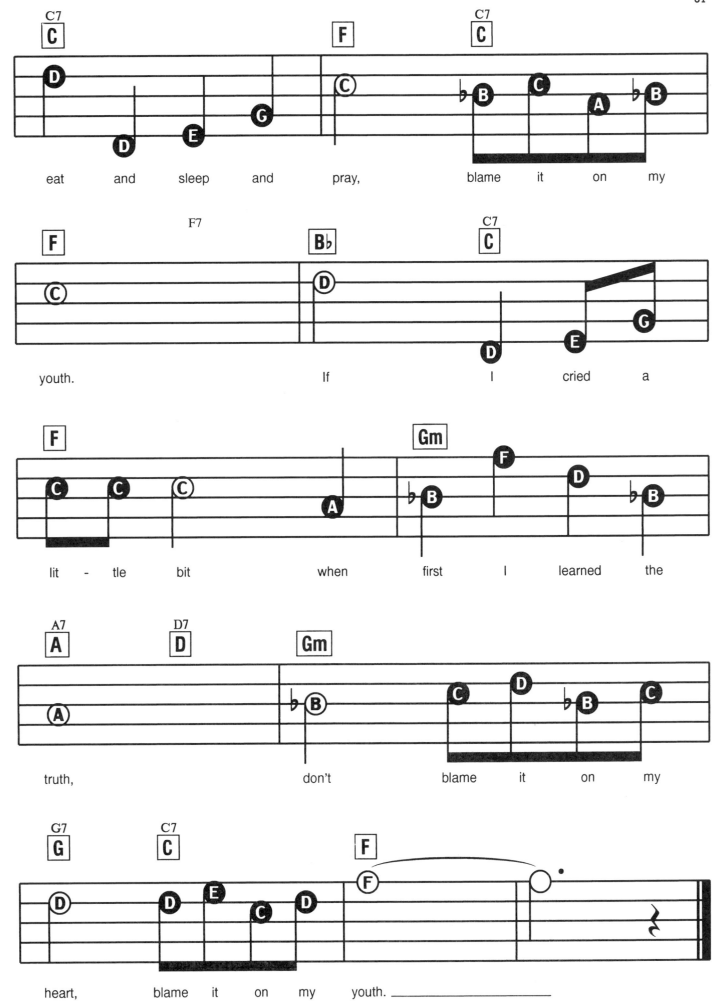

Born Free
from the Columbia Pictures' Release BORN FREE

Registration 4
Rhythm: Ballad or Slow Rock

Words by Don Black
Music by John Barry

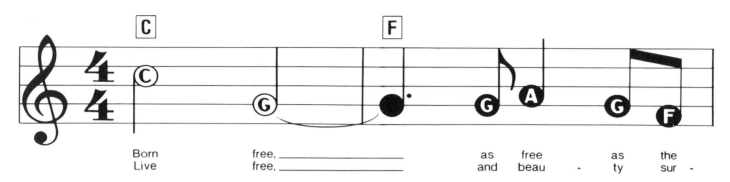

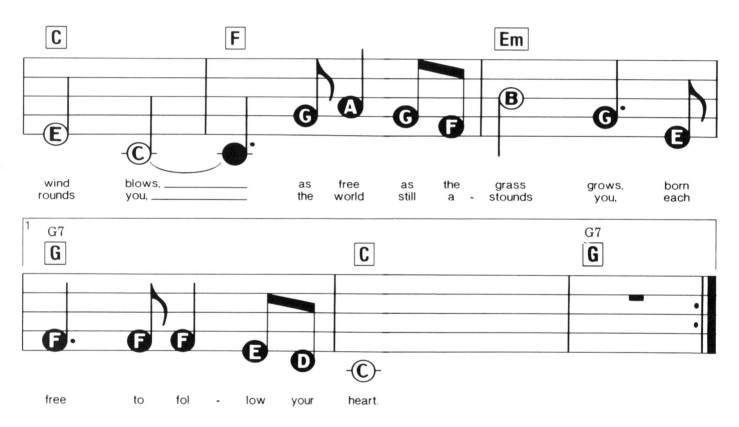

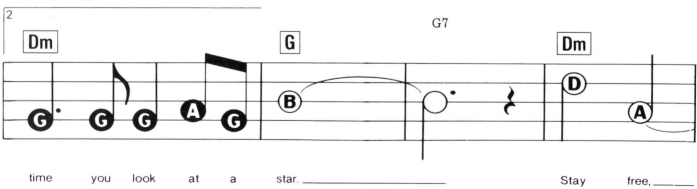

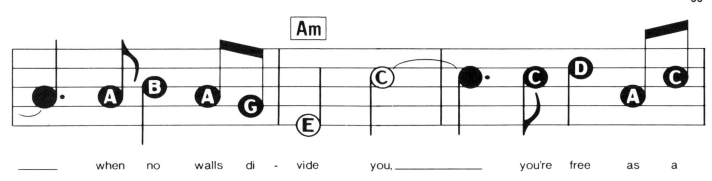

_____ when no walls di - vide you, _____ you're free as a

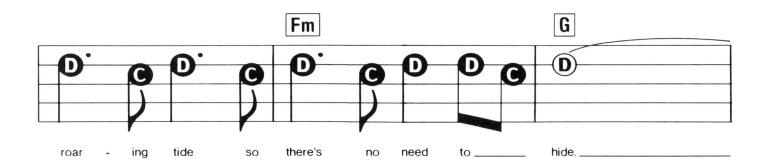

roar - ing tide so there's no need to _____ hide. _____

G7

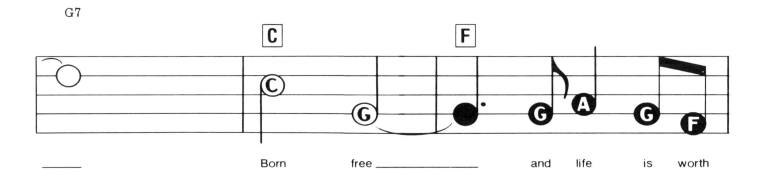

_____ Born free _____ and life is worth

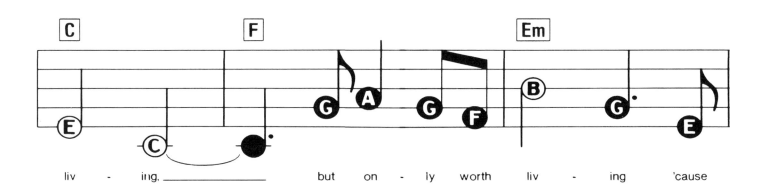

liv - ing, _____ but on - ly worth liv - ing 'cause

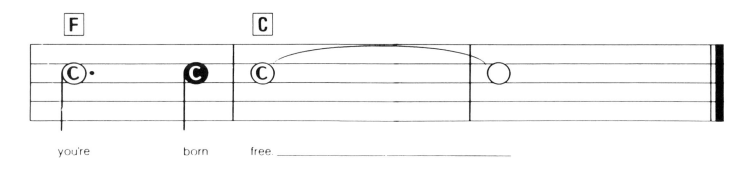

you're born free. _____

Call Me Irresponsible
from the Paramount Picture PAPA'S DELICATE CONDITION

Registration 8
Rhythm: Swing or Ballad

Words by Sammy Cahn
Music by James Van Heusen

Call me ir-re-spon-si-ble, call me un-re-li-a-ble, throw in un-de-pend-a-ble too._____ Do my fool-ish al-i-bis bore you? Well, I'm not too clev-er. I just a-dore you. Call me

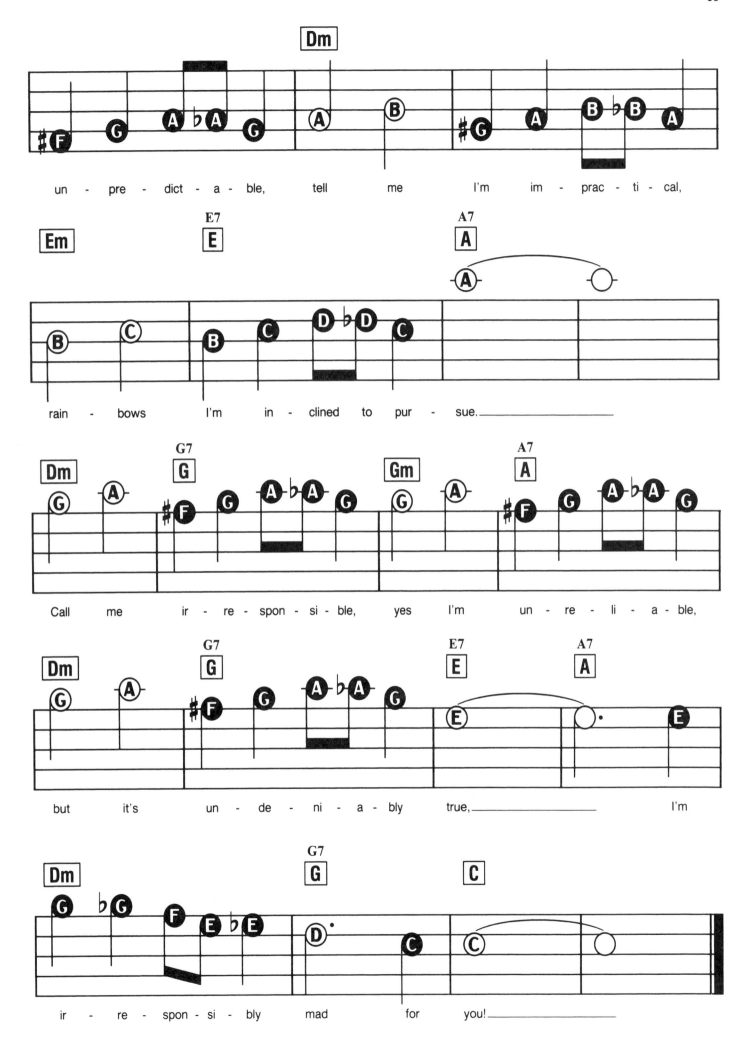

Count Your Blessings Instead of Sheep

from the Motion Picture Irving Berlin's WHITE CHRISTMAS

Registration 4
Rhythm: Swing

Words and Music by
Irving Berlin

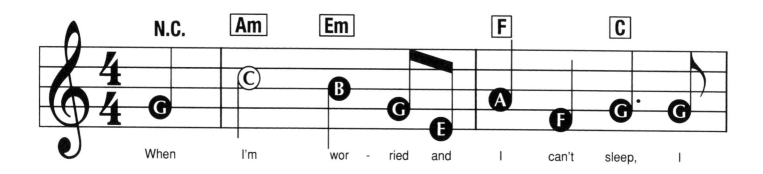

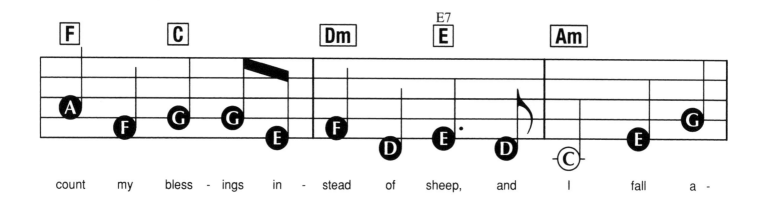

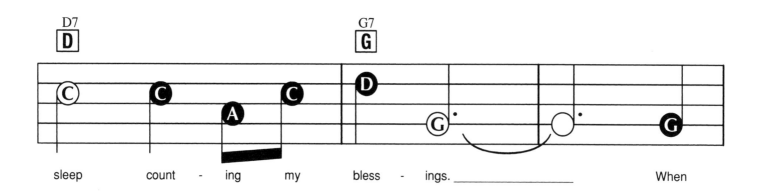

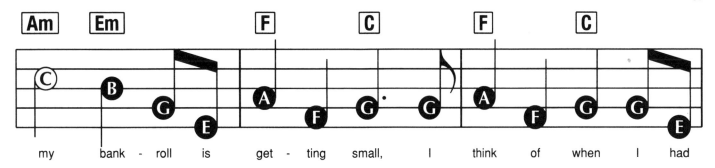

my bank - roll is get - ting small, I think of when I had

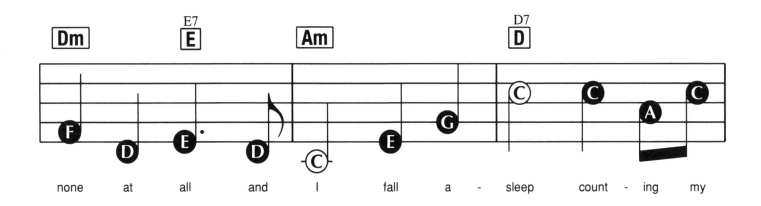

none at all and I fall a - sleep count - ing my

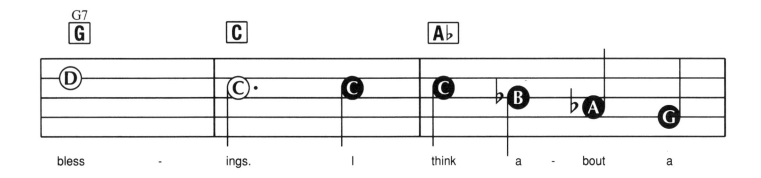

bless - ings. I think a - bout a

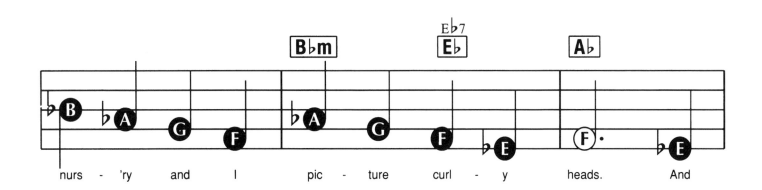

nurs - 'ry and I pic - ture curl - y heads. And

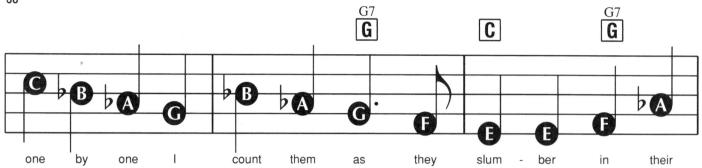

one by one I count them as they slum - ber in their

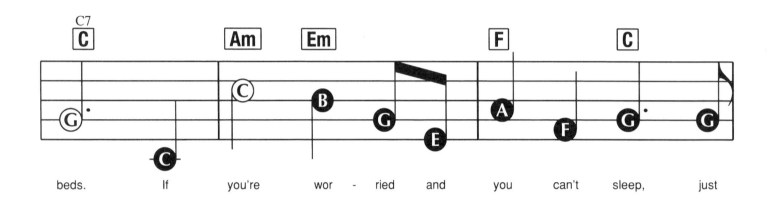

beds.   If you're wor - ried and you can't sleep, just

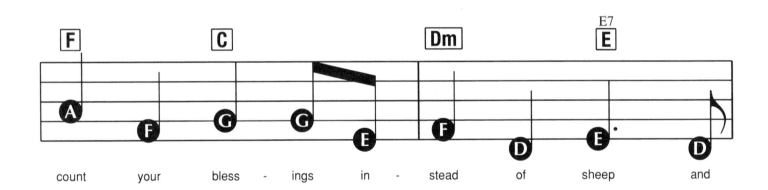

count your bless - ings in - stead of sheep and

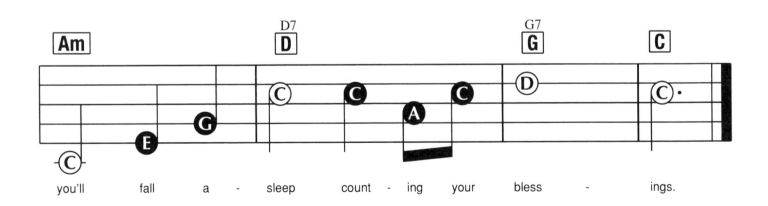

you'll fall a - sleep count - ing your bless - ings.

Day by Day
Theme from the Paramount Television Series DAY BY DAY

Registration 4
Rhythm: Swing

Words and Music by Sammy Cahn,
Axel Stordahl and Paul Weston

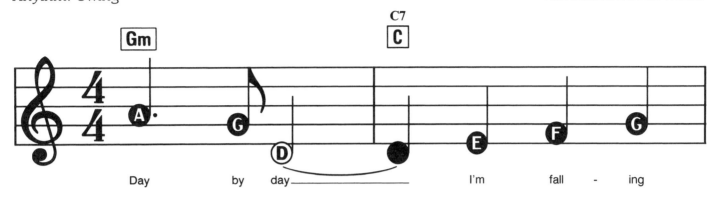

Day by day___ I'm fall - ing

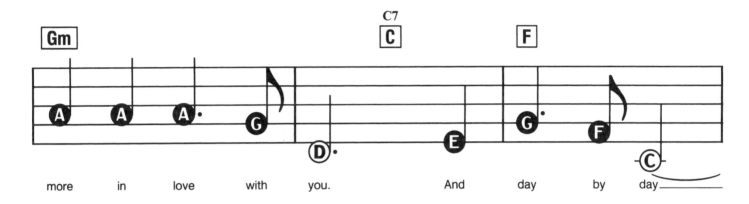

more in love with you. And day by day___

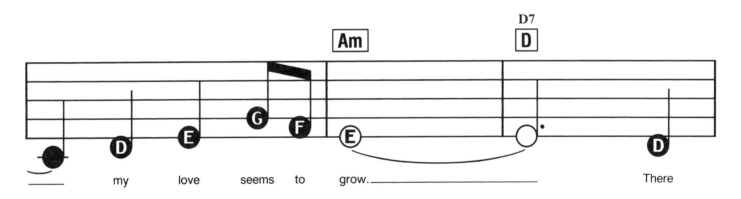

___ my love seems to grow.___ There

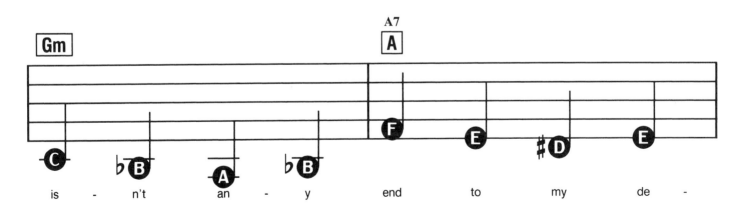

is - n't an - y end to my de -

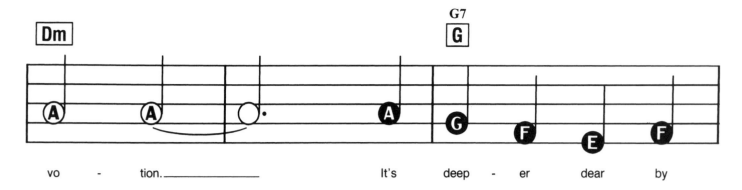

vo - tion._____ It's deep - er dear by

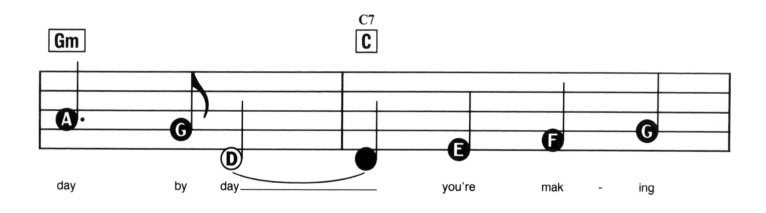

far than an - y o - cean._____ I find that

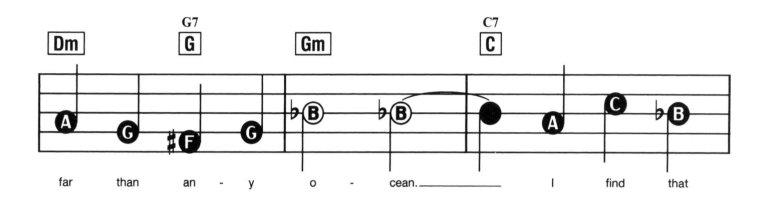

day by day_____ you're mak - ing

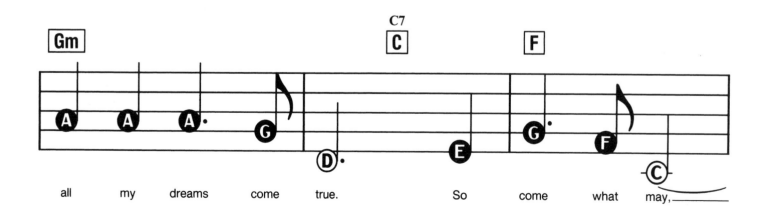

all my dreams come true. So come what may,_____

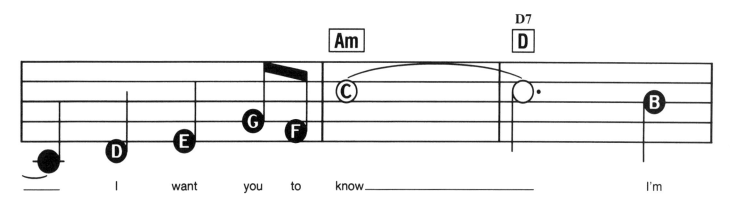

I want you to know _____ I'm

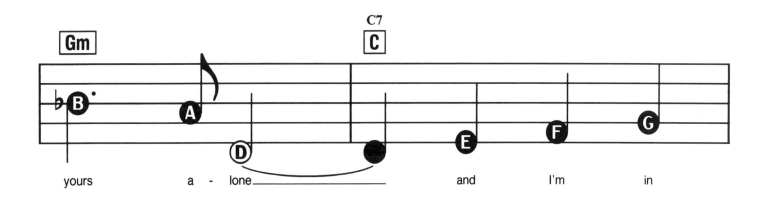

yours a - lone _____ and I'm in

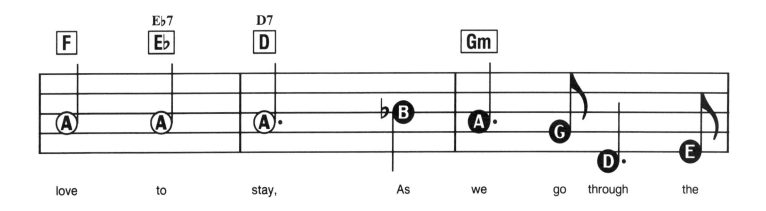

love to stay, As we go through the

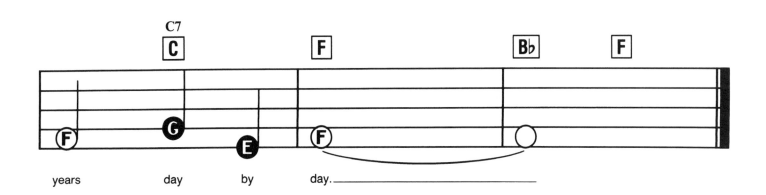

years day by day. _____

Cry Me a River

Registration 2
Rhythm: Fox Trot

Words and Music by
Arthur Hamilton

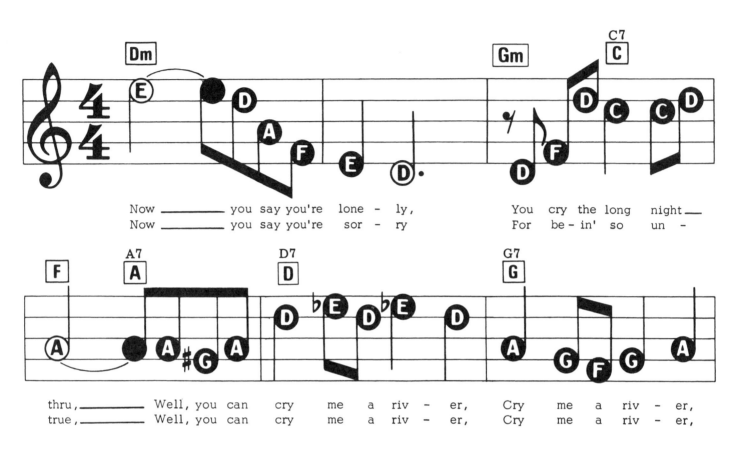

Now _____ you say you're lone - ly,   You cry the long night _____
Now _____ you say you're sor - ry   For be - in' so un -

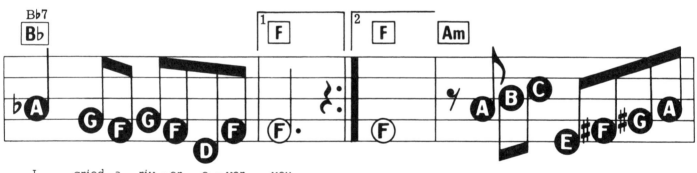

thru, _____ Well, you can cry me a riv - er, Cry me a riv - er,
true, _____ Well, you can cry me a riv - er, Cry me a riv - er,

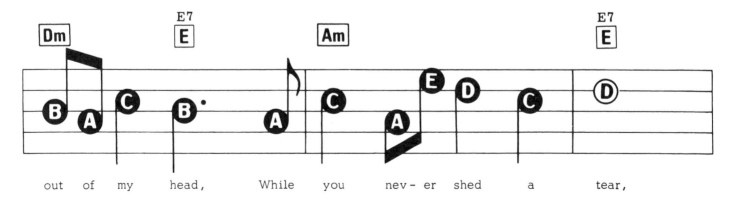

I cried a riv - er o - ver you.
I cried a riv - er o - ver you. You drove me, near - ly drove me

out of my head, While you nev - er shed a tear,

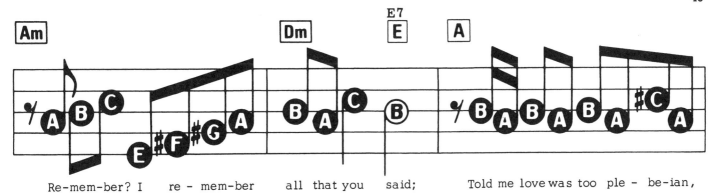

Re-mem-ber? I re - mem-ber all that you said; Told me love was too ple - be-ian,

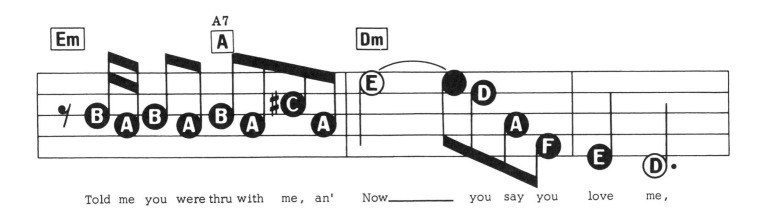

Told me you were thru with me, an' Now_____ you say you love me,

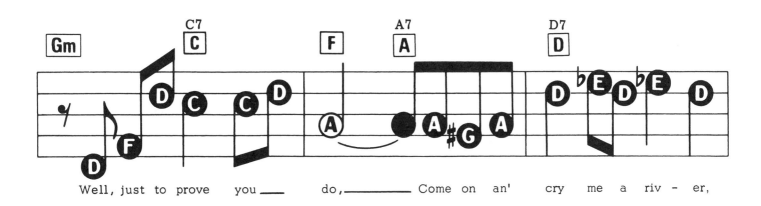

Well, just to prove you ___ do,_____ Come on an' cry me a riv - er,

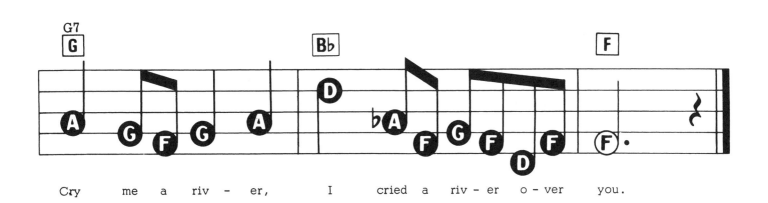

Cry me a riv - er, I cried a riv - er o - ver you.

Dancing on the Ceiling
from SIMPLE SIMON

Registration 5
Rhythm: Swing

Words by Lorenz Hart
Music by Richard Rodgers

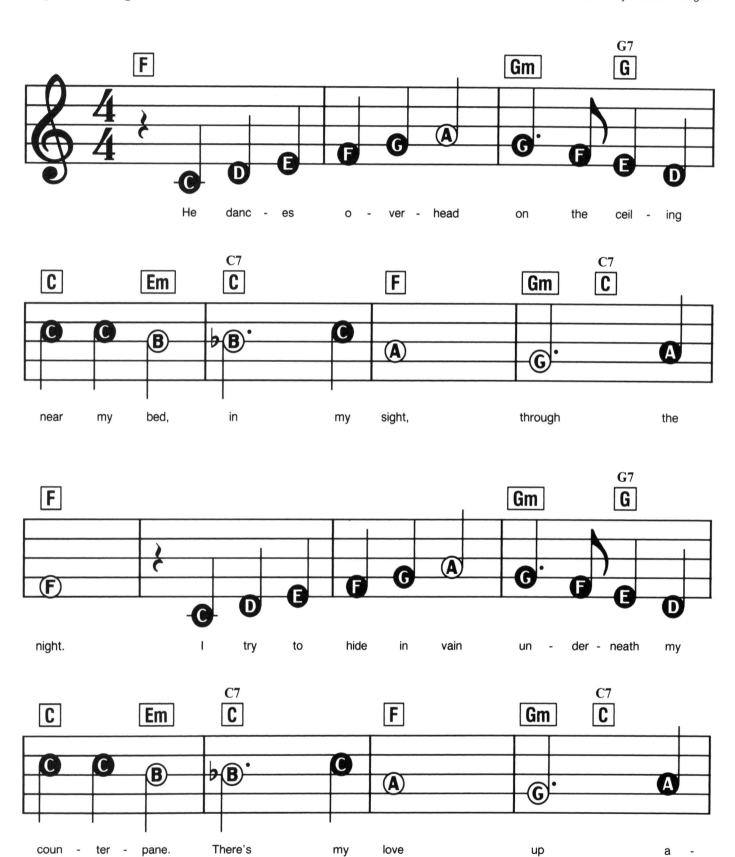

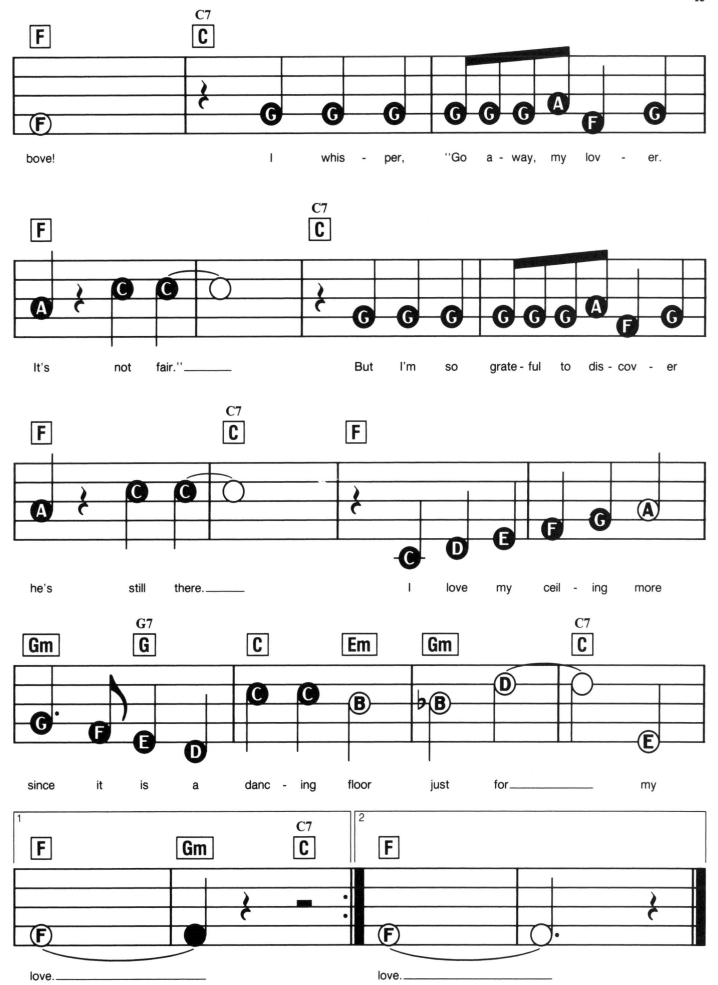

Dear Ruby
(Instrumentally known as "Ruby, My Dear")

Registration 8
Rhythm: Ballad or Blues

Music by Thelonious Monk
Lyrics by Sally Swisher

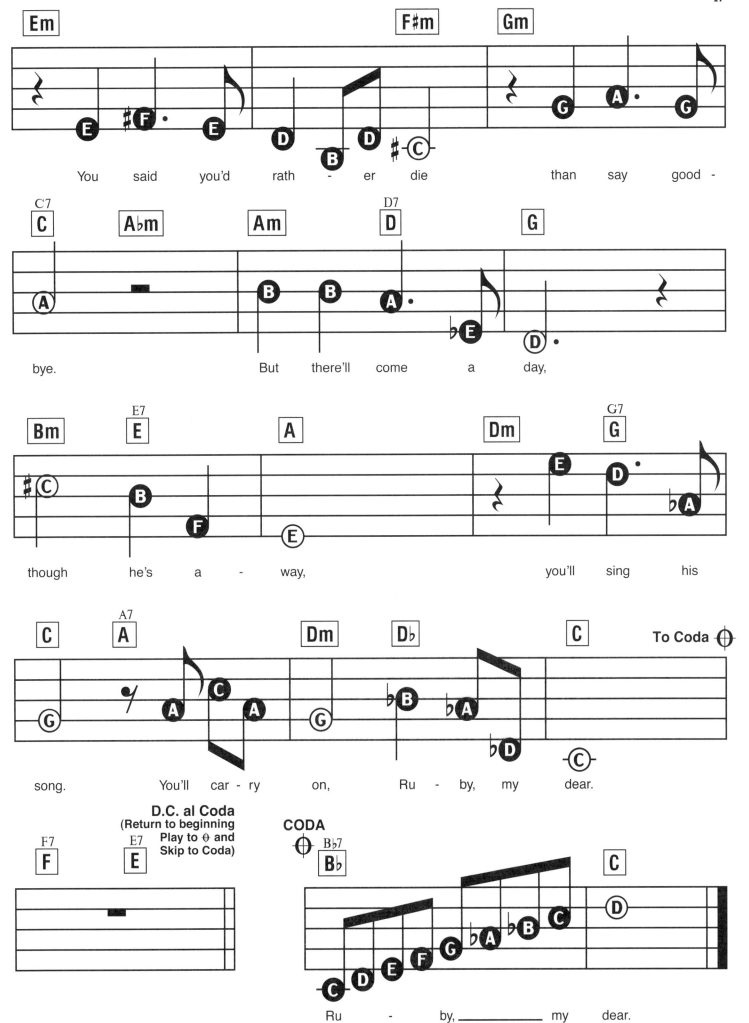

Dearly Beloved
from YOU WERE NEVER LOVELIER

Registration 1
Rhythm: Fox Trot or Swing

Music by Jerome Kern
Words by Johnny Mercer

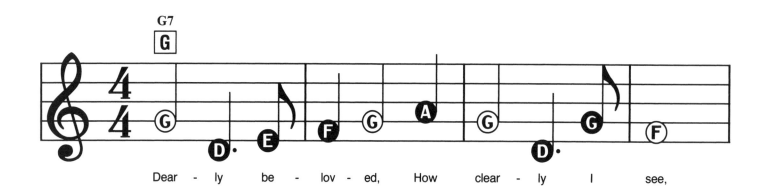

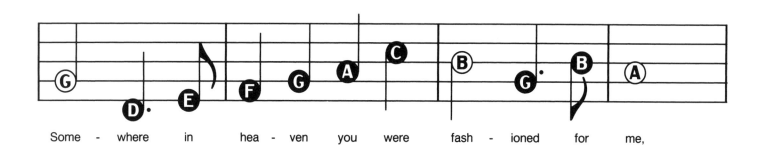

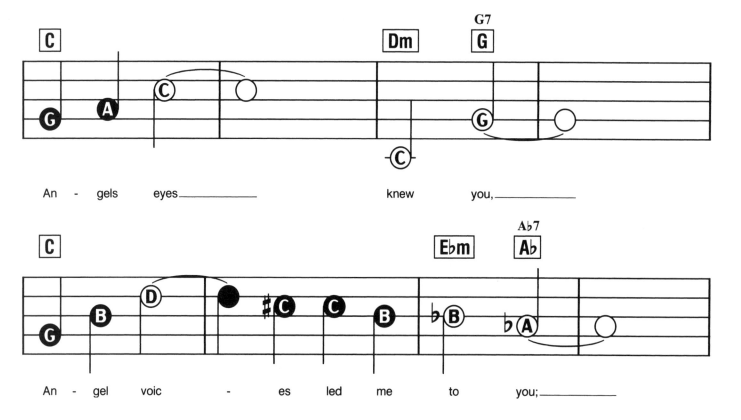

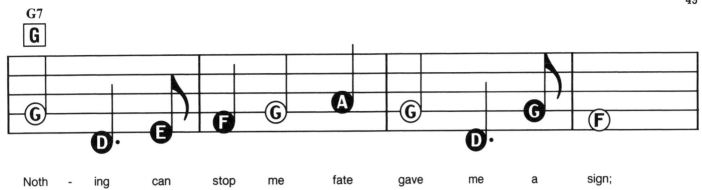

Noth - ing can stop me fate gave me a sign;

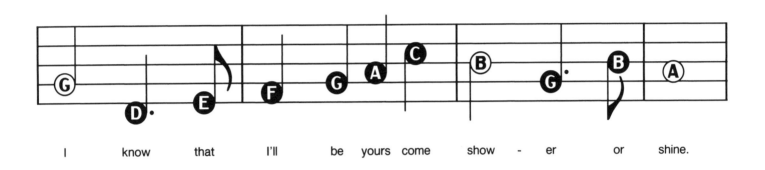

I know that I'll be yours come show - er or shine.

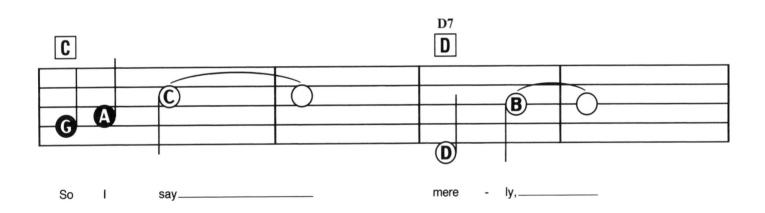

So I say_____ mere - ly,_____

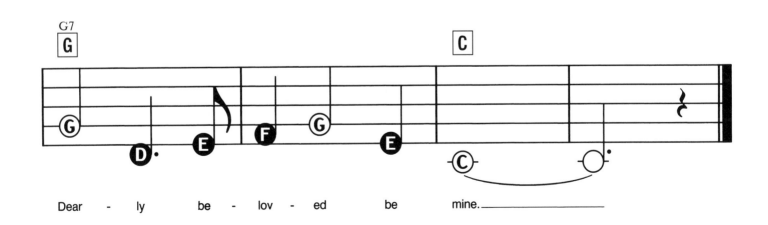

Dear - ly be - lov - ed be mine._____

Diamonds Are a Girl's Best Friend
from GENTLEMEN PREFER BLONDES

Registration 5
Rhythm: March or Polka

Words by Leo Robin
Music by Jule Styne

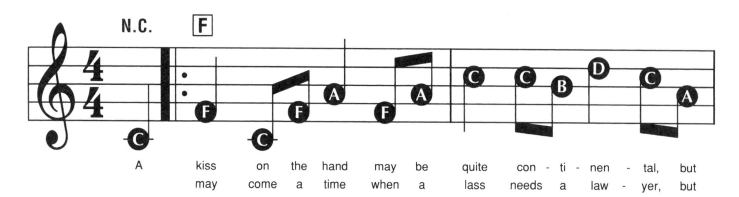

A   kiss   on   the   hand   may   be   quite   con - ti - nen - tal,   but
may   come   a   time   when   a   lass   needs   a   law - yer,   but

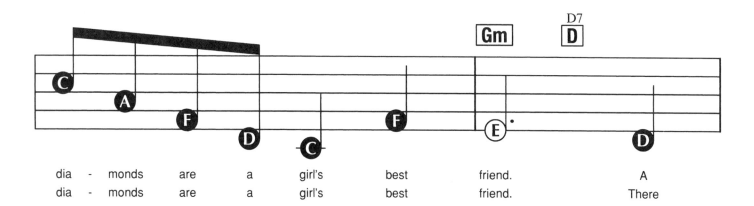

dia - monds   are   a   girl's   best   friend.   A
dia - monds   are   a   girl's   best   friend.   There

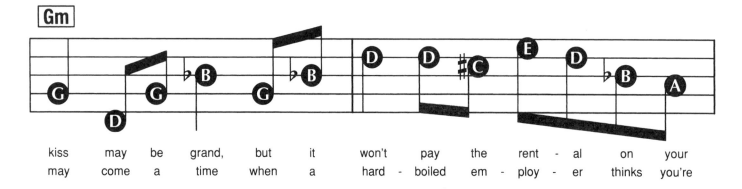

kiss   may   be   grand,   but   it   won't   pay   the   rent - al   on   your
may   come   a   time   when   a   hard - boiled   em - ploy - er   thinks   you're

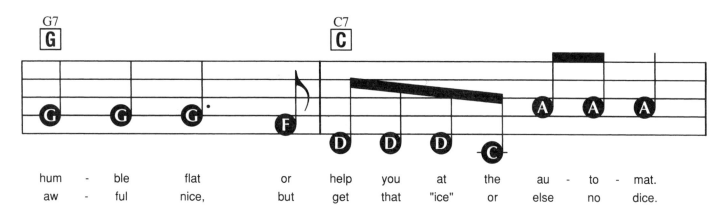

hum - ble   flat   or   help   you   at   the   au - to - mat.
aw - ful   nice,   but   get   that   "ice"   or   else   no   dice.

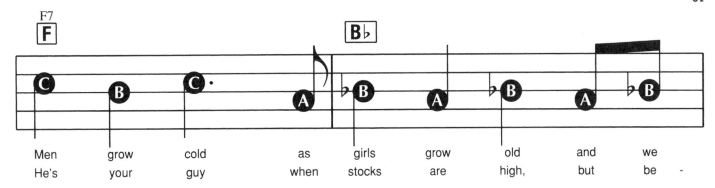

Men grow cold as girls grow old and we
He's your guy when stocks are high, but we be -

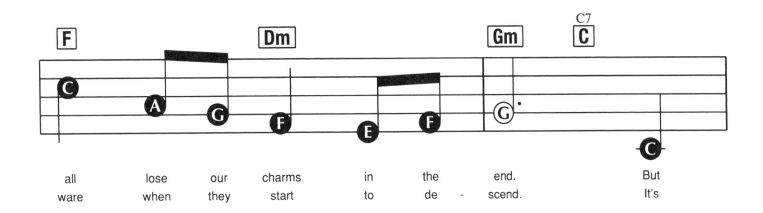

all lose our charms in the end. But
ware when they start to de - scend. It's

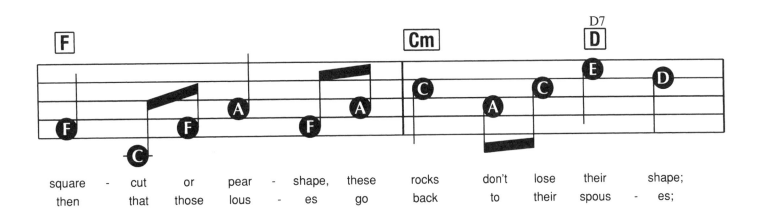

square - cut or pear - shape, these rocks don't lose their shape;
then that those lous - es go back to their spous - es;

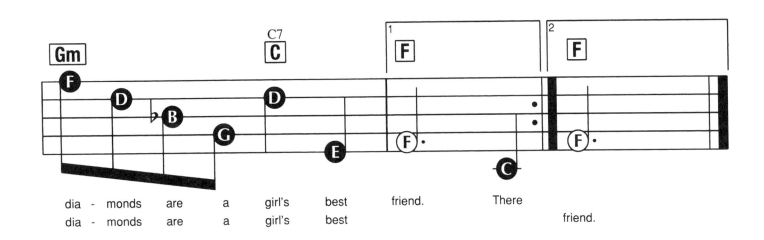

dia - monds are a girl's best friend. There
dia - monds are a girl's best friend.

Easy to Love
(You'd Be So Easy to Love)
from BORN TO DANCE

Registration 3
Rhythm: Swing or Fox Trot

Words and Music by
Cole Porter

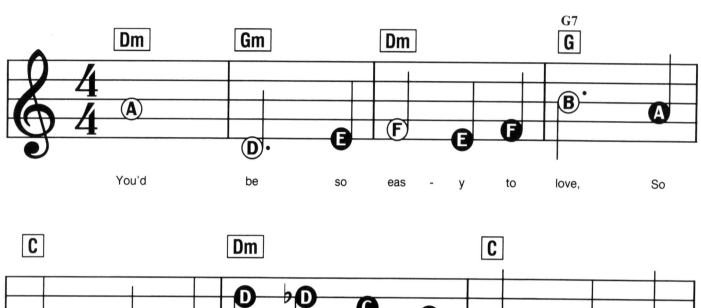

You'd be so eas - y to love, So

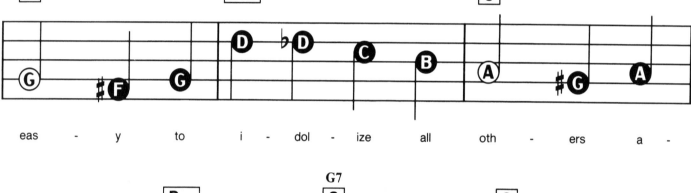

eas - y to i - dol - ize all oth - ers a -

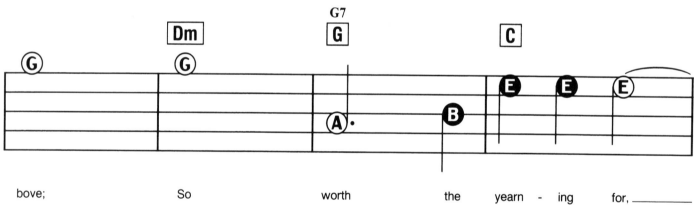

bove; So worth the yearn - ing for, _____

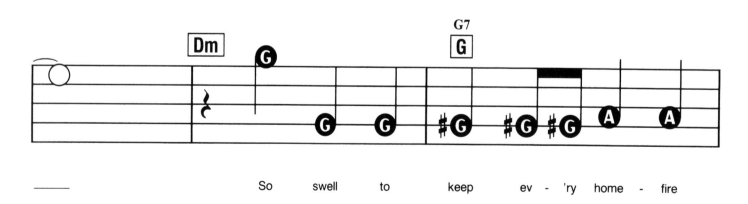

_____ So swell to keep ev - 'ry home - fire

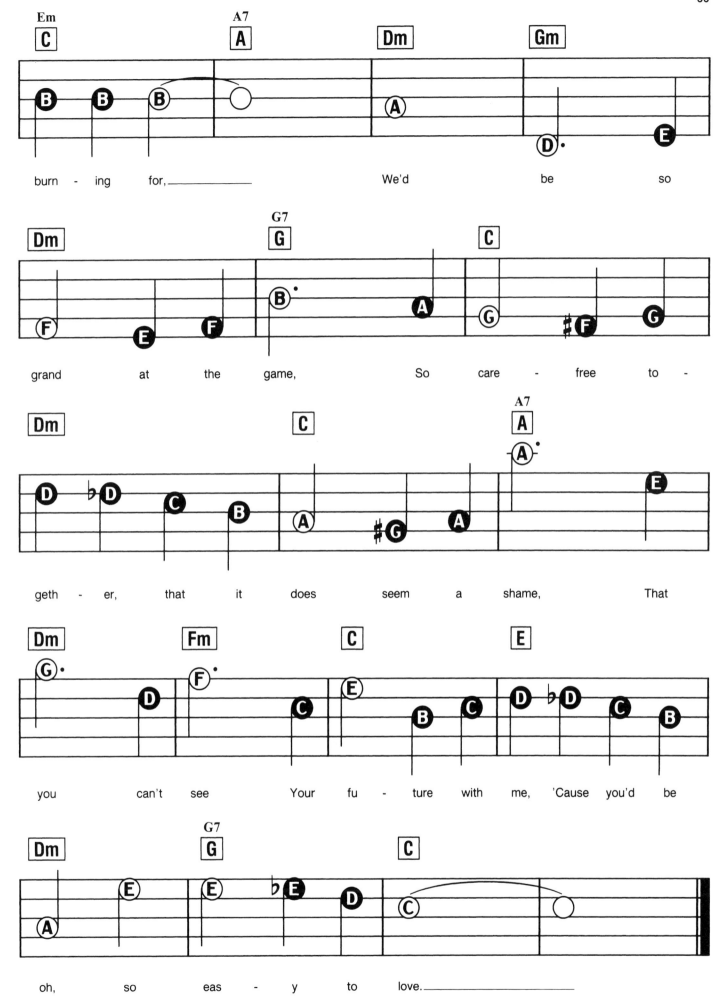

Far Away Places

Registration 1
Rhythm: Waltz

Words and Music by Alex Kramer
and Joan Whitney

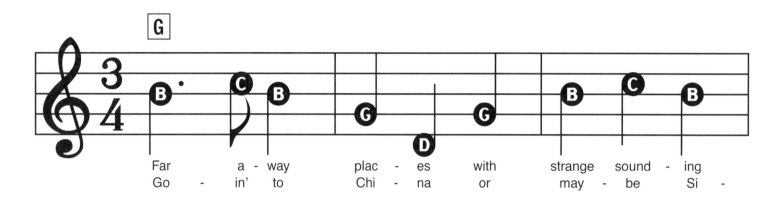

Far a - way plac - es with strange sound - ing
Go - in' to Chi - na or may - be Si -

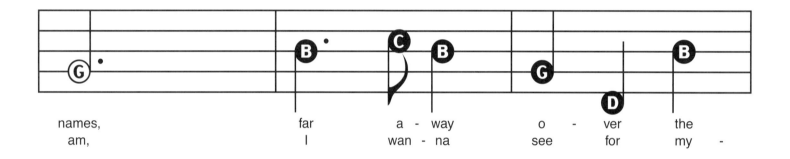

names, far a - way o - ver the
am, I wan - na see for my -

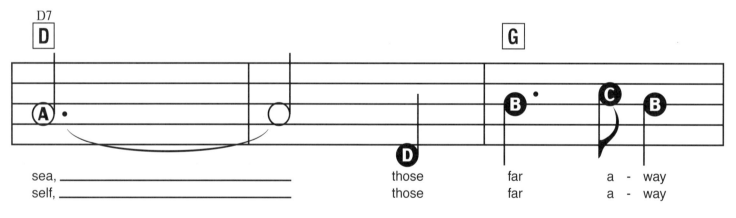

sea, _____ those far a - way
self, _____ those far a - way

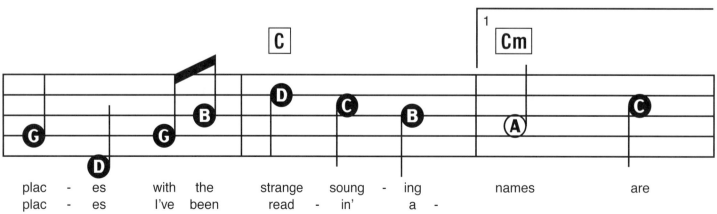

plac - es with the strange soung - ing names are
plac - es I've been read - in' a -

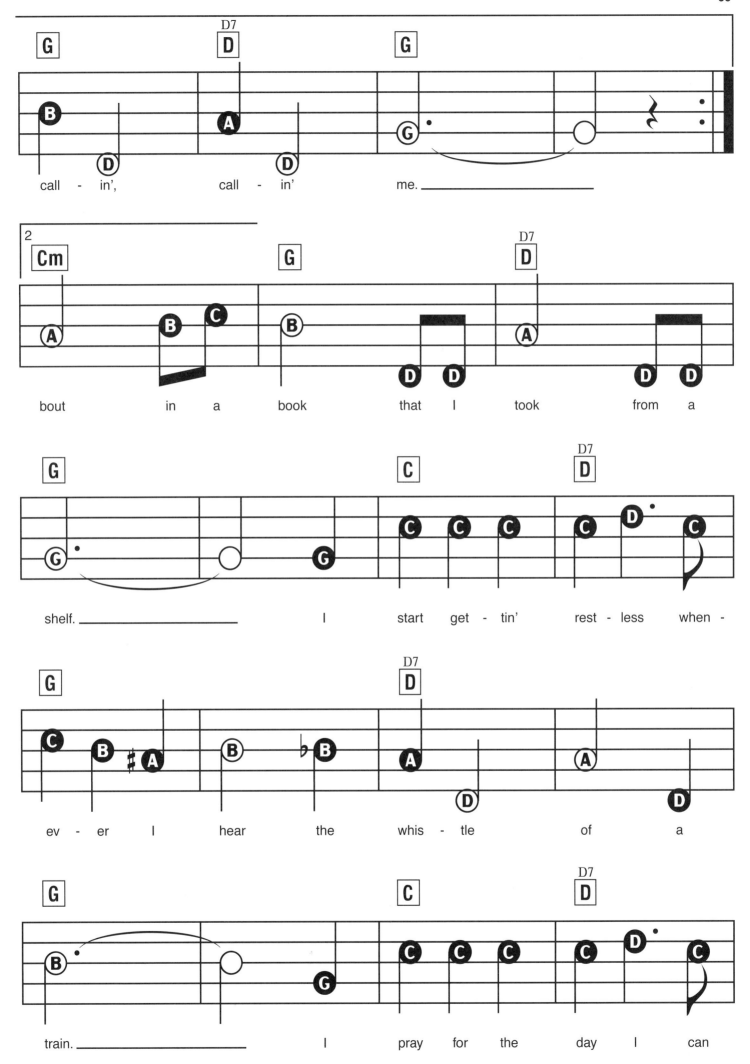

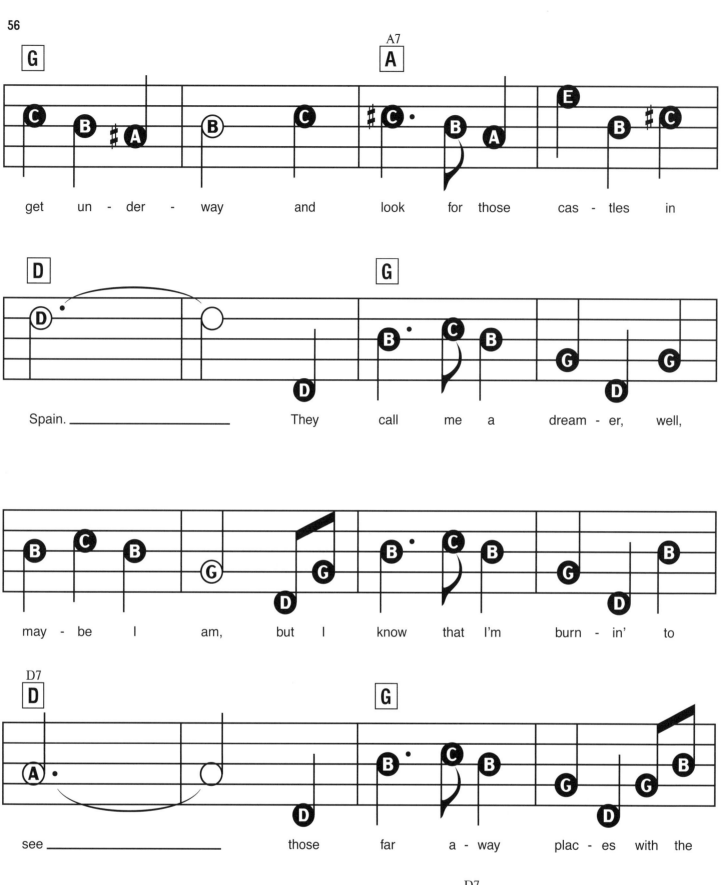

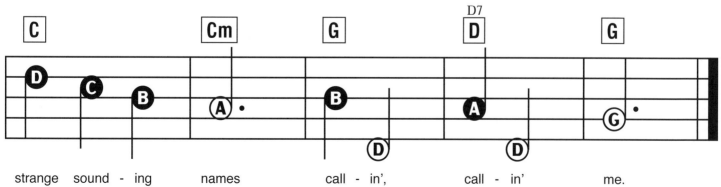

Everybody Loves Somebody

Registration 4
Rhythm: Swing or Shuffle

Words by Irving Taylor
Music by Ken Lane

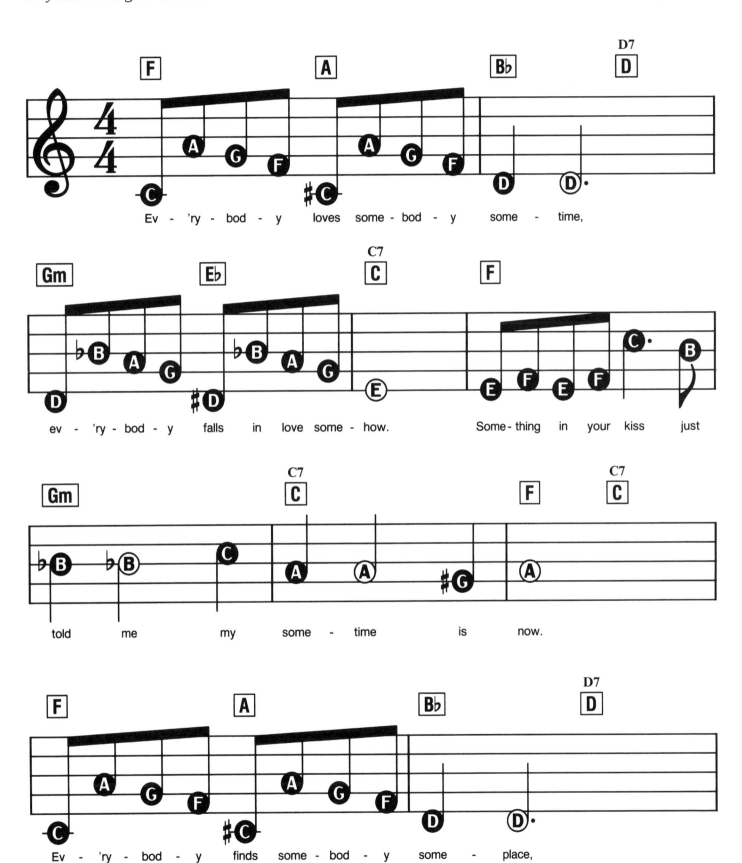

58

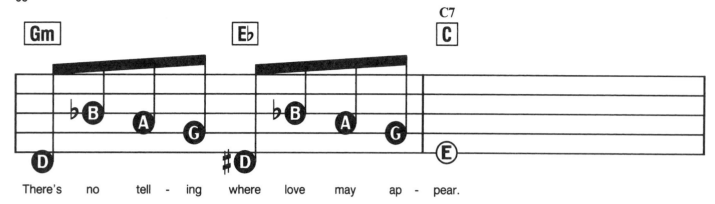

There's no tell - ing where love may ap - pear.

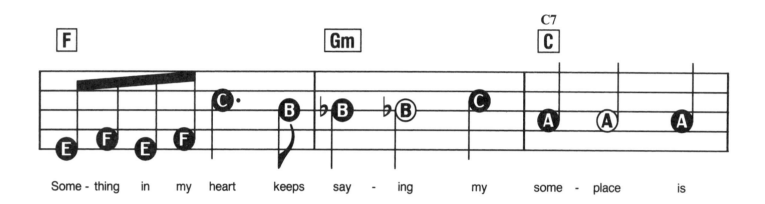

Some - thing in my heart keeps say - ing my some - place is

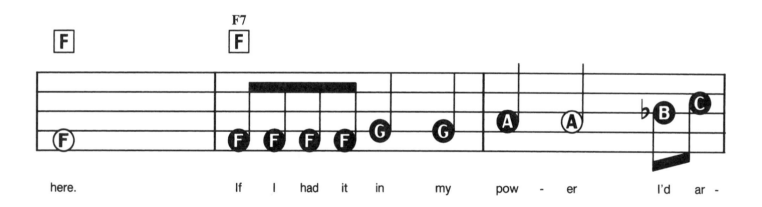

here. If I had it in my pow - er I'd ar -

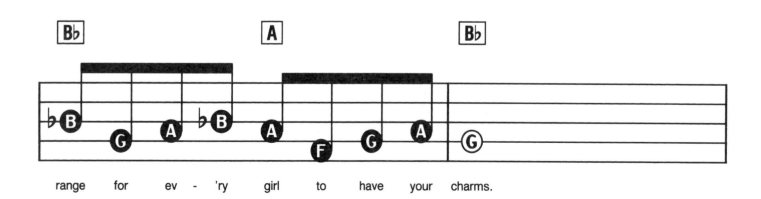

range for ev - 'ry girl to have your charms.

Fever

Registration 9
Rhythm: Fox Trot or Swing

Words and Music by John Davenport
and Eddie Cooley

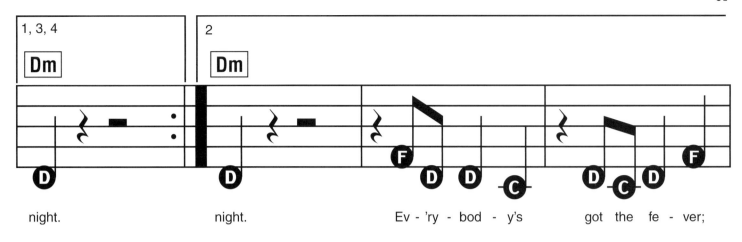

night.   night.   Ev - 'ry - bod - y's   got the fe - ver;

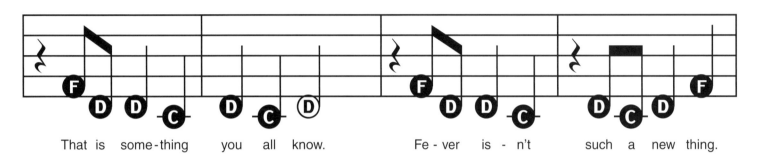

That is some-thing you all know.   Fe - ver is - n't such a new thing.

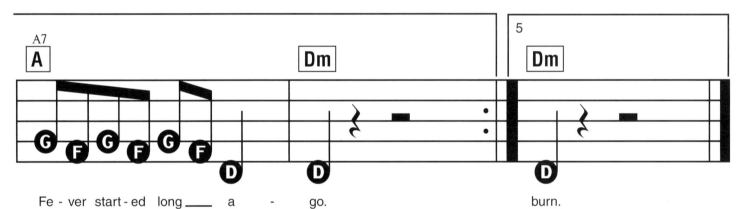

Fe - ver start-ed long ___ a - go.   burn.

Additional Verses

Verse 3
Romeo loved Juliet,
Juliet, she felt the same.
When he put his arms around her, he said,
"Julie, baby, you're my flame."

Chorus
Thou givest fever when we kisseth,
Fever with thy flaming youth.
Fever — I'm afire,
Fever, yea I burn forsooth.

Verse 4
Captain Smith and Pocahontas
Had a very mad affair.
When her daddy tried to kill him, she said,
"Daddy-o, don't you dare."

Chorus
Give me fever with his kisses,
Fever when he holds me tight.
Fever — I'm his Missus,
Oh, Daddy, won't you treat him right.

Verse 5
Now you've listened to my story,
Here's the point that I have made.
Chicks were born to give you fever,
Be it fahrenheit or centigrade.

Chorus
They give you fever when you kiss them,
Fever if you live and learn.
Fever — till you sizzle,
What a lovely way to burn.

The Folks Who Live on the Hill
from HIGH, WIDE AND HANDSOME

Registration 3
Rhythm: Fox Trot or Swing

Lyrics by Oscar Hammerstein II
Music by Jerome Kern

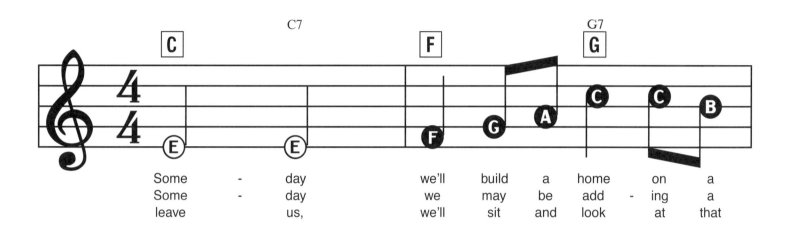

Some - day we'll build a home on a
Some - day we may be add - ing a
leave us, we'll sit and look at that

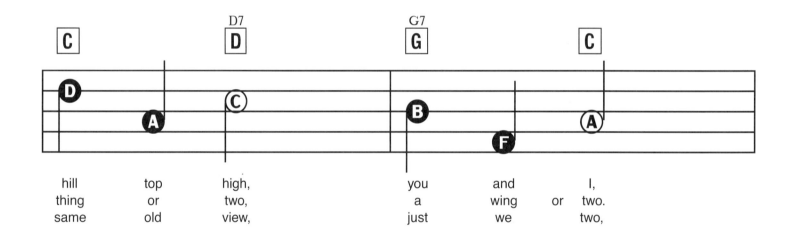

hill top high, you and I,
thing or two, a wing or two.
same old view, just we two,

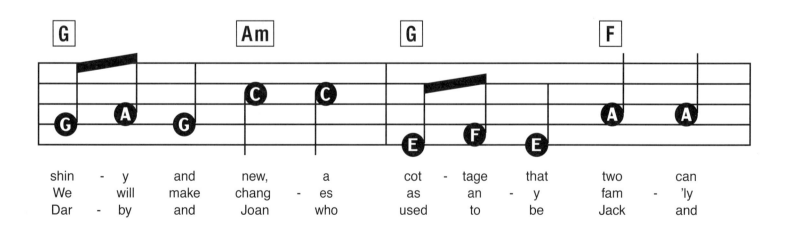

shin - y and new, a cot - tage that two can
We will make chang - es as an - y fam - 'ly
Dar - by and Joan who used to be Jack and

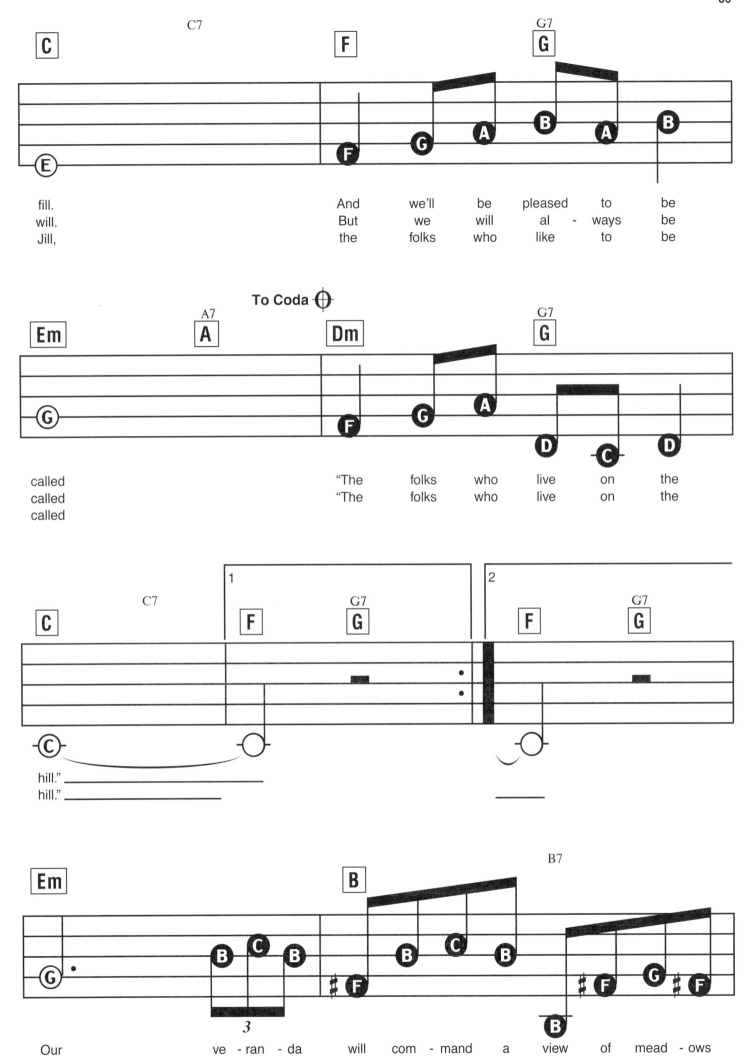

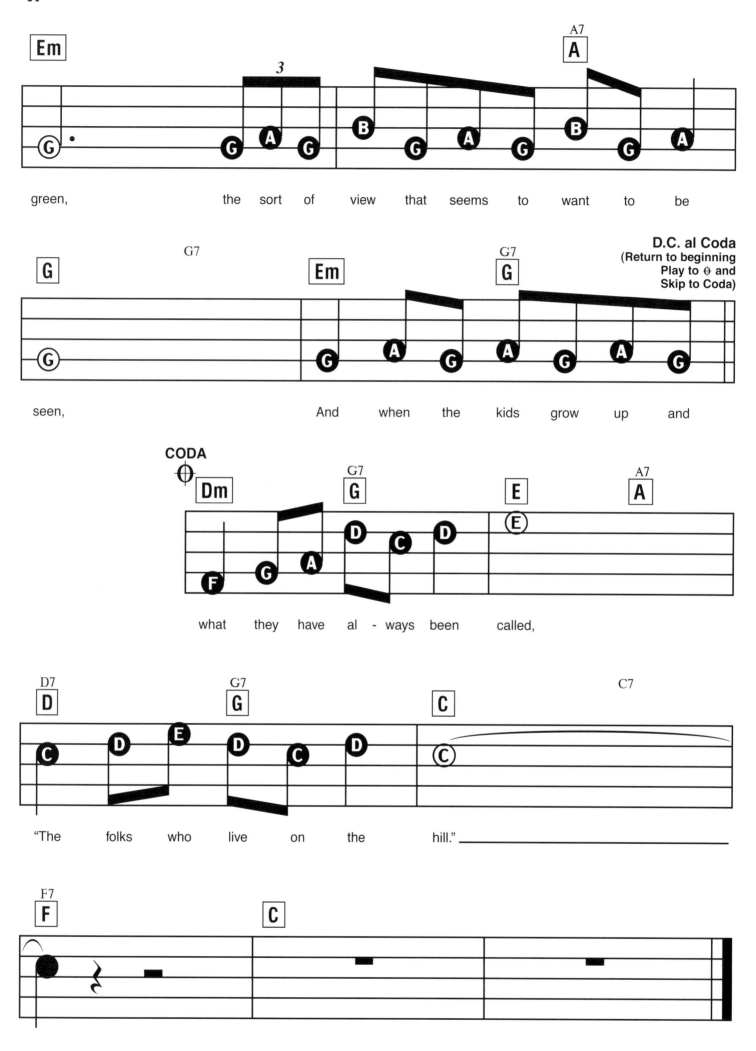

Gypsy in My Soul

Registration 9
Rhythm: Swing

Words by Moe Jaffe and Clay Boland
Music by Clay Boland

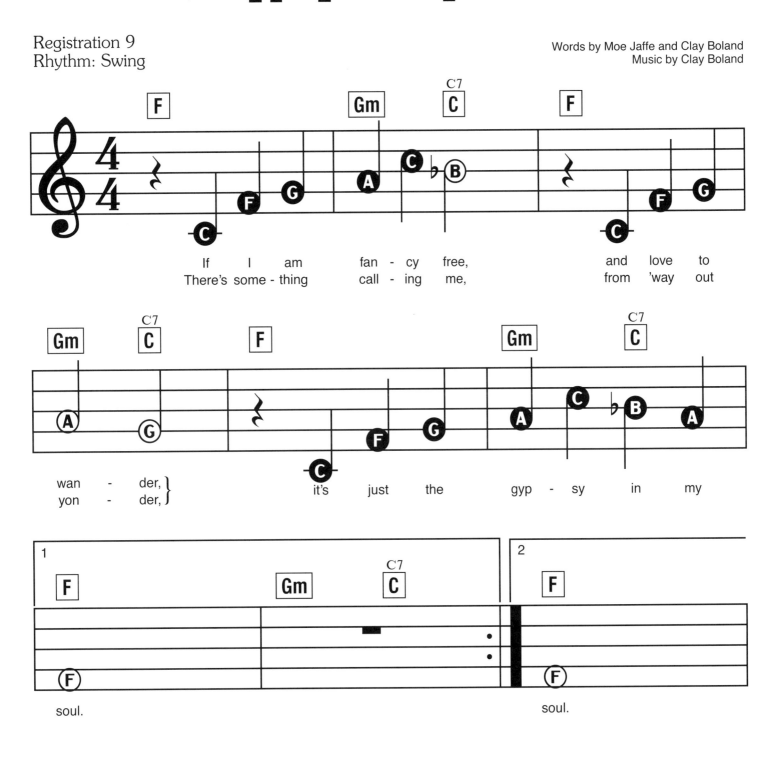

If I am fan - cy free, and love to
There's some - thing call - ing me, from 'way out

wan - der,
yon - der,
it's just the gyp - sy in my

1.
soul.

2.
soul.

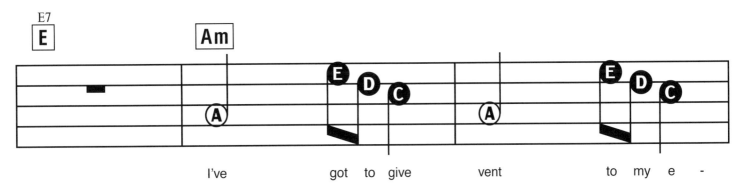

I've got to give vent to my e -

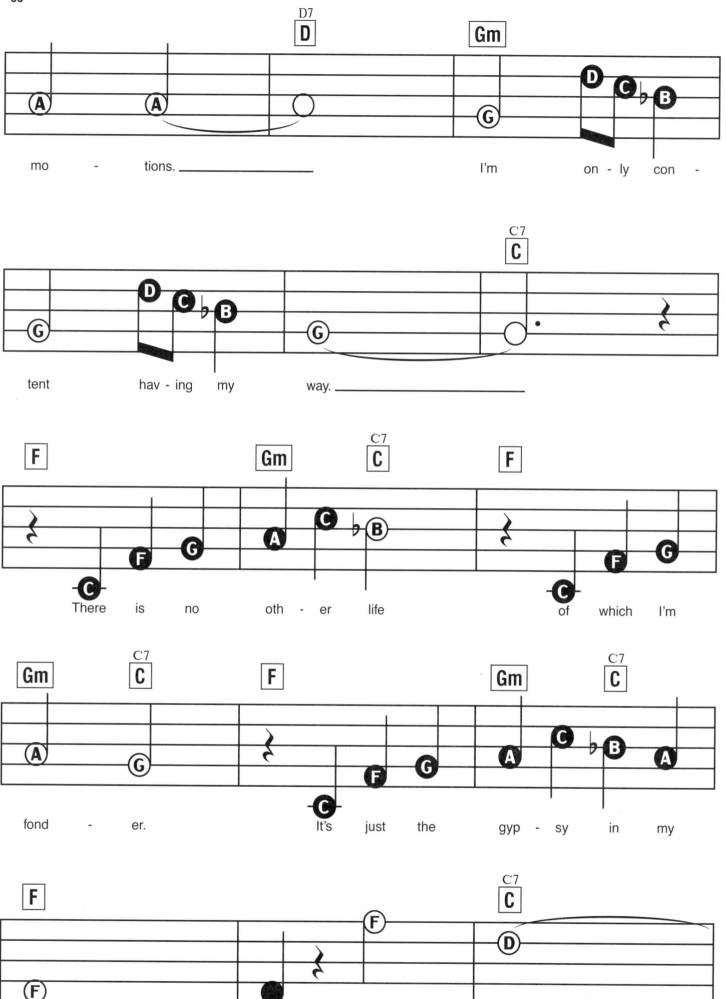

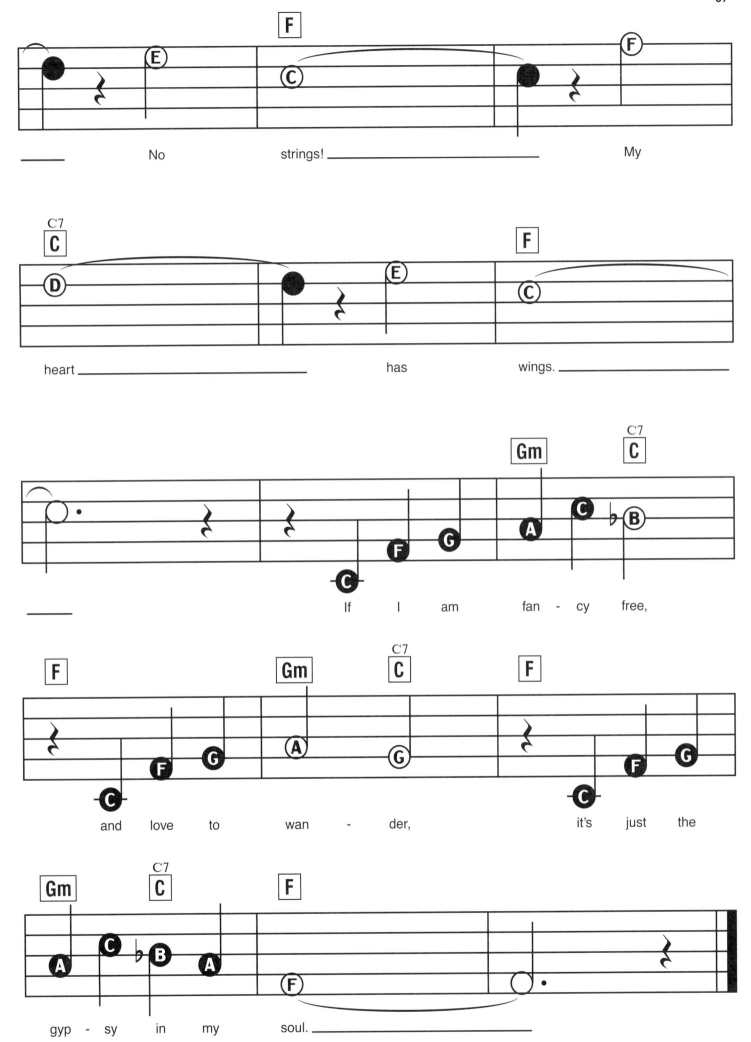

For All We Know

Registration 1
Rhythm: Swing

Words by Sam M. Lewis
Music by J. Fred Coots

For all we know we may nev - er meet a - gain, Be - fore you go make this mo - ment sweet a - gain, We won't say good - night un - til the last min - ute, I'll hold out my hand and my

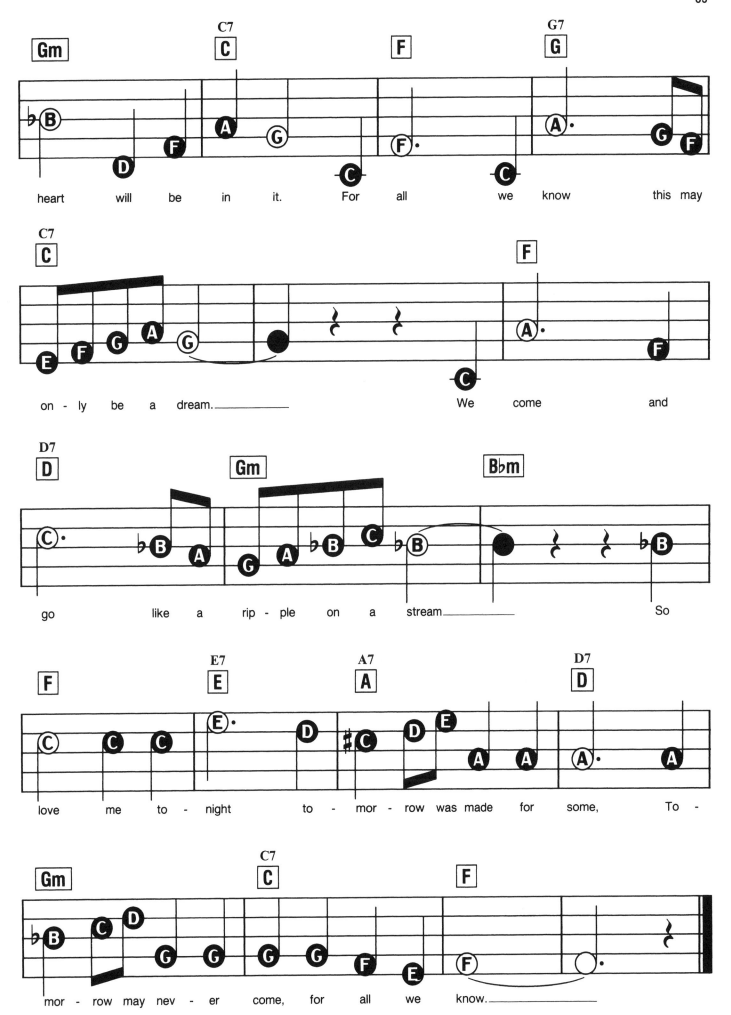

The Girl That I Marry
from the Stage Production ANNIE GET YOUR GUN

Registration 3
Rhythm: Waltz

Words and Music by
Irving Berlin

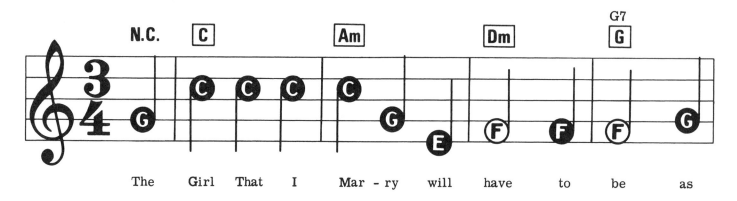

The Girl That I Mar - ry will have to be as

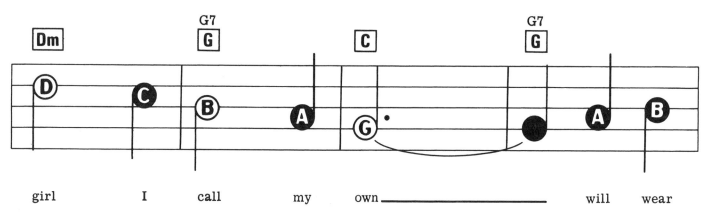

soft and as pink as a nurs - er - y. The

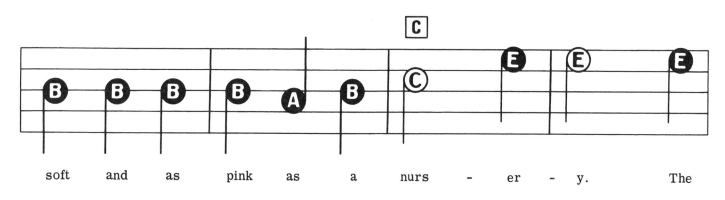

girl I call my own _____ will wear

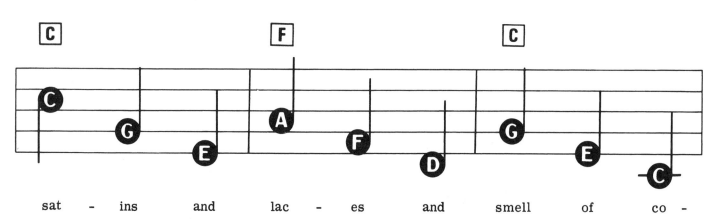

sat - ins and lac - es and smell of co -

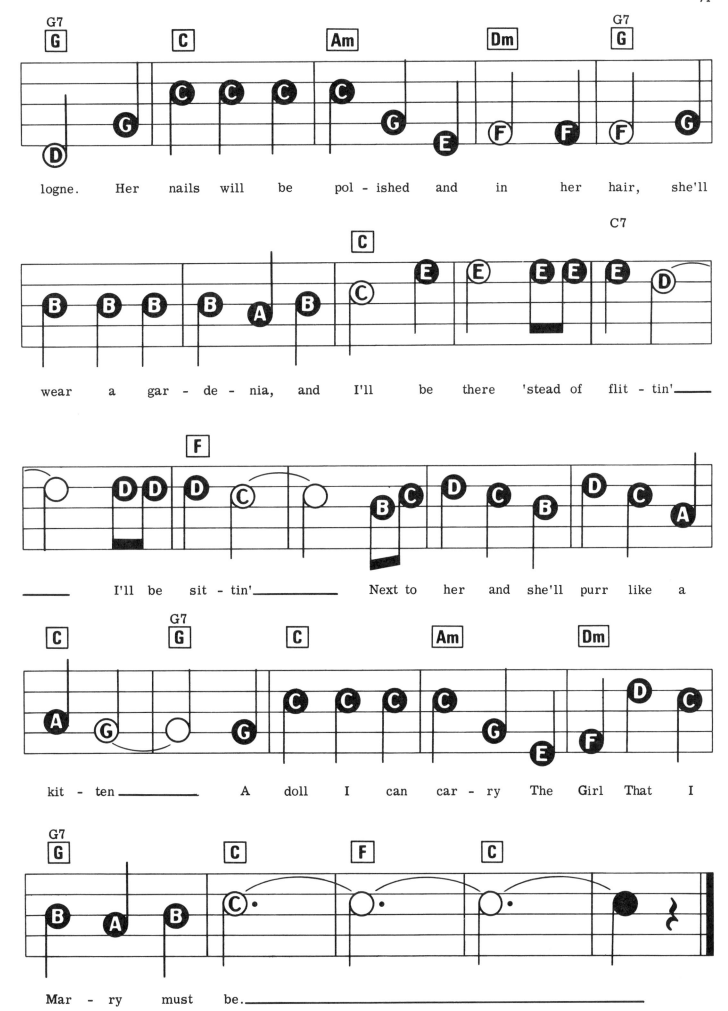

Gone with the Wind

Registration 2
Rhythm: Swing

Words and Music by Herb Magidson
and Allie Wrubel

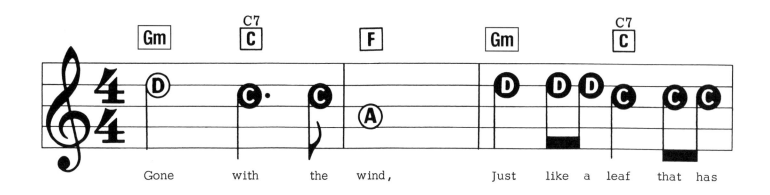

Gone with the wind, Just like a leaf that has

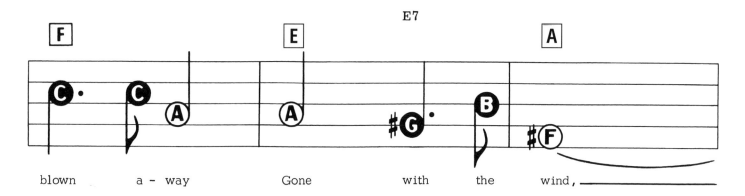

blown a - way Gone with the wind, _____

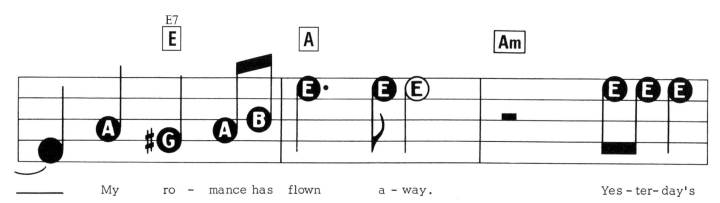

_____ My ro - mance has flown a - way. Yes - ter - day's

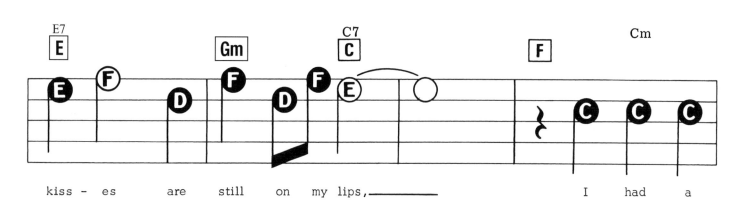

kiss - es are still on my lips, _____ I had a

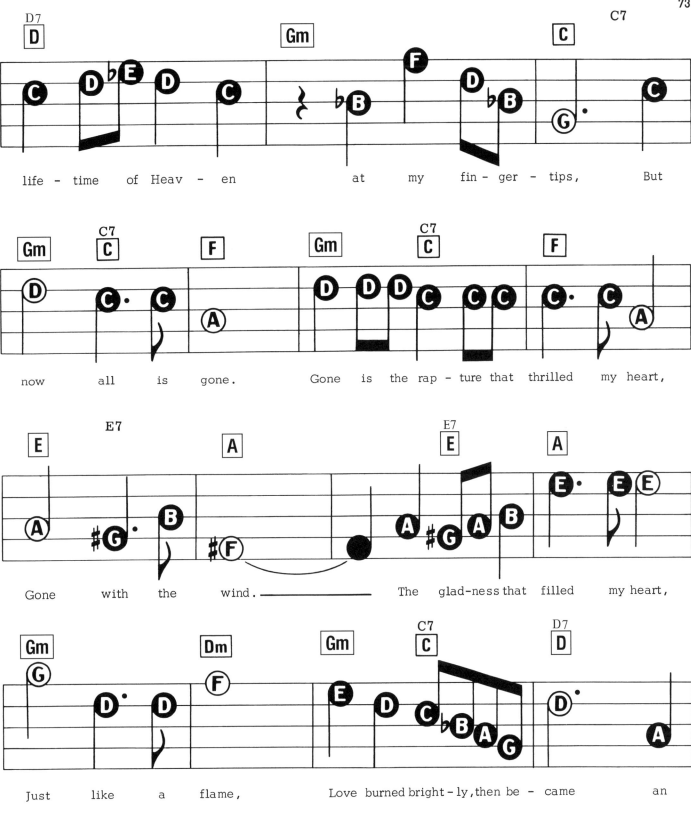

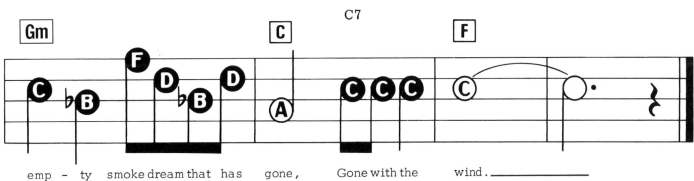

Half as Much

Registration 2
Rhythm: Fox Trot or Swing

Words and Music by
Curley Williams

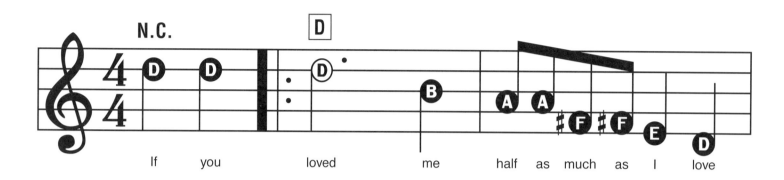

If you loved me half as much as I love

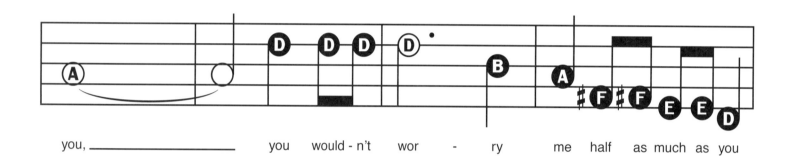

you, _____ you would-n't wor — ry me half as much as you

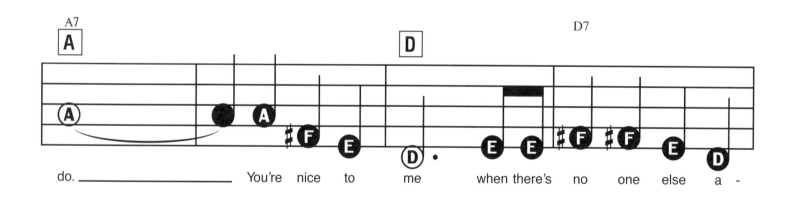

do. _____ You're nice to me when there's no one else a -

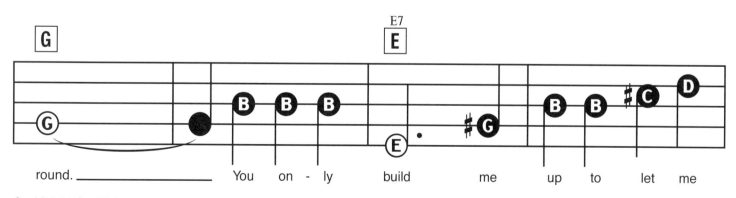

round. _____ You on — ly build me up to let me

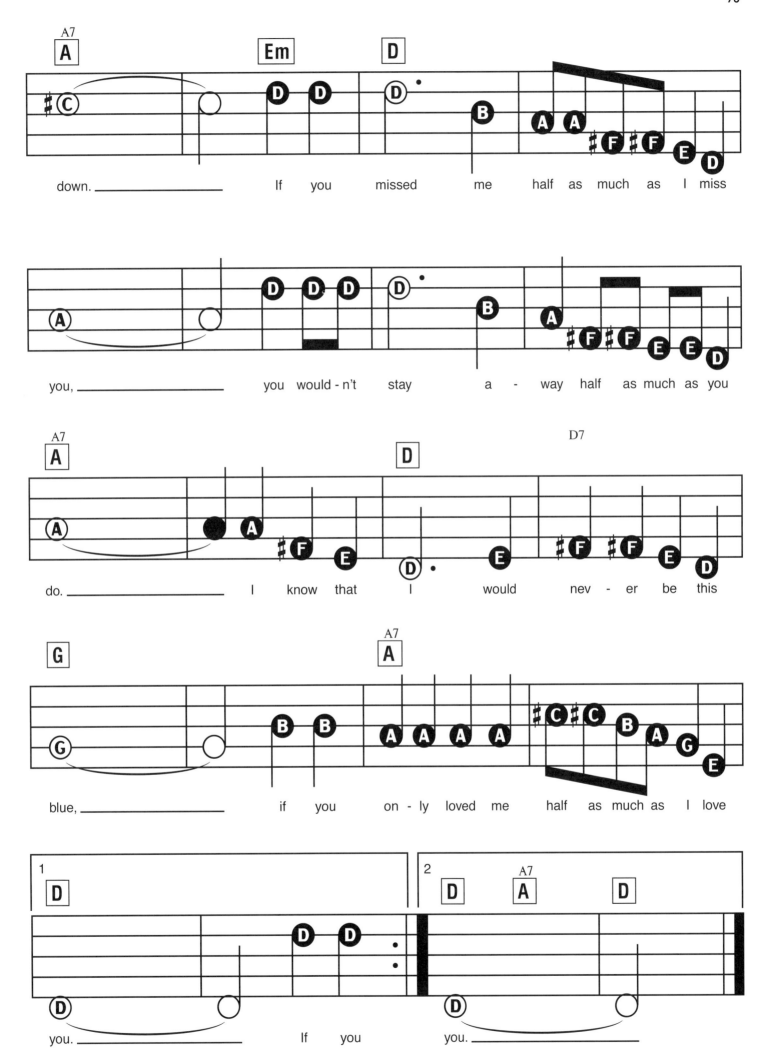

Haunted Heart
from INSIDE U.S.A.

Registration 4
Rhythm: Fox Trot

Words by Howard Dietz
Music by Arthur Schwartz

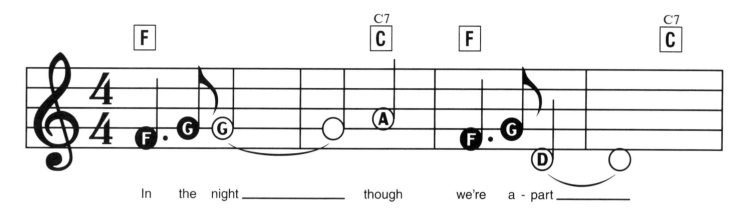

In the night _____ though we're a - part _____

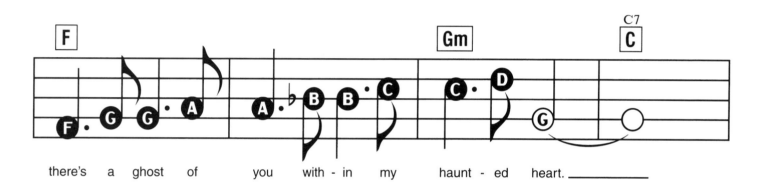

there's a ghost of you with - in my haunt - ed heart. _____

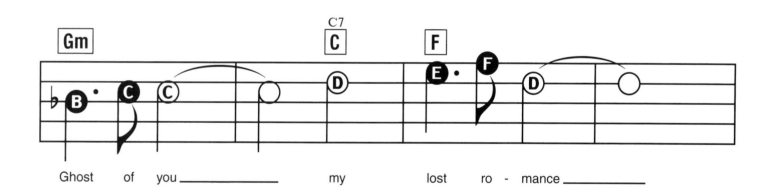

Ghost of you _____ my lost ro - mance _____

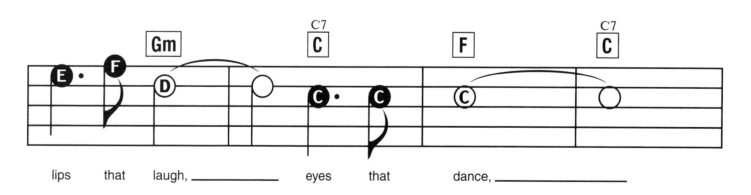

lips that laugh, _____ eyes that dance, _____

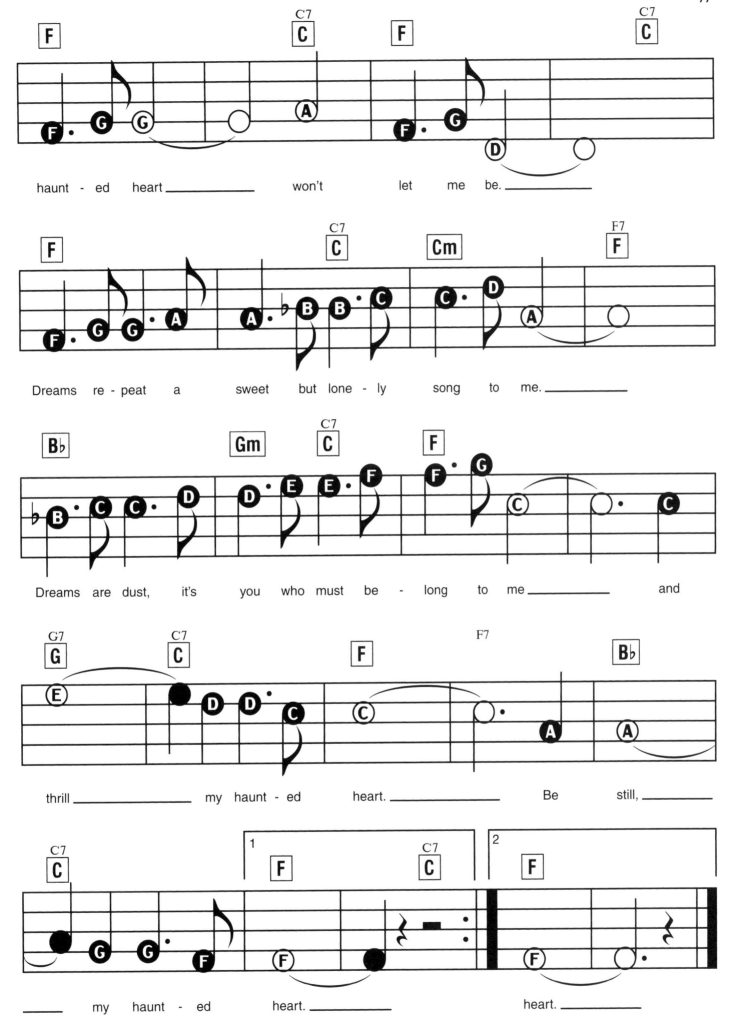

Heart and Soul
from the Paramount Short Subject A SONG IS BORN

Registration 8
Rhythm: Swing

Words by Frank Loesser
Music by Hoagy Carmichael

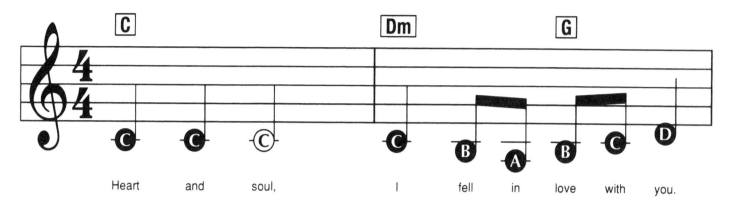

Heart and soul, I fell in love with you.

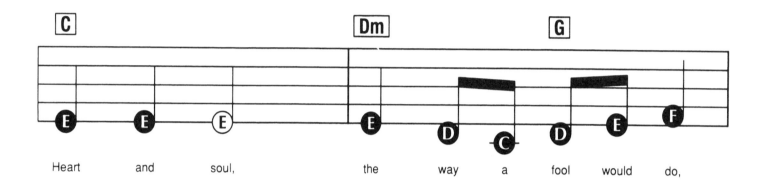

Heart and soul, the way a fool would do,

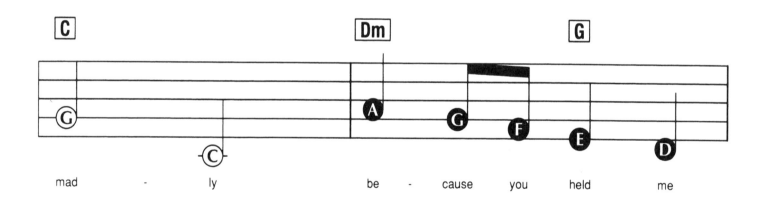

mad - ly be - cause you held me

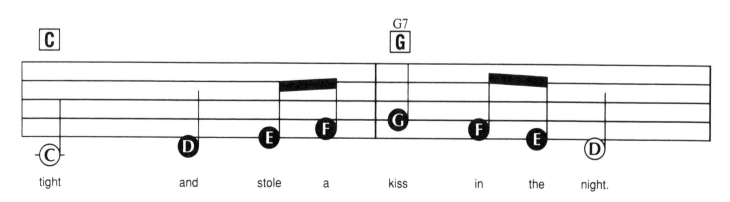

tight and stole a kiss in the night.

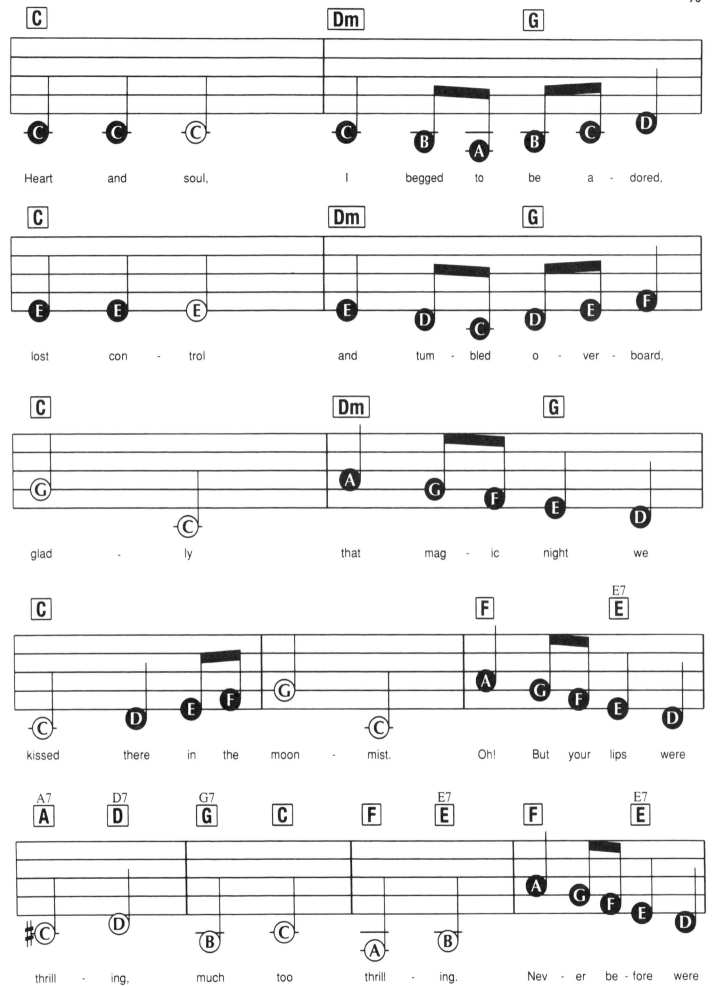

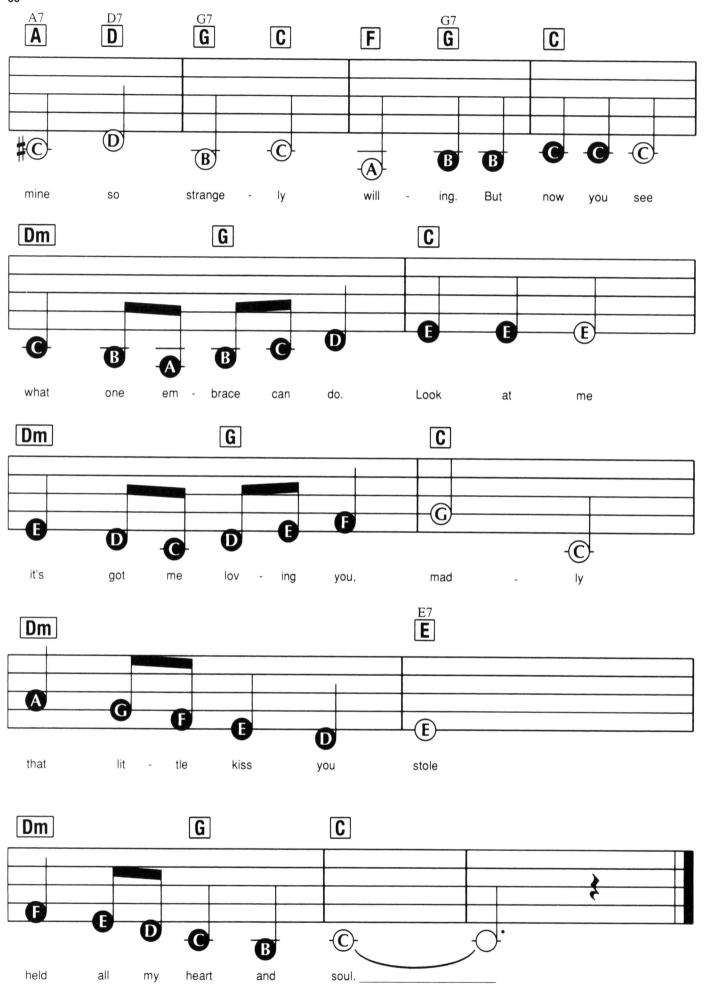

Heat Wave
from THERE'S NO BUSINESS LIKE SHOW BUSINESS

Registration 2
Rhythm: Latin

Words and Music by
Irving Berlin

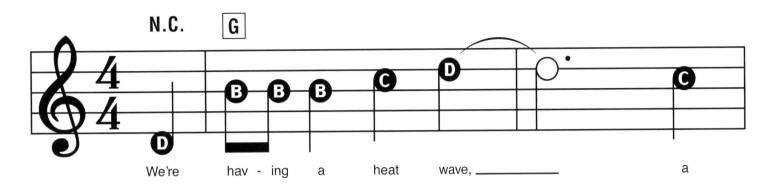

We're hav-ing a heat wave, _____ a

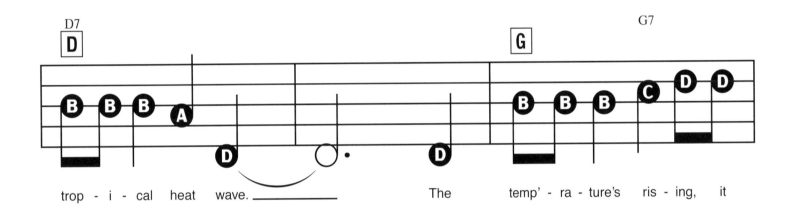

trop - i - cal heat wave. _____ The temp' - ra - ture's ris - ing, it

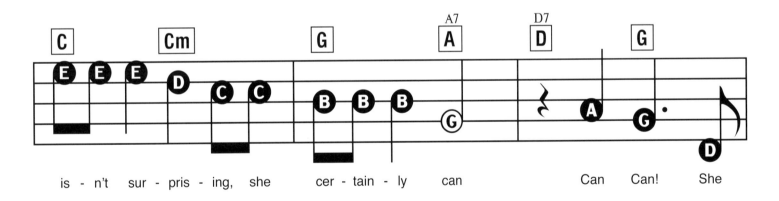

is - n't sur - pris - ing, she cer - tain - ly can Can Can! She

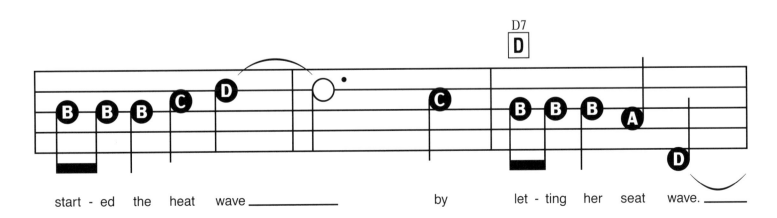

start - ed the heat wave _____ by let - ting her seat wave. _____

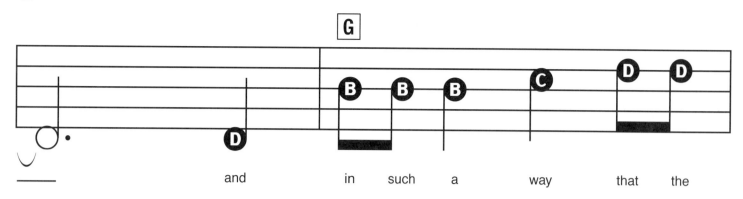

and   in   such   a   way   that   the

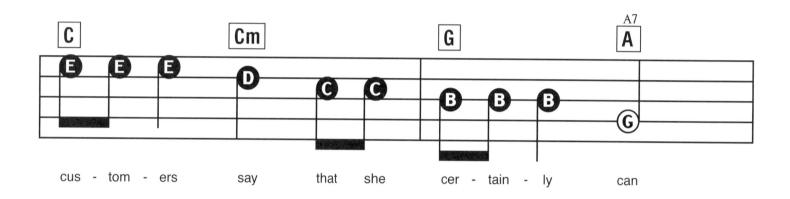

cus - tom - ers   say   that   she   cer - tain - ly   can

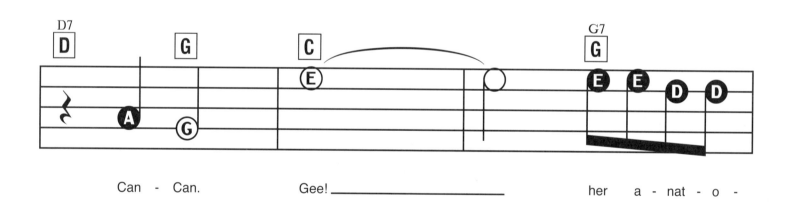

Can - Can.   Gee! _____   her   a - nat - o -

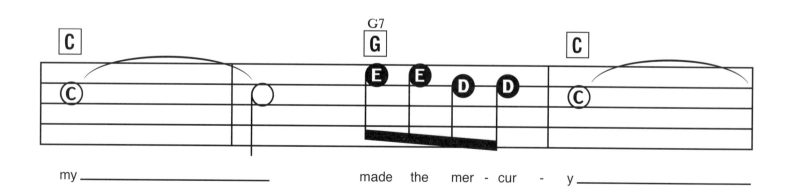

my _____   made   the   mer - cur - y _____

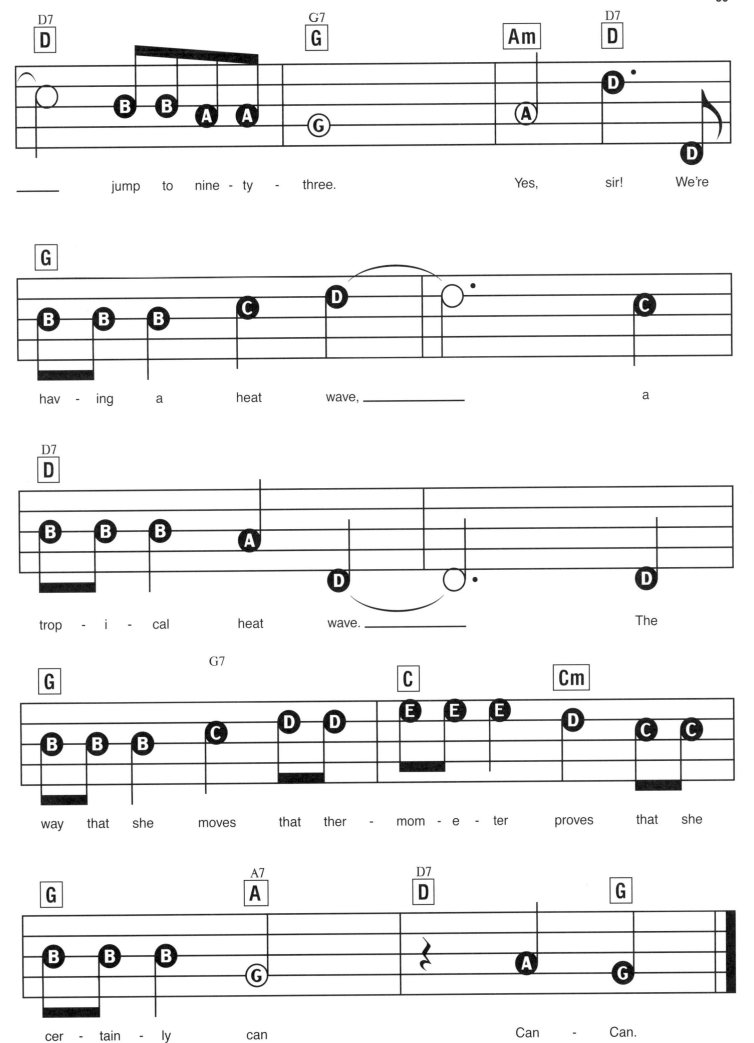

Hello, Dolly!
from HELLO, DOLLY!

Registration 7
Rhythm: Swing

Music and Lyric by
Jerry Herman

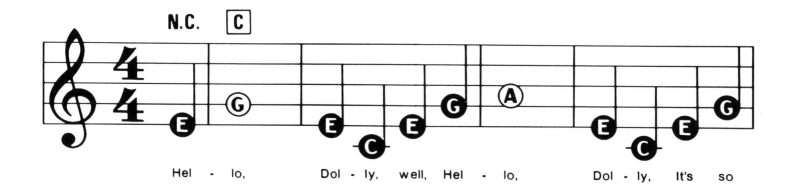

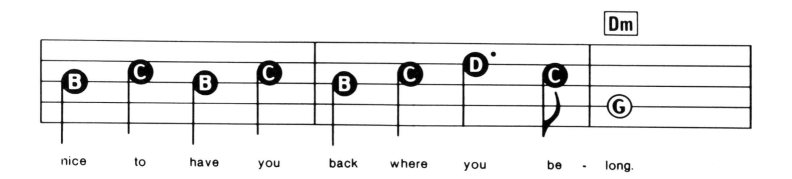

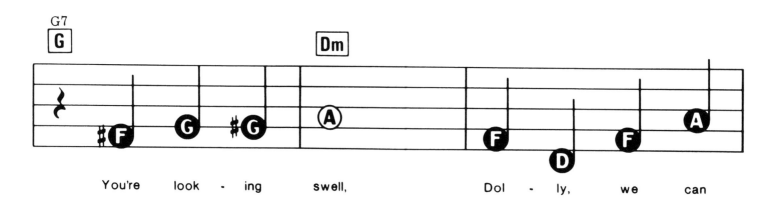

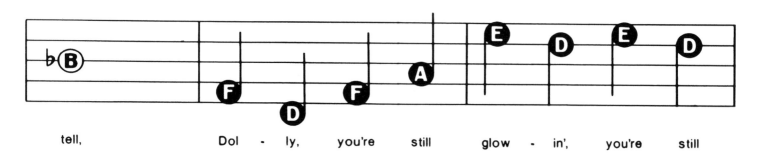

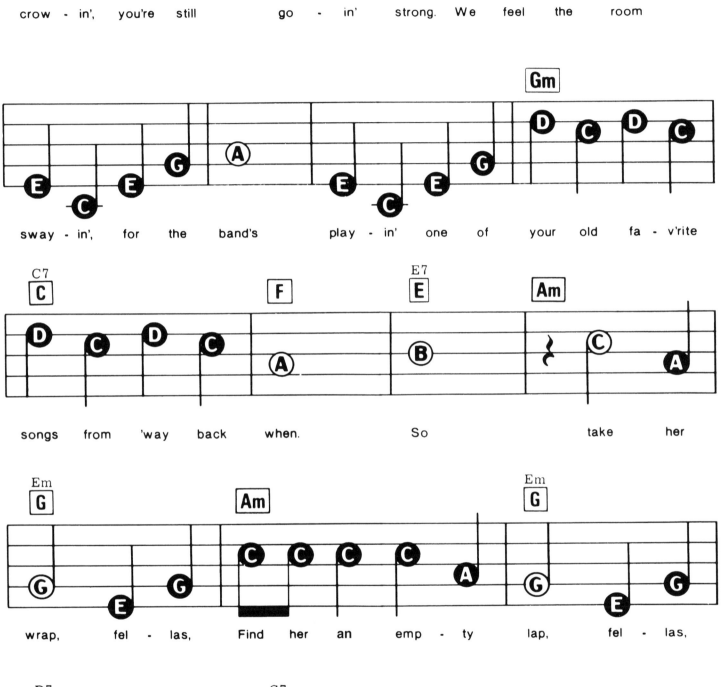

crow - in', you're still go - in' strong. We feel the room

sway - in', for the band's play - in' one of your old fa - v'rite

songs from 'way back when. So take her

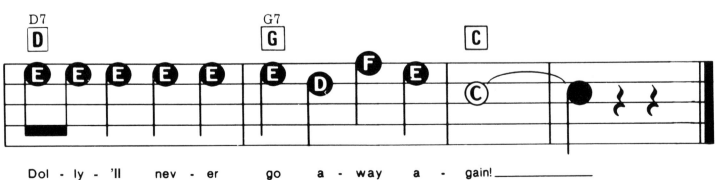

wrap, fel - las, Find her an emp - ty lap, fel - las,

Dol - ly - 'll nev - er go a - way a - gain!_____

How High the Moon
from TWO FOR THE SHOW

Registration 3
Rhythm: Ballad or Fox Trot

Lyrics by Nancy Hamilton
Music by Morgan Lewis

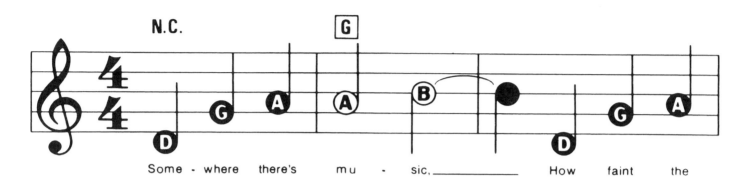

Some - where there's mu - sic, ___ How faint the

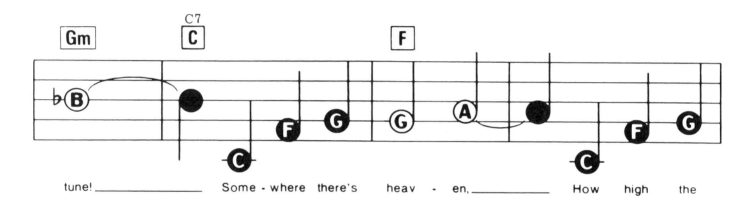

tune! ___ Some - where there's heav - en, ___ How high the

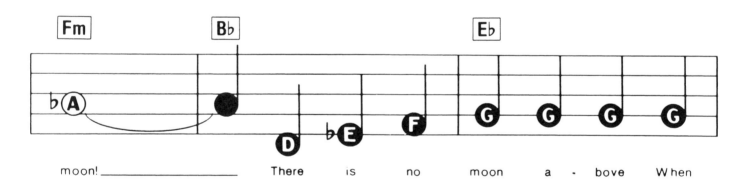

moon! ___ There is no moon a - bove When

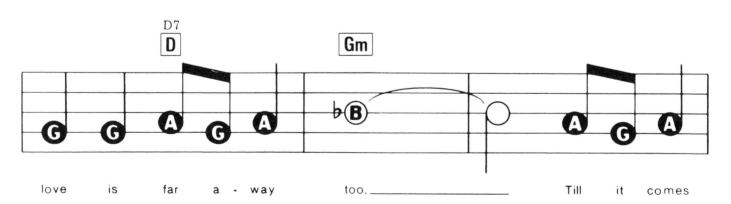

love is far a - way too. ___ Till it comes

87

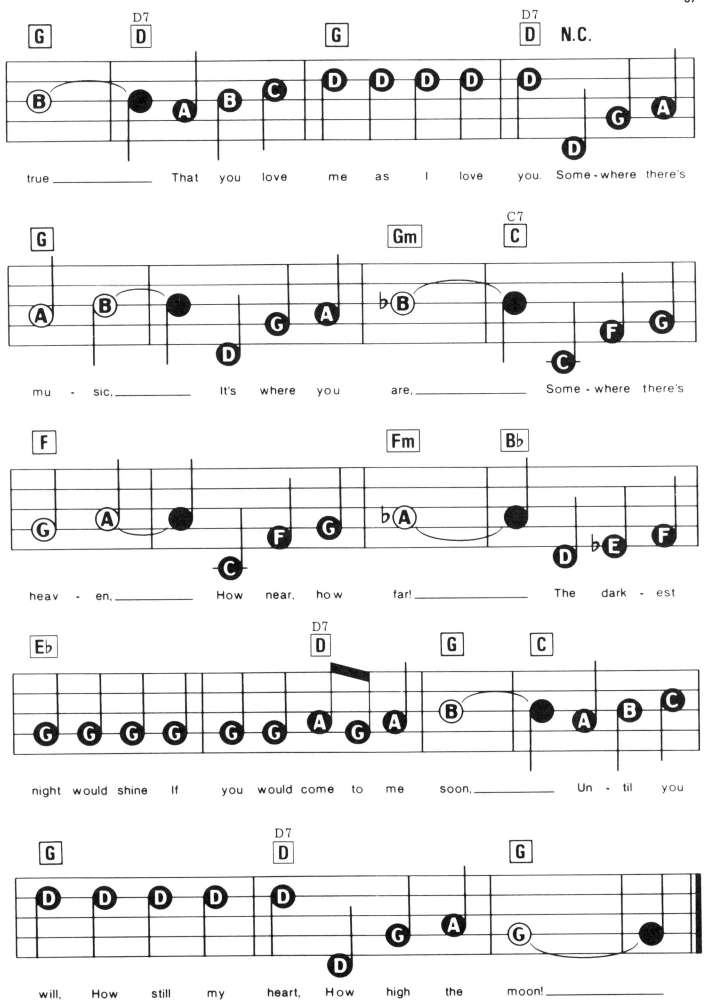

I Could Write a Book
from PAL JOEY

Registration 7
Rhythm: Fox Trot or Swing

Words by Lorenz Hart
Music by Richard Rodgers

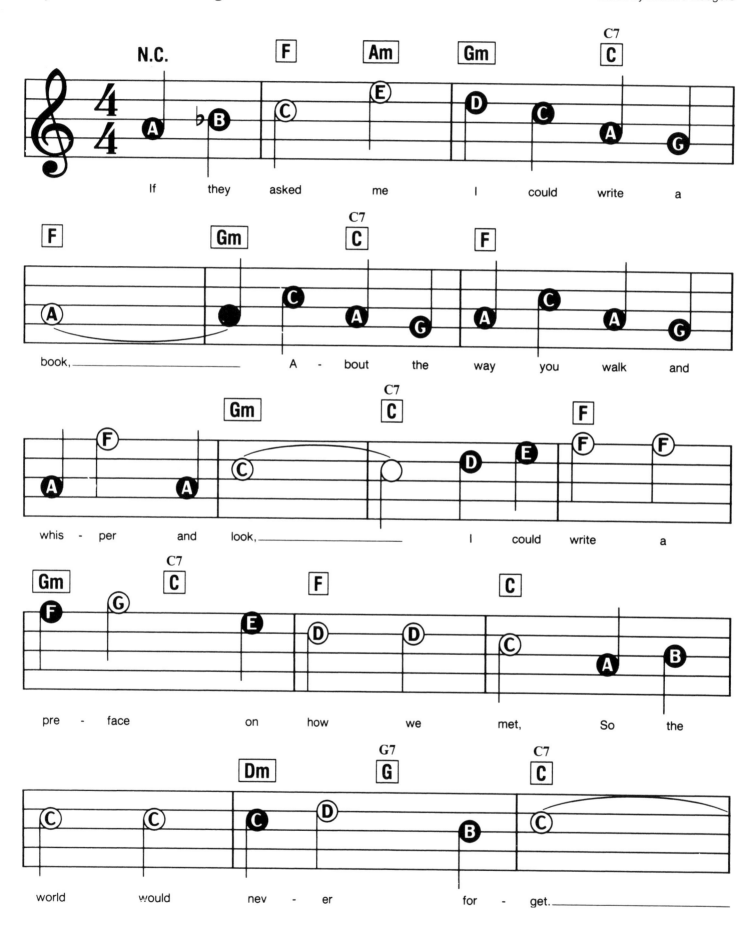

89

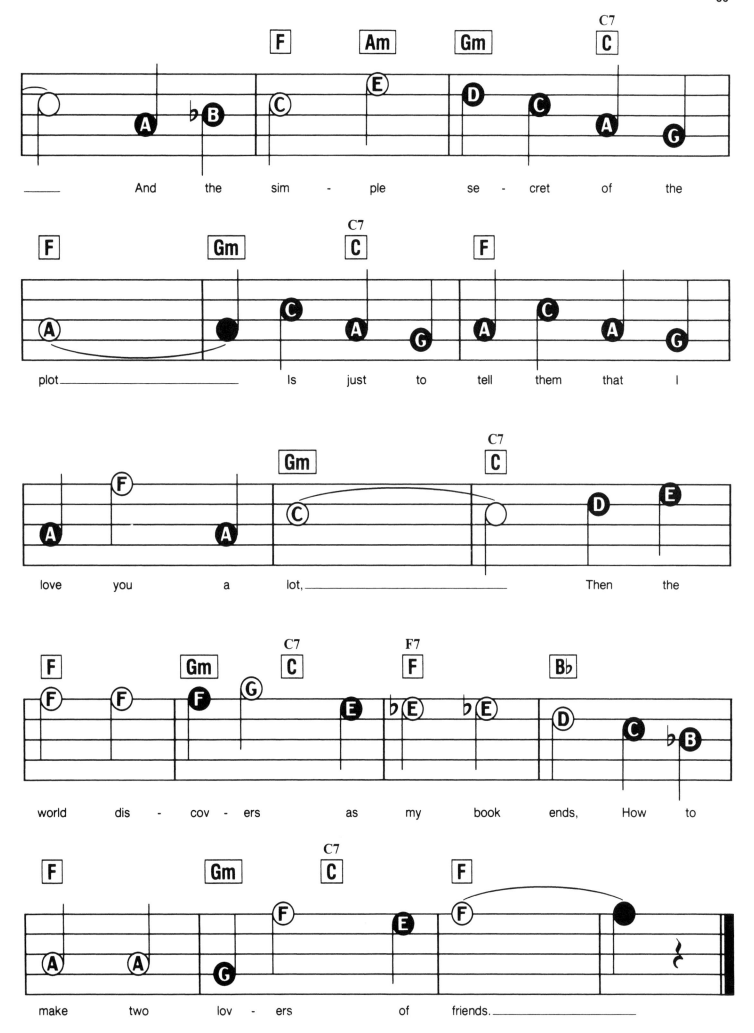

I Don't Want to Walk Without You
from the Paramount Picture SWEATER GIRL

Registration 1
Rhythm: Swing

Words by Frank Loesser
Music by Jule Styne

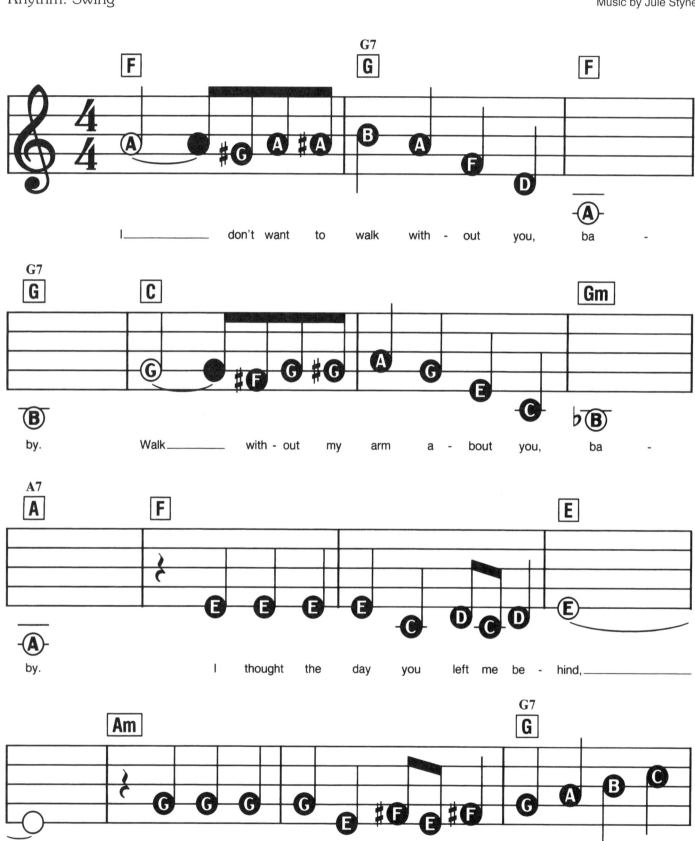

91

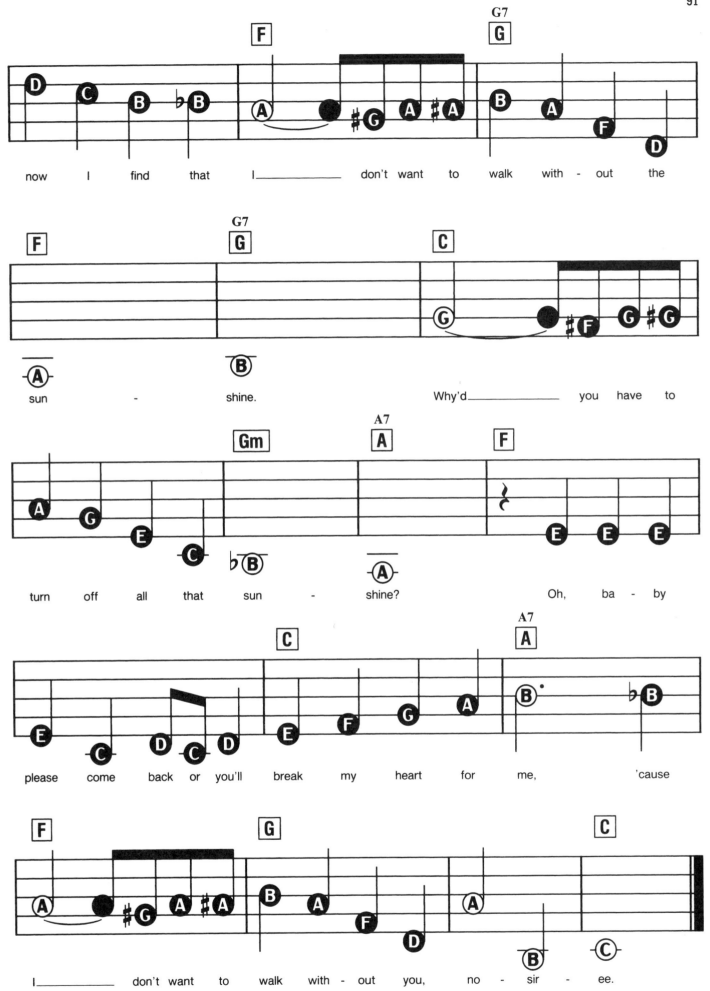

I Left My Heart in San Francisco

Registration 9
Rhythm: Fox Trot

Words by Douglass Cross
Music by George Cory

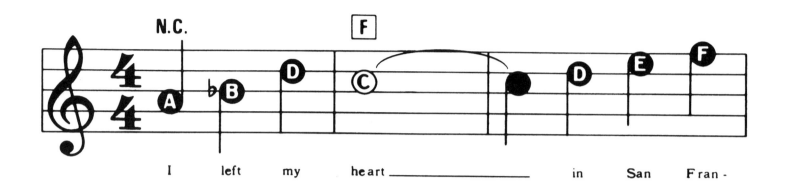

I left my heart _____ in San Fran -

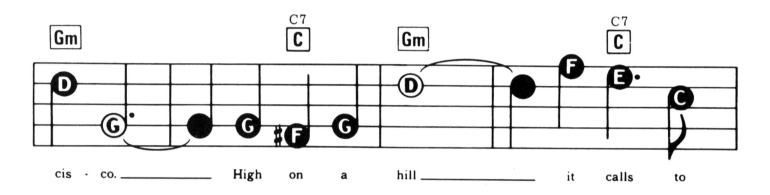

cis - co. _____ High on a hill _____ it calls to

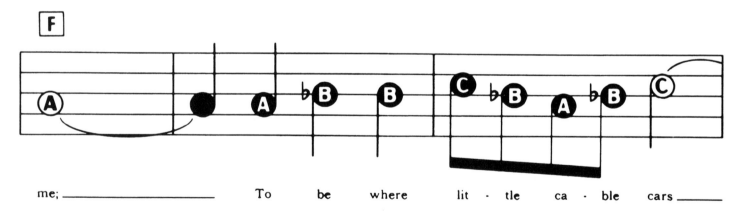

me; _____ To be where lit - tle ca - ble cars _____

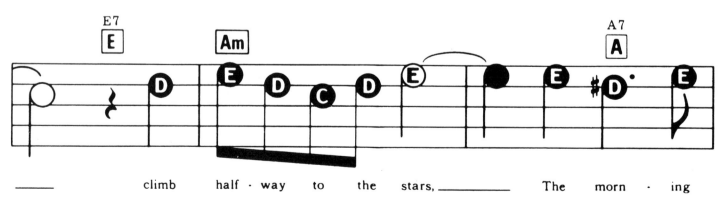

_____ climb half · way to the stars, _____ The morn - ing

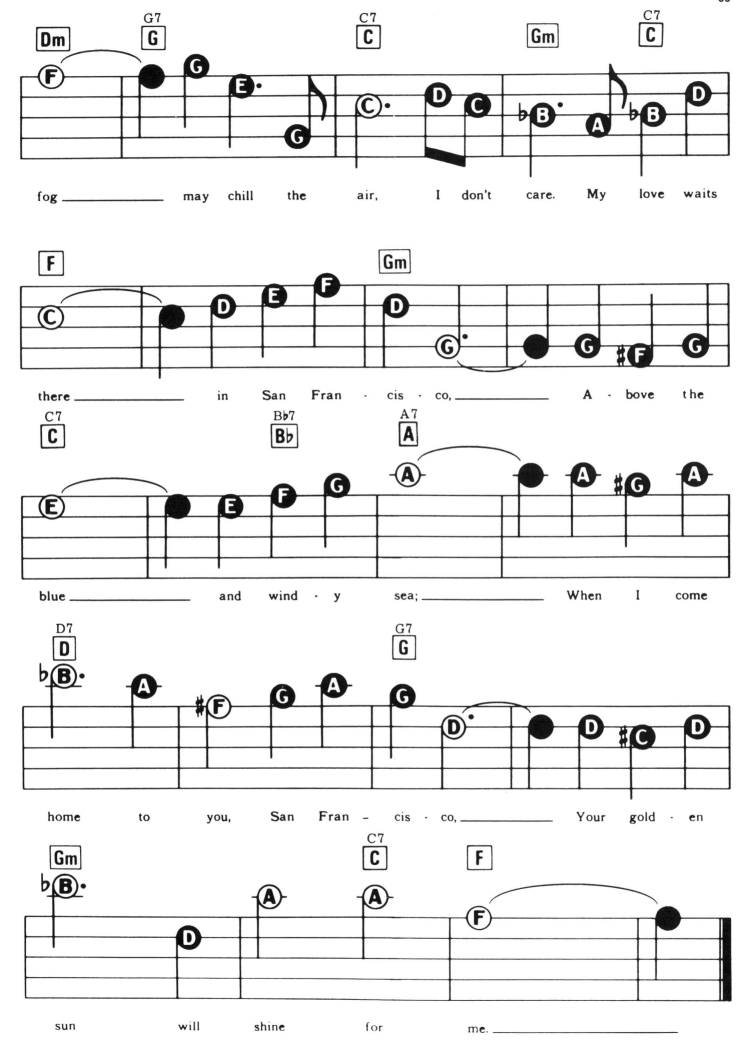

I Love Being Here with You

Registration 7
Rhythm: Swing

Words and Music by Peggy Lee
and Bill Schluger

N.C.

F

C D F
F D C A

I love the east   I love the
dance   by Fred A -

F7   B♭   B♭7

F C D F   F D F G ♭A C

west   and   north   or   south   they're   both   the   best,   but
staire   and   Bran - do's   eyes   they're   Yul   Bryn - ner's   hair,   but

F   E♭7   E♭   D7   D   G7   G   C7   C

A A #G A #G A ♭B   C ♯C D   ♭A G F G F

I'll   on - ly   go   there   as   a   guest   'cause   I   love   be - ing   here   with
I   think   to   tell   you's   on - ly   fair   that   I   love   be - ing   here   with

F   C7   C   F   F7

F C D F   F D C A   F C D F

you.   I   love   the   sea   I   love   the   shore   I   love   the
you.   And   Ca - ry   Grant   oh   do - dah - day   his   ut - ter

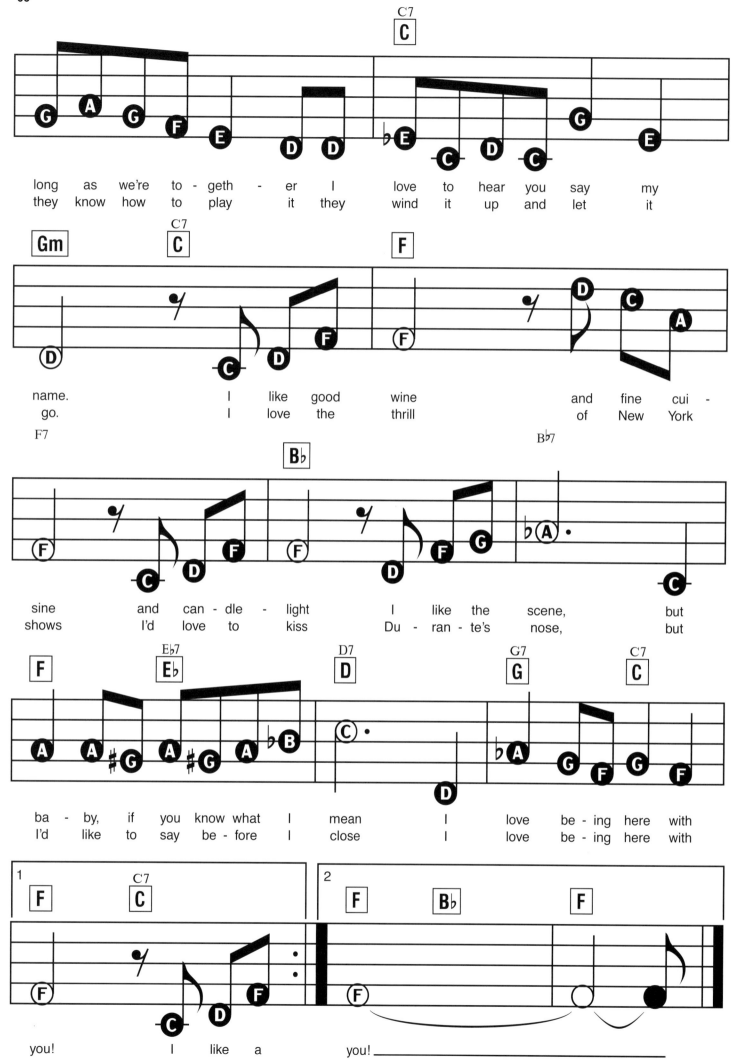

I Wanna Be Loved

Registration 2
Rhythm: Fox Trot or Swing

Words by Billy Rose and Edward Heyman
Music by John Green

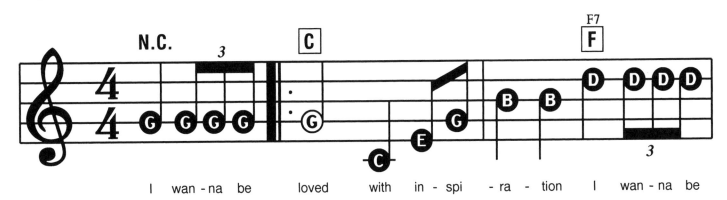

I wan-na be loved with in-spi-ra-tion I wan-na be

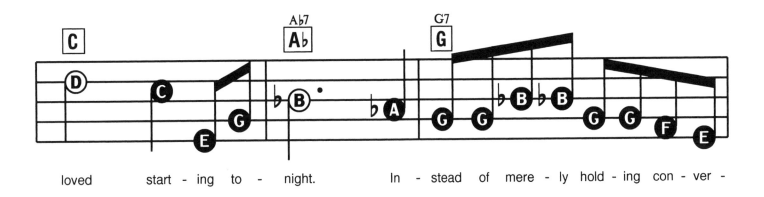

loved start-ing to - night. In - stead of mere - ly hold-ing con-ver-

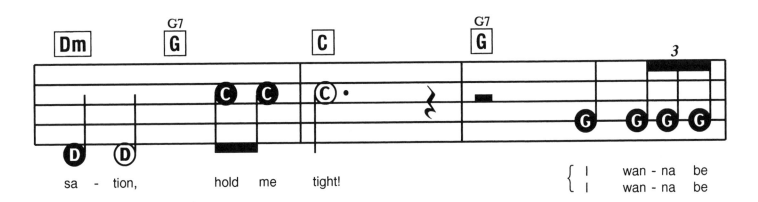

sa - tion, hold me tight! I wan-na be / I wan-na be

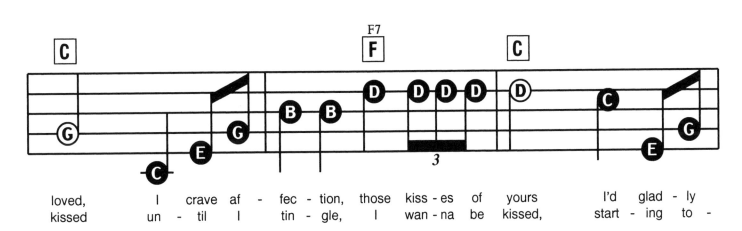

loved, I crave af-fec-tion, those kiss-es of yours I'd glad-ly
kissed un - til I tin-gle, I wan-na be kissed, start-ing to -

I Should Care

Registration 3
Rhythm: Swing

Words by Sammy Cahn and Paul Weston
Music by Alex Stordahl and Paul Weston

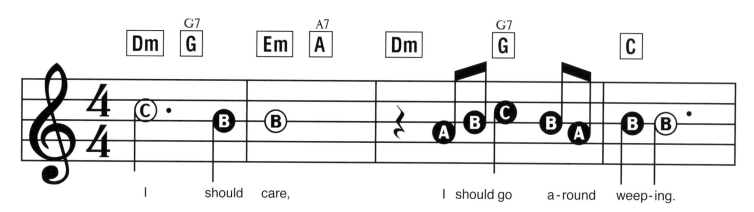

I should care, I should go a-round weep-ing.

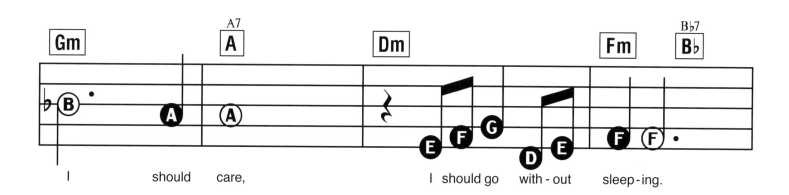

I should care, I should go with-out sleep-ing.

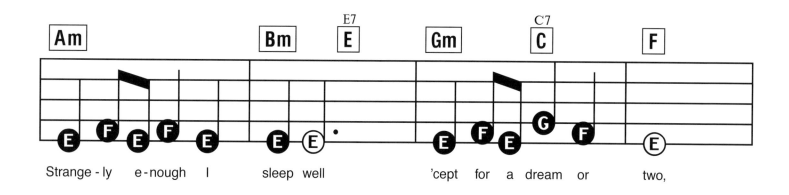

Strange-ly e-nough I sleep well 'cept for a dream or two,

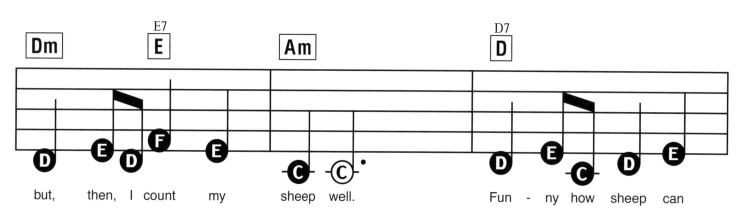

but, then, I count my sheep well. Fun-ny how sheep can

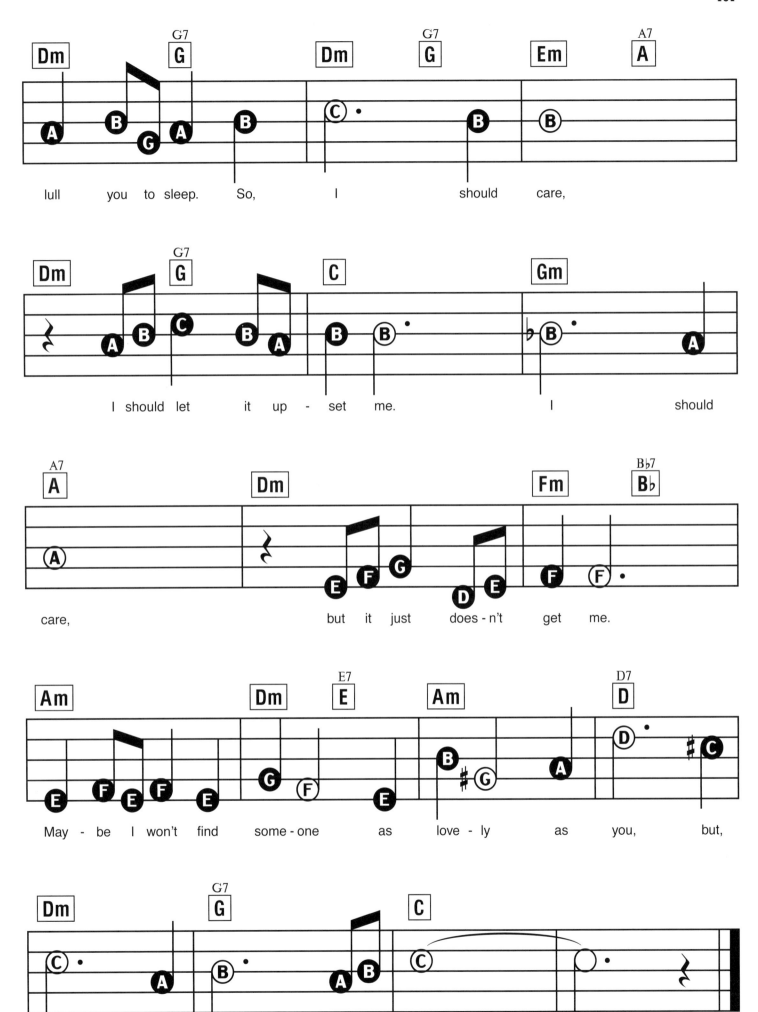

I Wish You Love

Registration 8
Rhythm: Latin

English Words by Albert Beach
French Words and Music by Charles Trenet

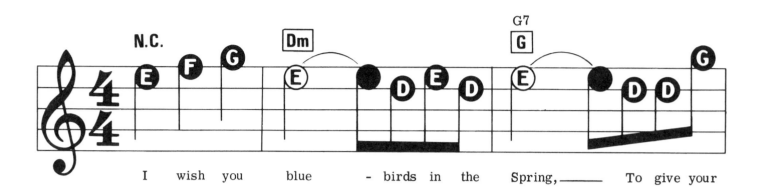

I wish you blue - birds in the Spring, _____ To give your

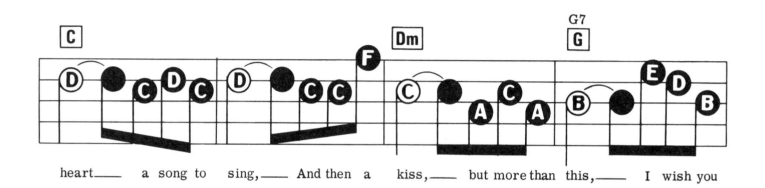

heart_____ a song to sing,_____ And then a kiss,_____ but more than this,_____ I wish you

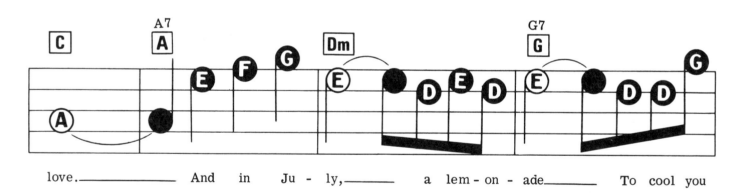

love._____ And in Ju - ly,_____ a lem - on - ade_____ To cool you

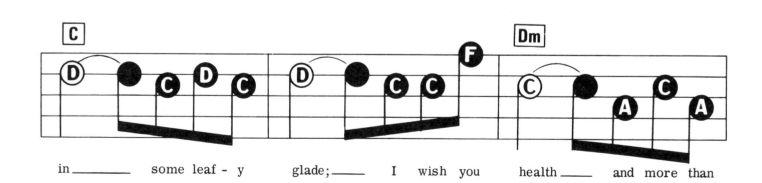

in _____ some leaf - y glade;_____ I wish you health _____ and more than

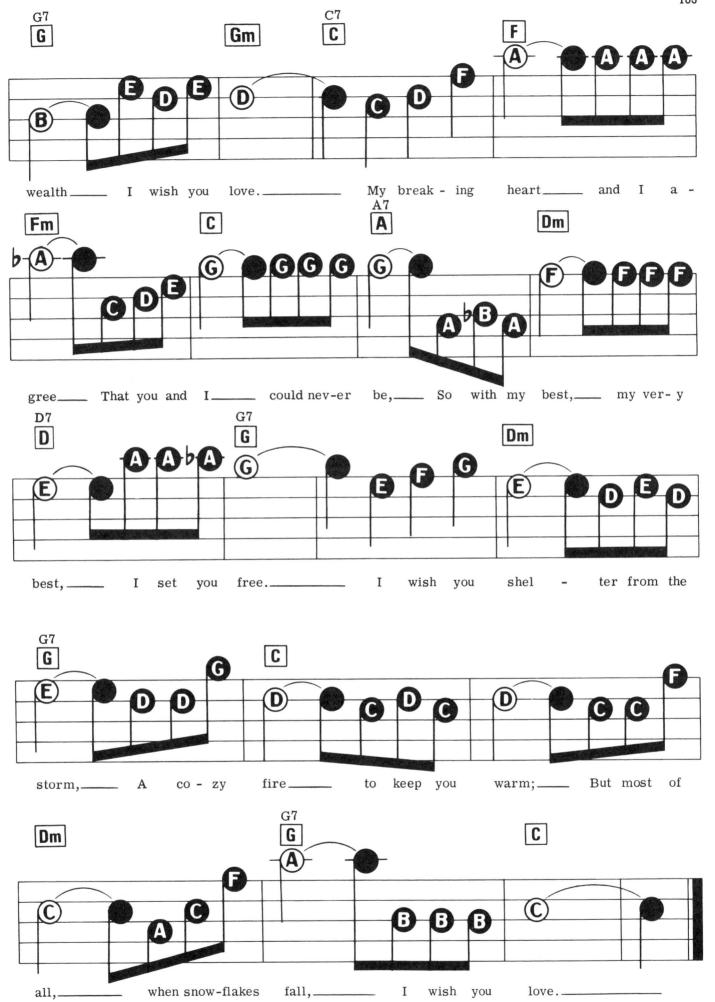

I'll Take Romance

Registration 3
Rhythm: Waltz

Lyrics by Oscar Hammerstein II
Music by Ben Oakland

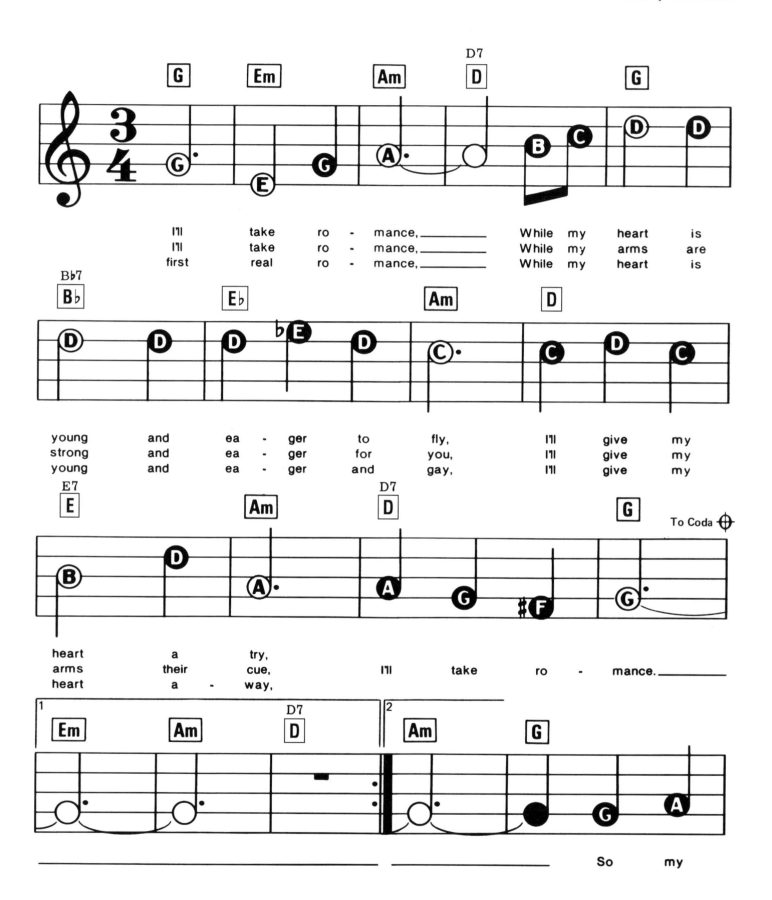

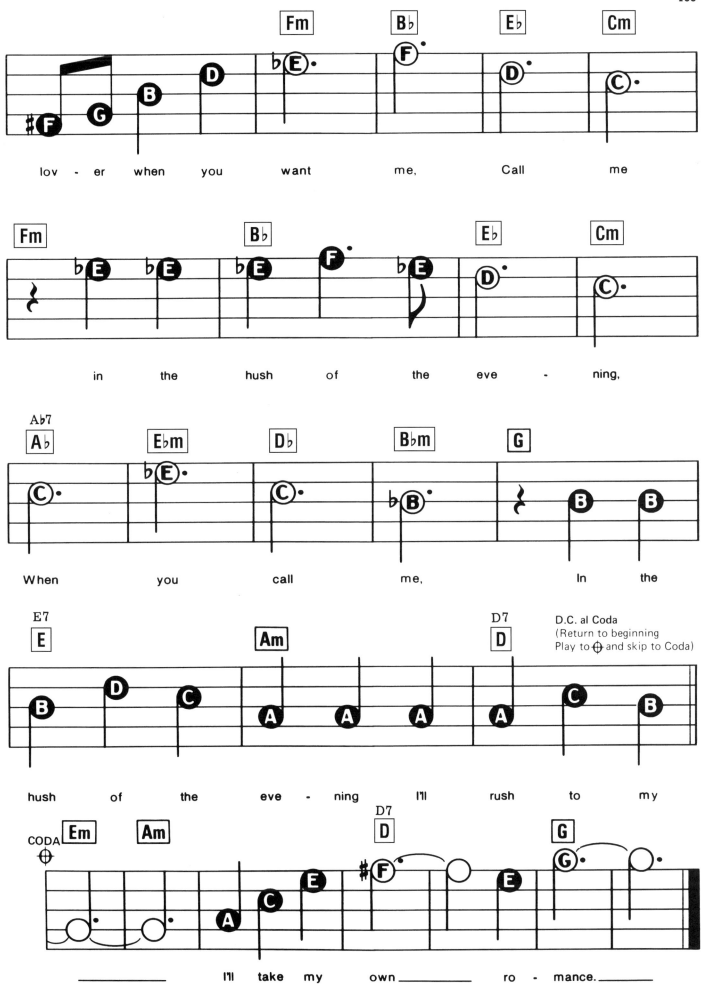

I'll Walk Alone
from WITH A SONG IN MY HEART

Registration 1
Rhythm: Ballad or Swing

Lyric by Sammy Cahn
Music by Jule Styne

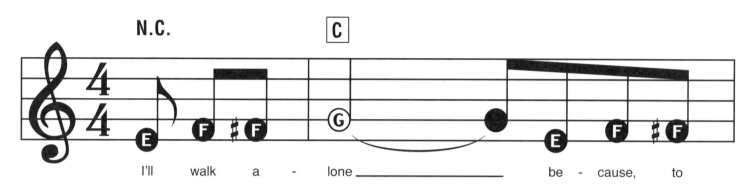

I'll walk a - lone _____ be - cause, to

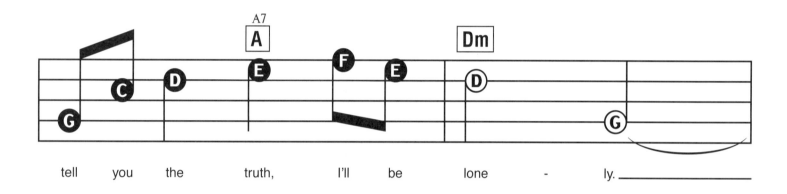

tell you the truth, I'll be lone - ly. _____

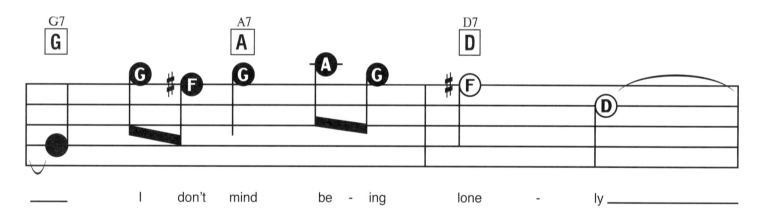

_____ I don't mind be - ing lone - ly _____

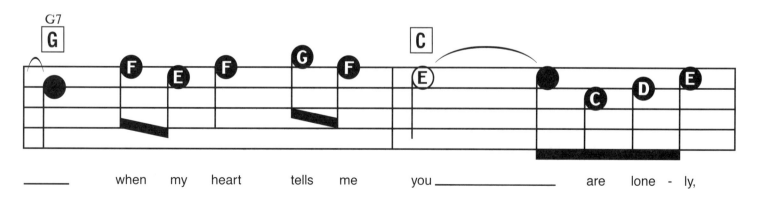

_____ when my heart tells me you _____ are lone - ly,

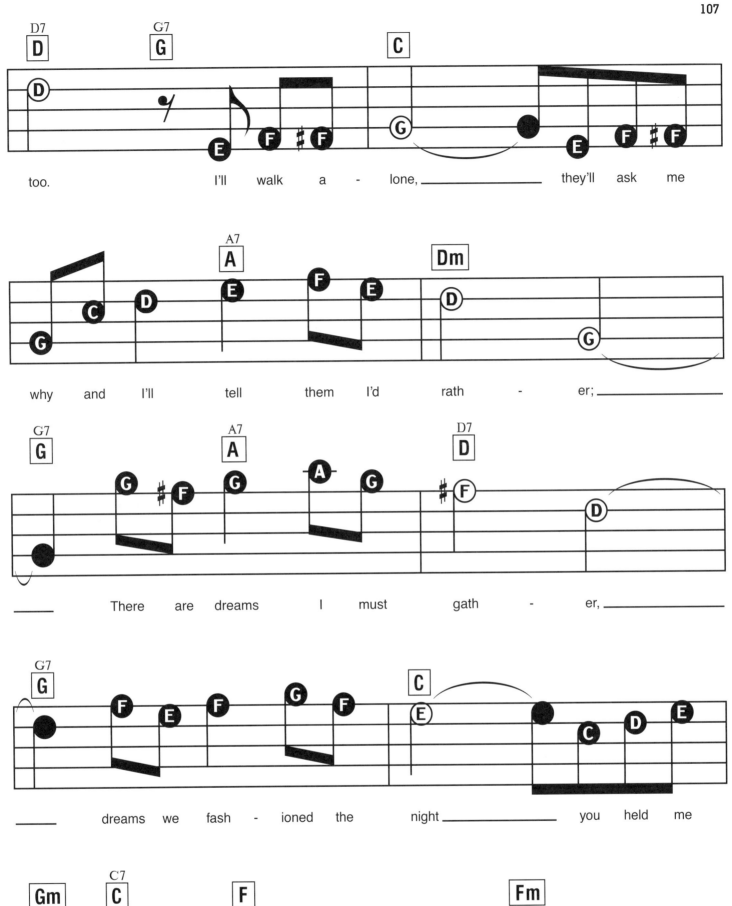

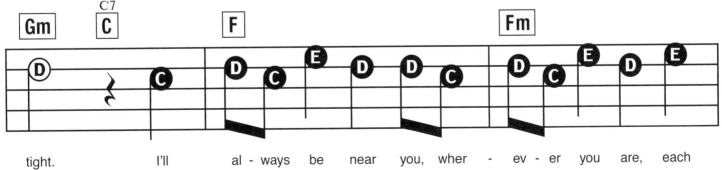

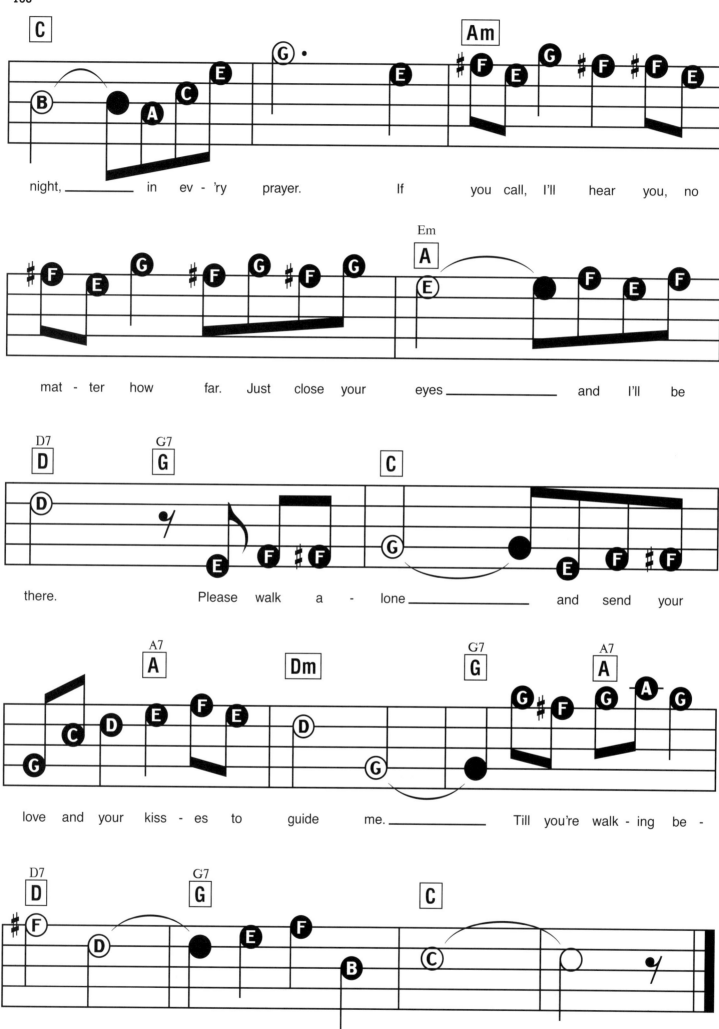

The Impossible Dream
(The Quest)
from MAN OF LA MANCHA

Registration 3
Rhythm: Waltz

Lyric by Joe Darion
Music by Mitch Leigh

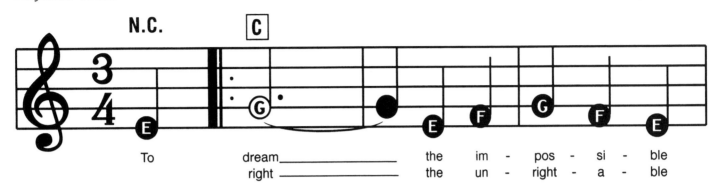

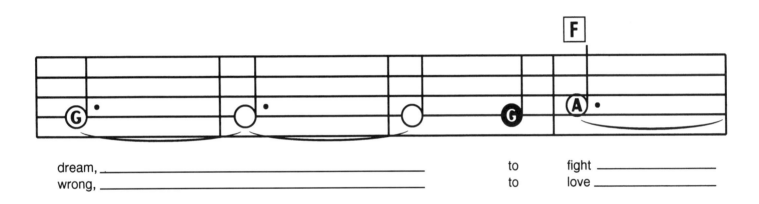

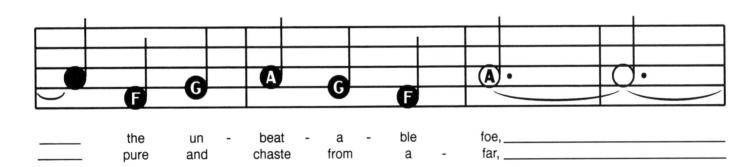

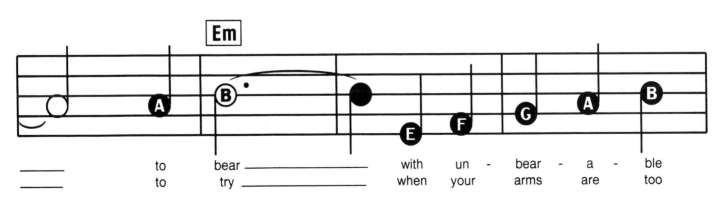

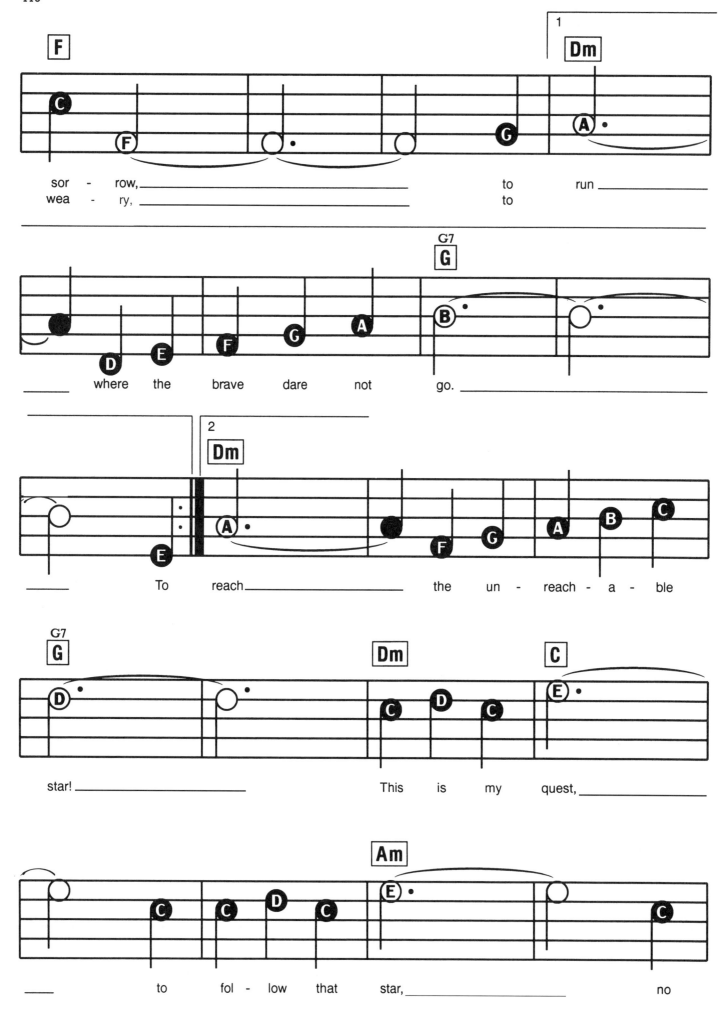

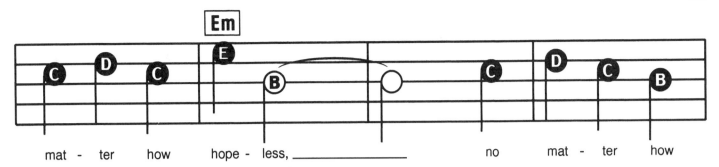

mat - ter how hope - less, _____ no mat - ter how

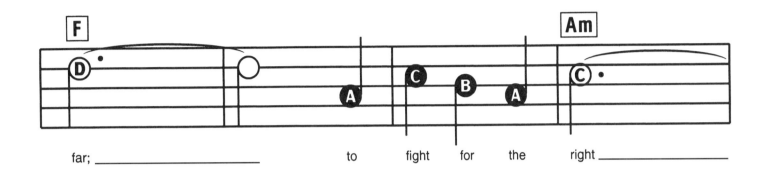

far; _____ to fight for the right _____

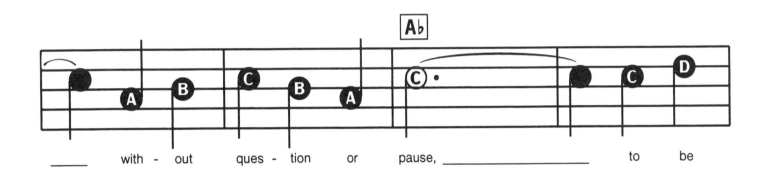

_____ with - out ques - tion or pause, _____ to be

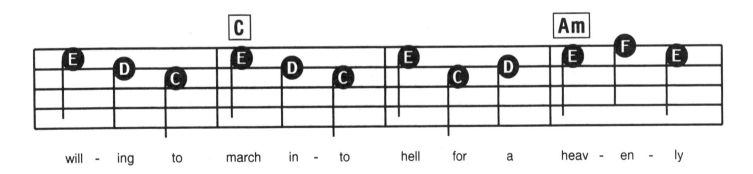

will - ing to march in - to hell for a heav - en - ly

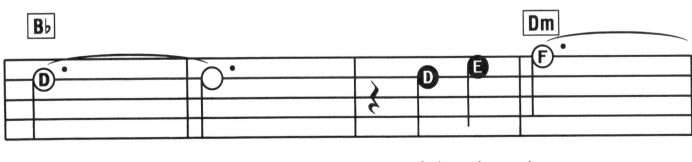

cause! _____ And I know, _____

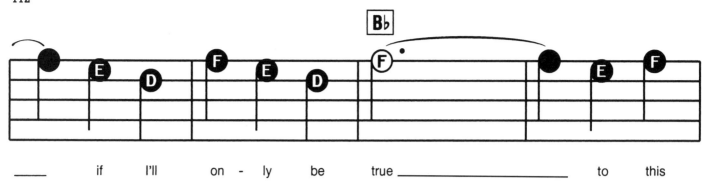

_____ if I'll on - ly be true _____ to this

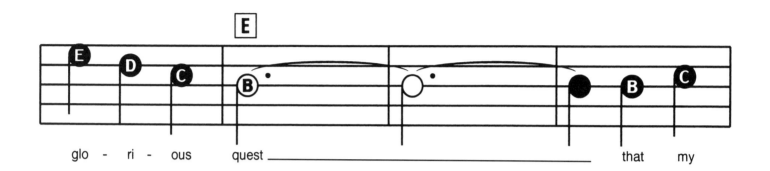

glo - ri - ous quest _____ that my

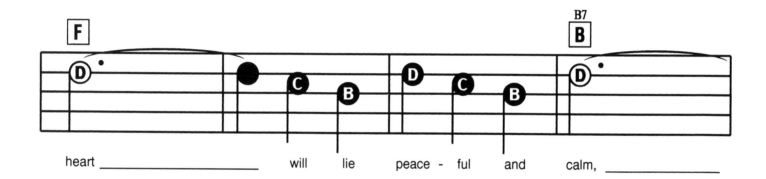

heart _____ will lie peace - ful and calm, _____

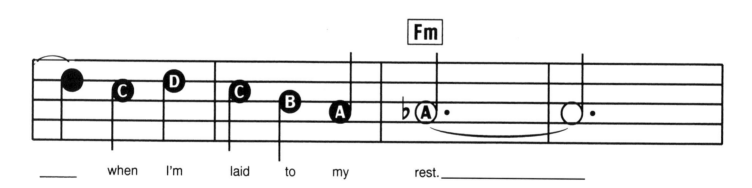

_____ when I'm laid to my rest. _____

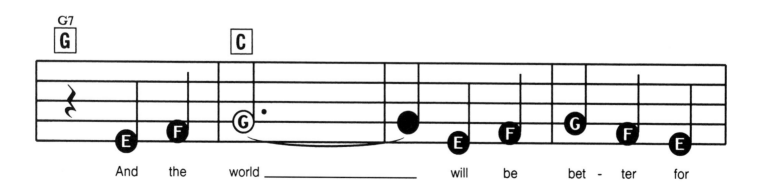

And the world _____ will be bet - ter for

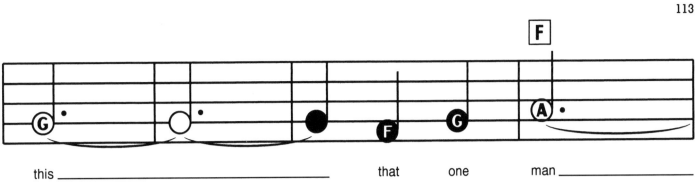

this _____ that one man _____

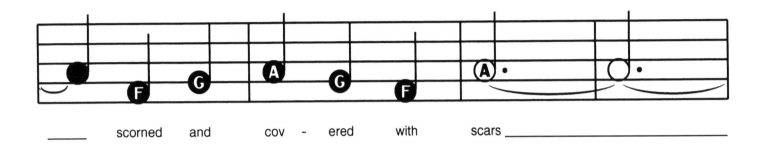

____ scorned and cov - ered with scars _____

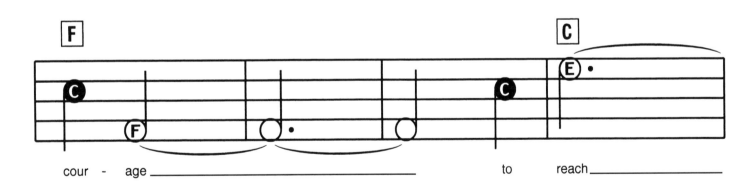

____ still ____ strove _____ with his last ounce of

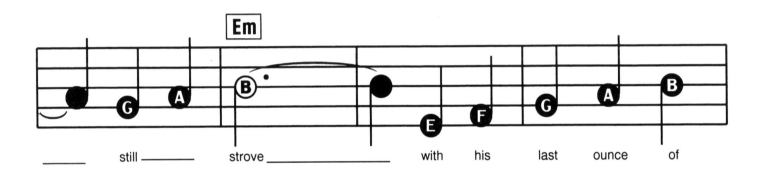

cour - age _____ to reach _____

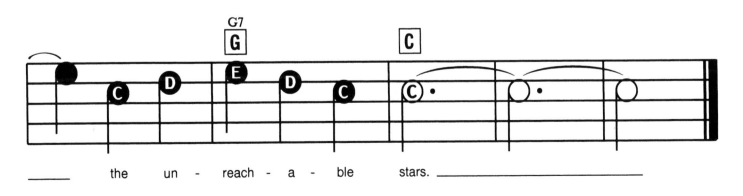

____ the un - reach - a - ble stars. _____

I'm Old Fashioned
from YOU WERE NEVER LOVELIER

Registration 5
Rhythm: Fox Trot or Ballad

Lyrics by Johnny Mercer
Music by Jerome Kern

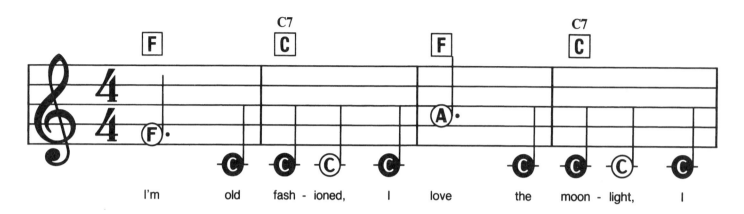

I'm old fash - ioned, I love the moon - light, I

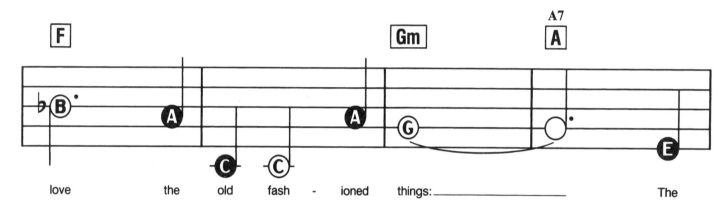

love the old fash - ioned things:_____ The

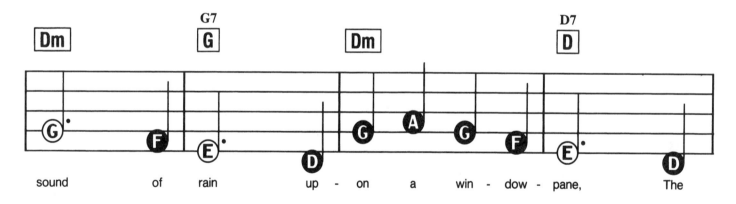

sound of rain up - on a win - dow - pane, The

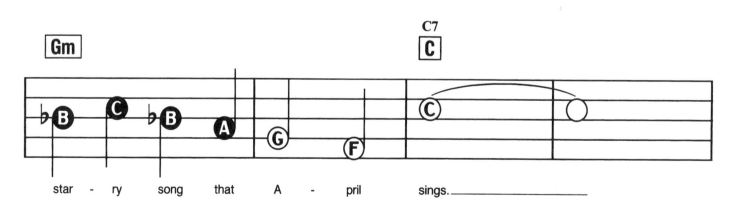

star - ry song that A - pril sings._____

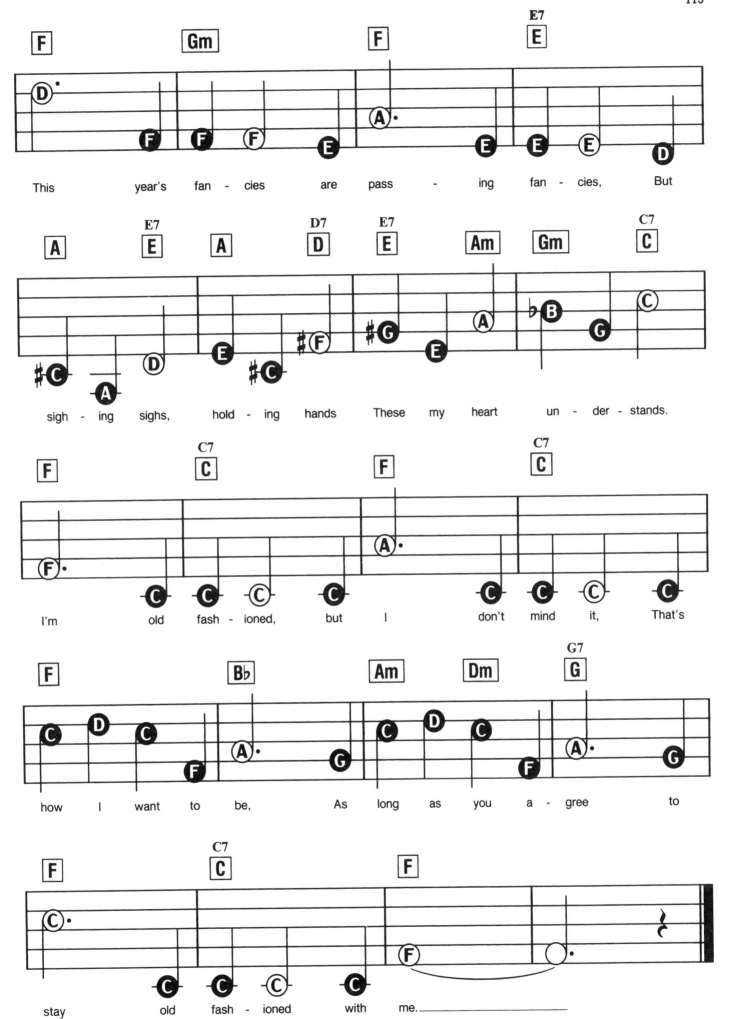

I've Got My Love to Keep Me Warm
from the 20th Century Fox Motion Picture ON THE AVENUE

Registration 4
Rhythm: Fox Trot or Swing

Words and Music by
Irving Berlin

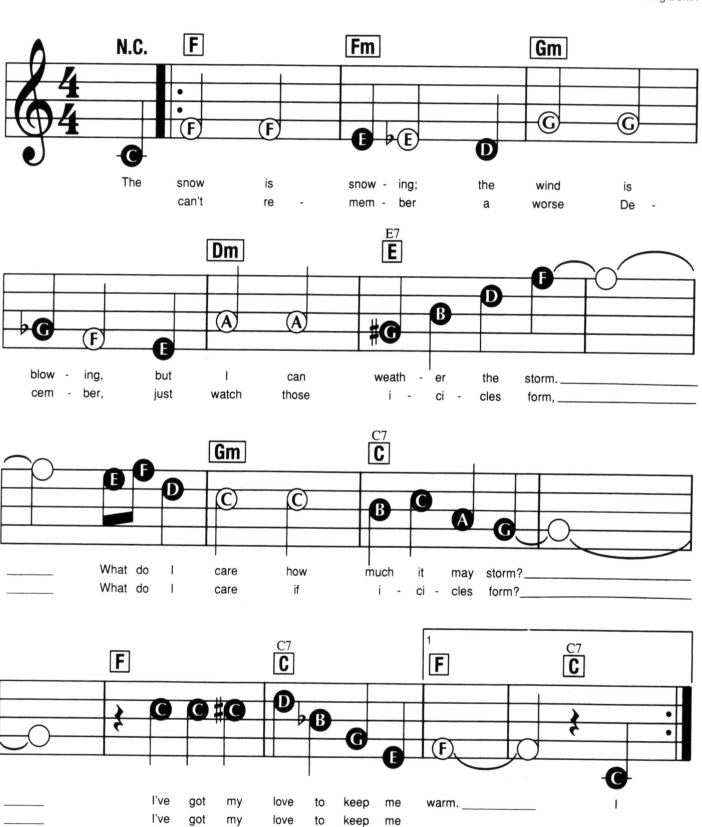

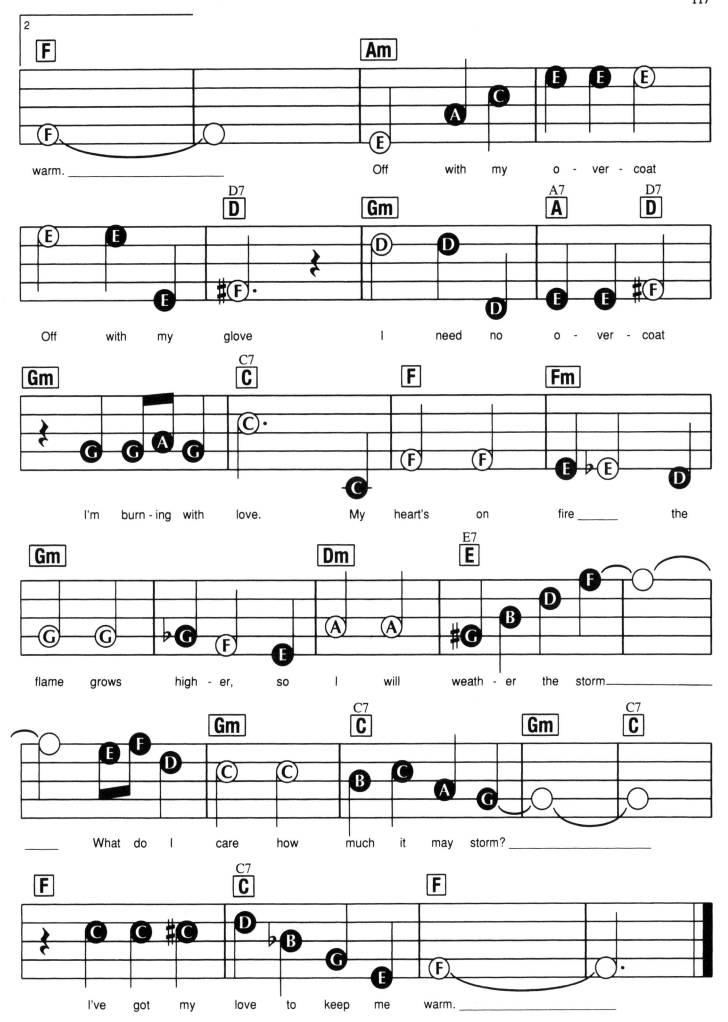

If

Registration 9
Rhythm: Waltz

Words by Robert Hargreaves and Stanley J. Damerell
Music by Tolchard Evans

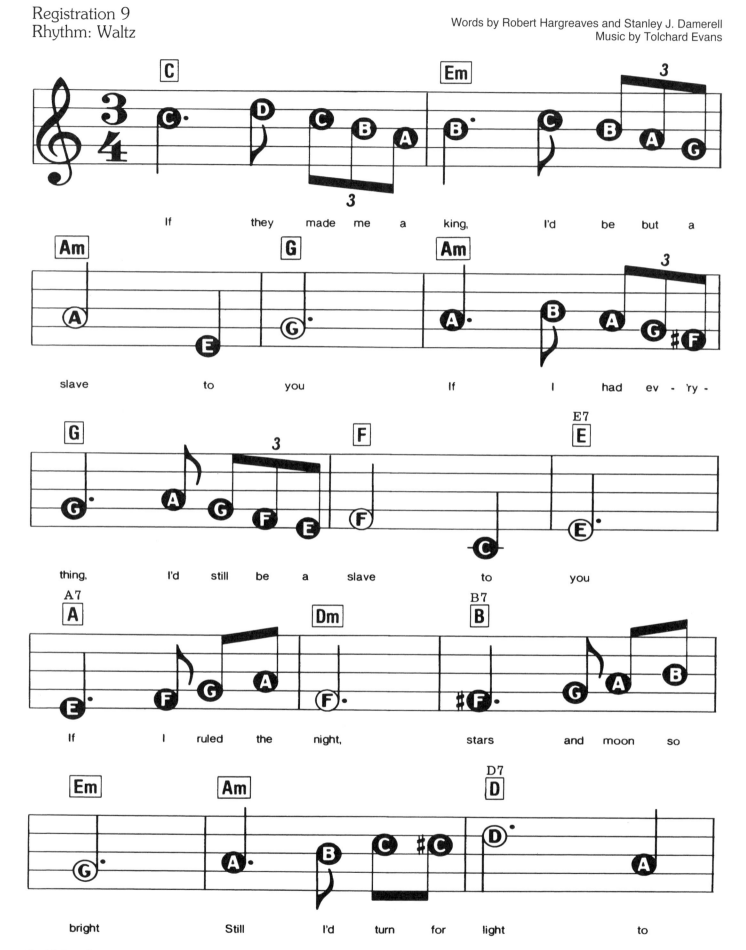

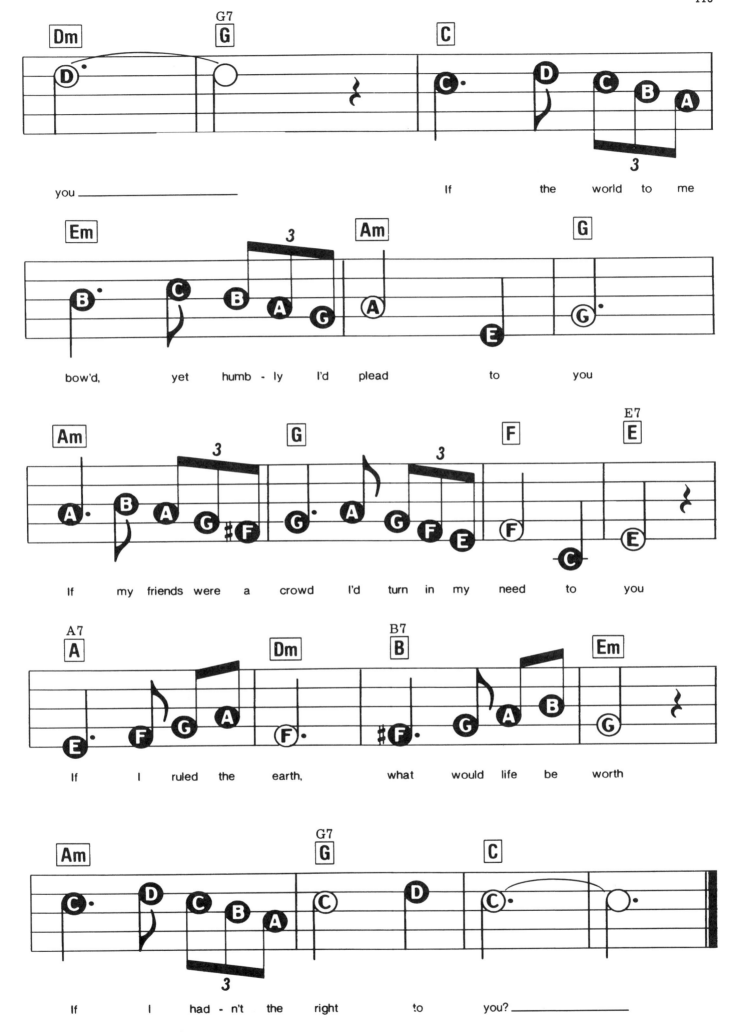

In the Wee Small Hours
of the Morning

Registration 2
Rhythm: Ballad

Words by Bob Hilliard
Music by David Mann

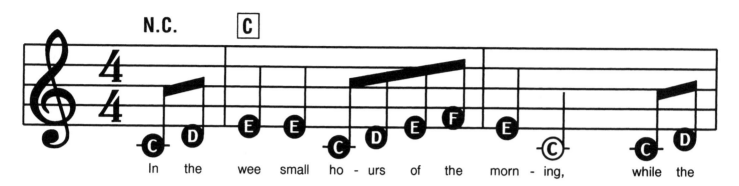

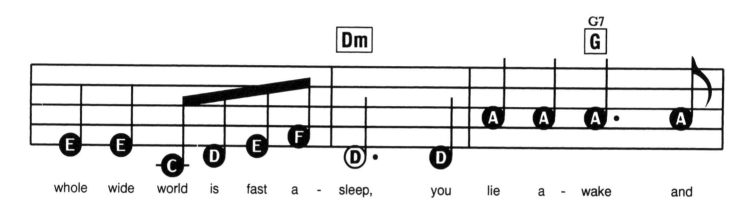

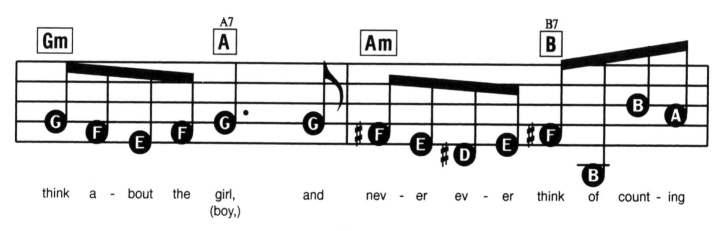

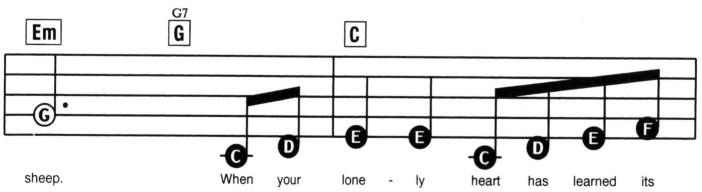

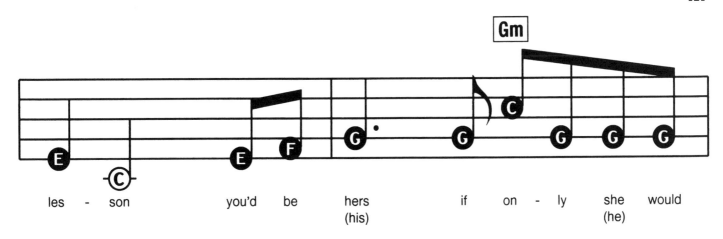

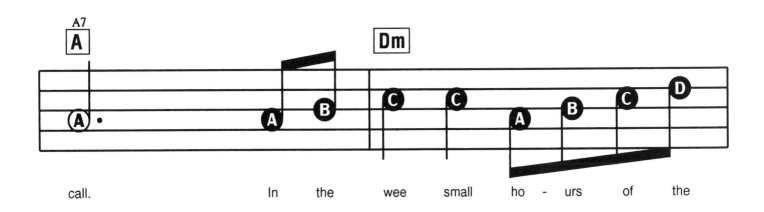

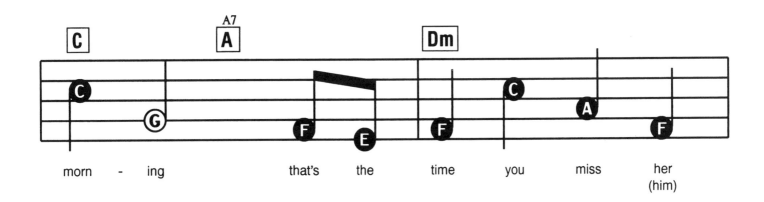

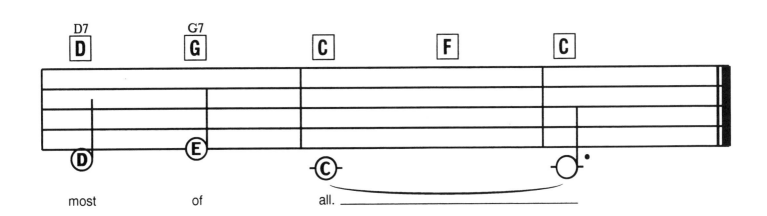

It's a Most Unusual Day
from A DATE WITH JUDY

Registration 7
Rhythm: Waltz

Words by Harold Adamson
Music by Jimmy McHugh

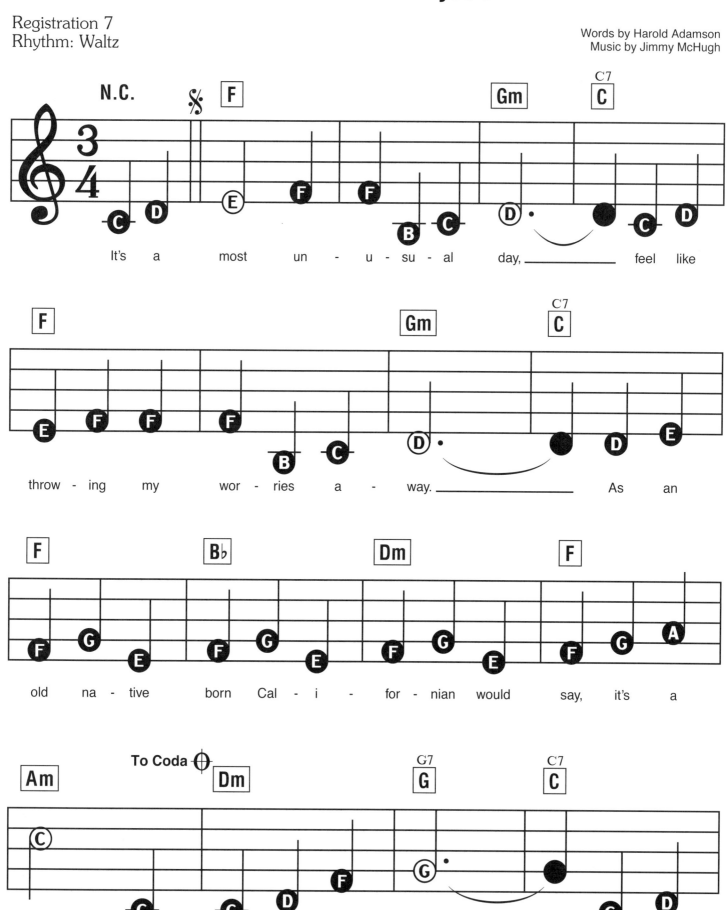

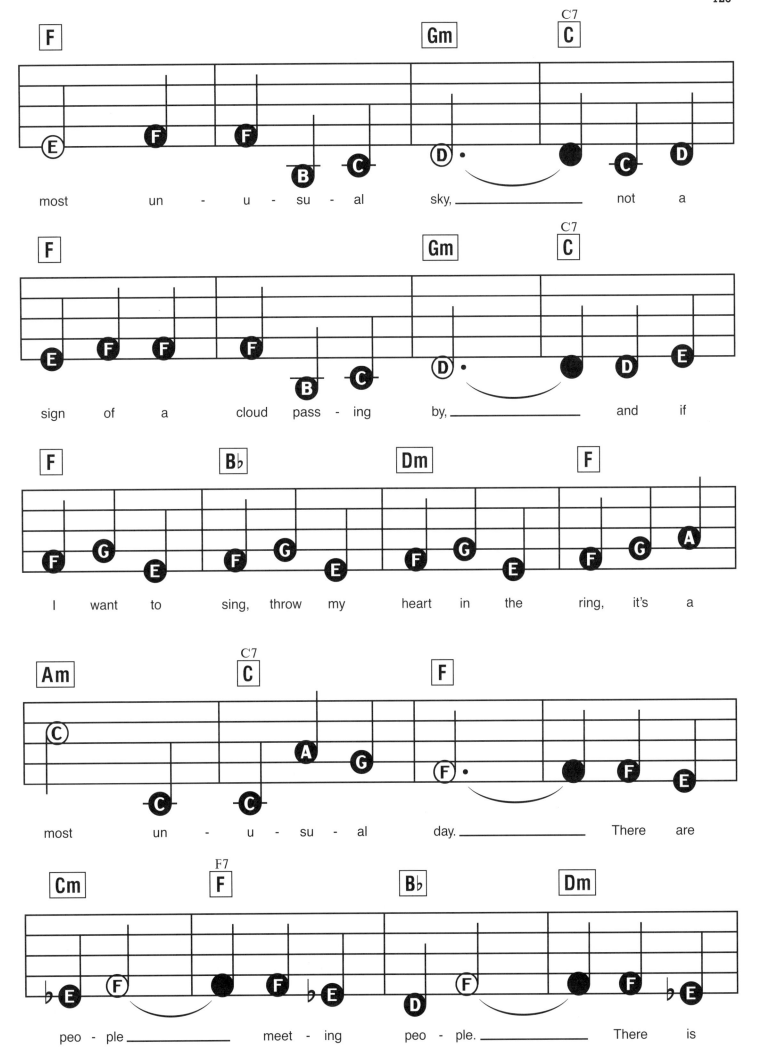

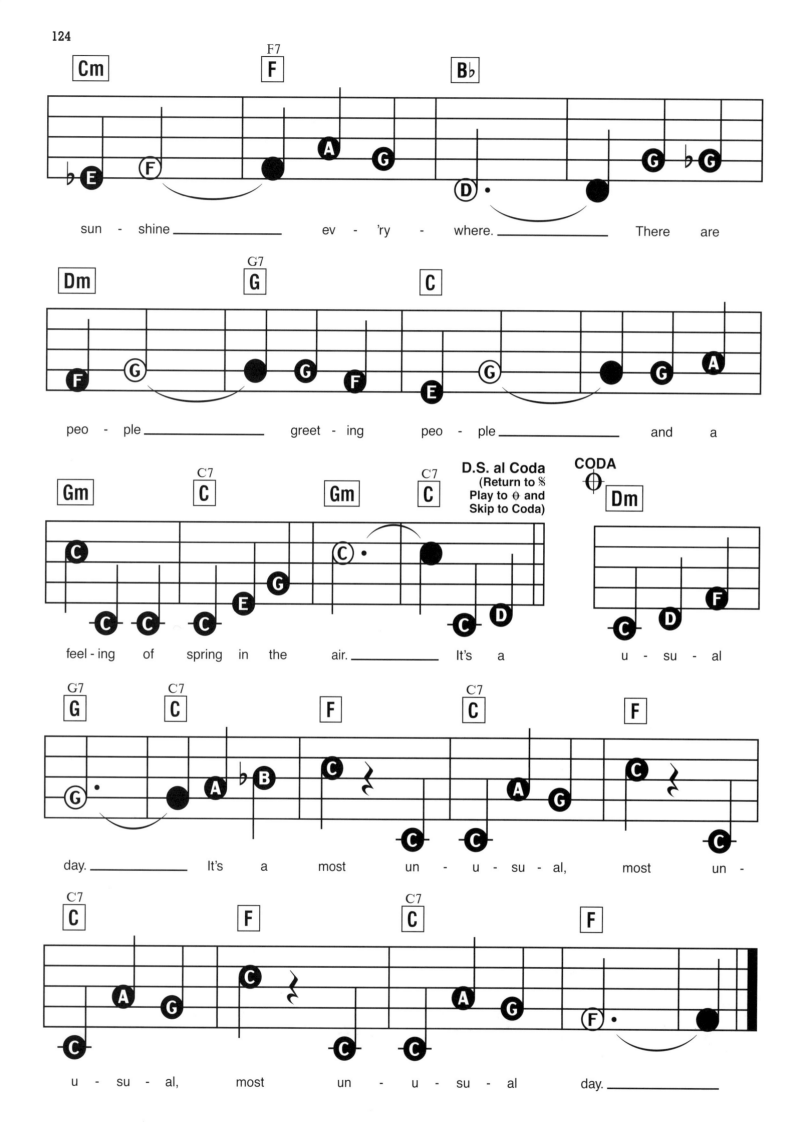

It's Impossible
(Somos novios)

Registration 4
Rhythm: Rhumba or Latin

English Lyric by Sid Wayne
Spanish Words and Music by
Armando Manzanero

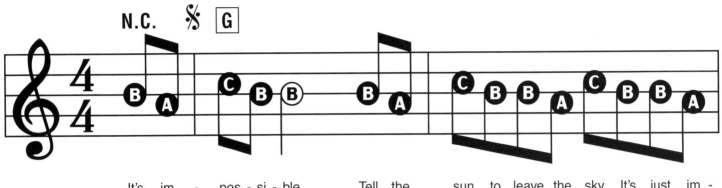

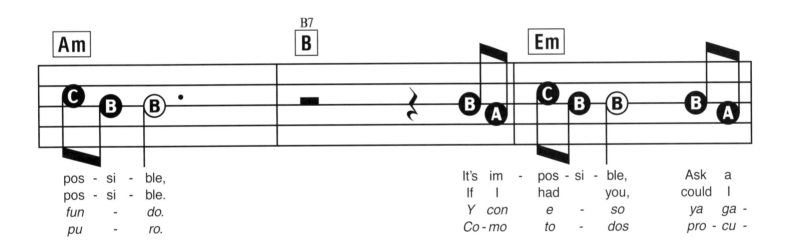

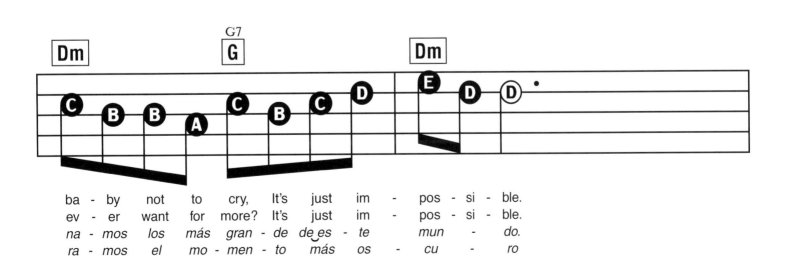

126

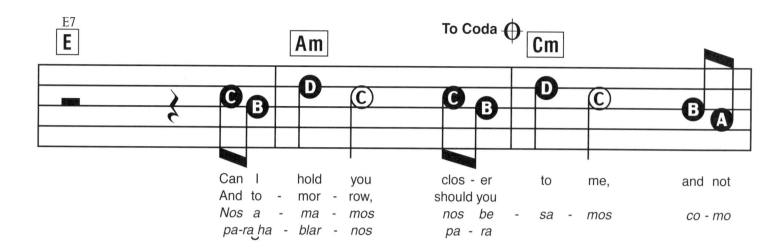

Can I hold you clos - er to me, and not
And to - mor - row, should you
Nos a - ma - mos nos be - sa - mos co - mo
pa-ra ha - blar - nos pa - ra

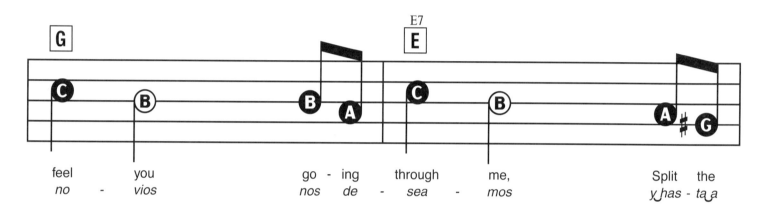

feel you go - ing through me, Split the
no - vios nos de - sea - mos
y has - ta a

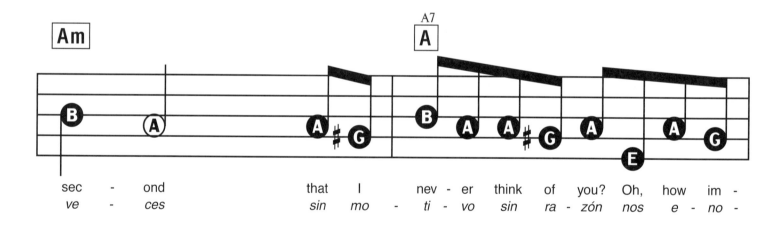

sec - ond that I nev - er think of you? Oh, how im -
ve - ces sin mo - ti - vo sin ra - zón nos e - no -

D.S. al Coda
(Return to 𝄋
Play to ⊕ and
Skip to Coda)

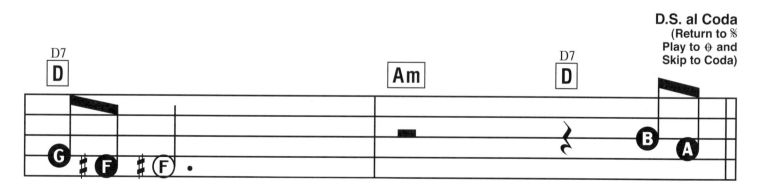

pos - si - ble. Can the
ja - mos. So - mos

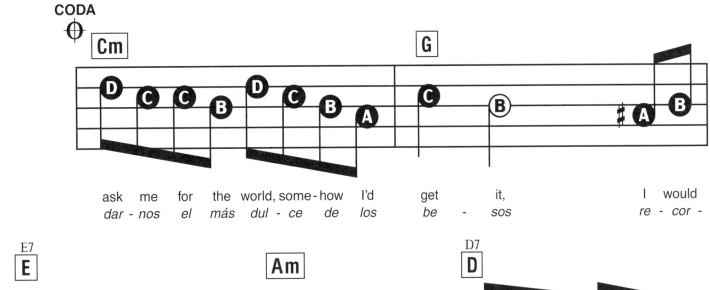

ask me for the world, some-how I'd get it, I would
dar - nos el más dul - ce de los be - sos re - cor -

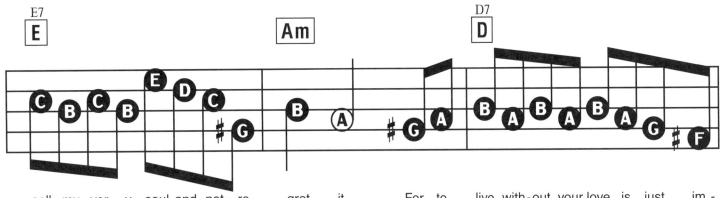

sell my ver - y soul and not re - gret it, For to live with-out your love is just im -
dar de que co - lor son los ce - re - zos sin ha - cer más co - men - ta - rios so - mos

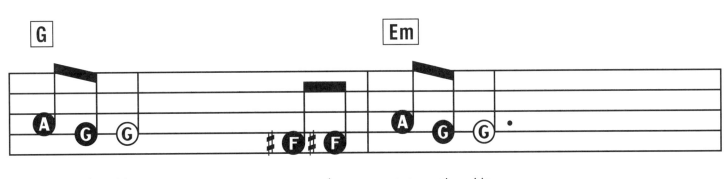

pos - si - ble, im - pos - si - ble.
no - vios so - mos no - vios

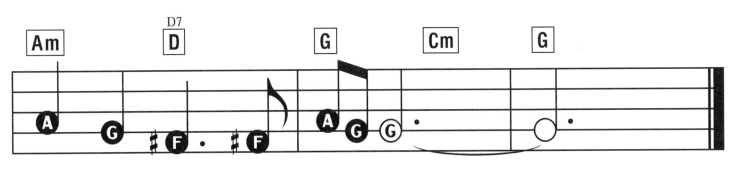

Mm, _____ im - pos - si - ble. _____
siem - pre no - vios. _____

The Lady Is a Tramp
from BABES IN ARMS

Registration 7
Rhythm: Fox Trot or Swing

Words by Lorenz Hart
Music by Richard Rodgers

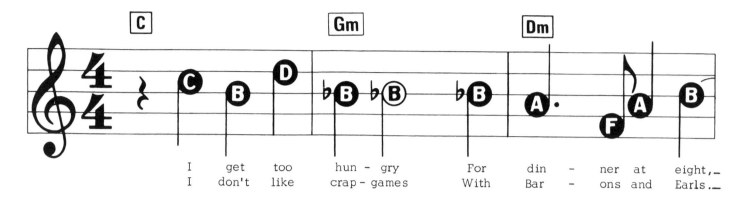

I get too hun - gry For din - ner at eight,
I don't like crap - games With Bar - ons and Earls.

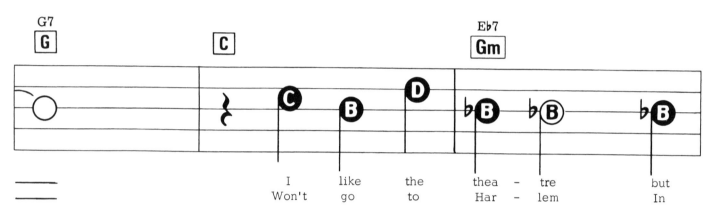

I like the thea - tre but
Won't go to Har - lem In

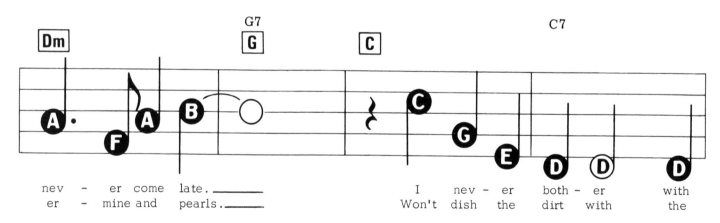

nev - er come late.
er - mine and pearls.

I nev - er both - er with
Won't dish the dirt with the

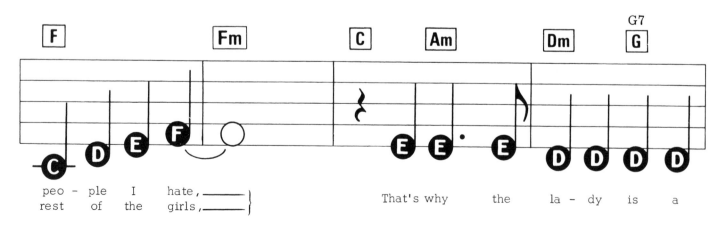

peo - ple I hate,
rest of the girls,

That's why the la - dy is a

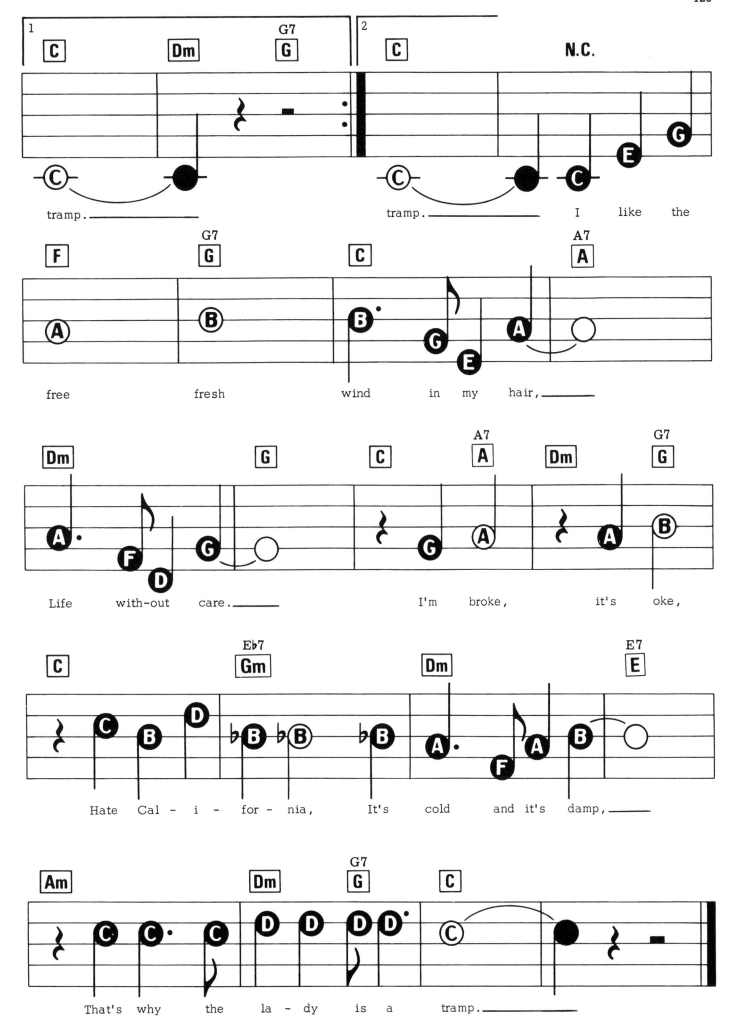

Like Someone in Love

Registration 2
Rhythm: Ballad

Words by Johnny Burke
Music by Jimmy Van Heusen

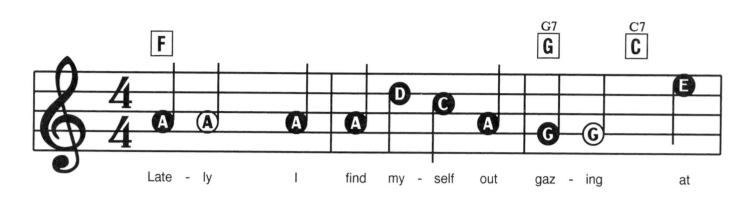

Late - ly   I   find   my - self   out   gaz - ing   at

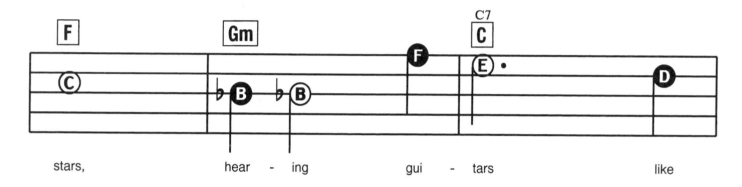

stars,   hear - ing   gui - tars   like

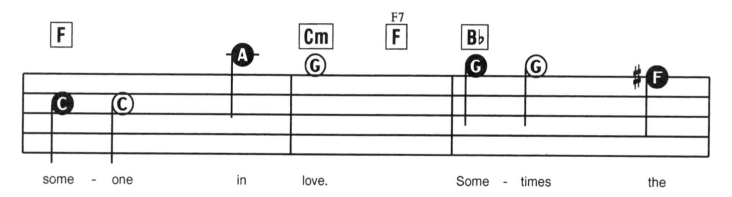

some - one   in   love.   Some - times   the

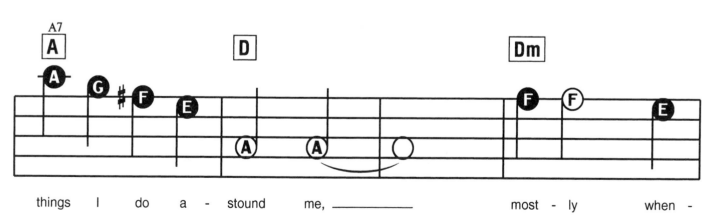

things   I   do   a - stound   me, _____   most - ly   when -

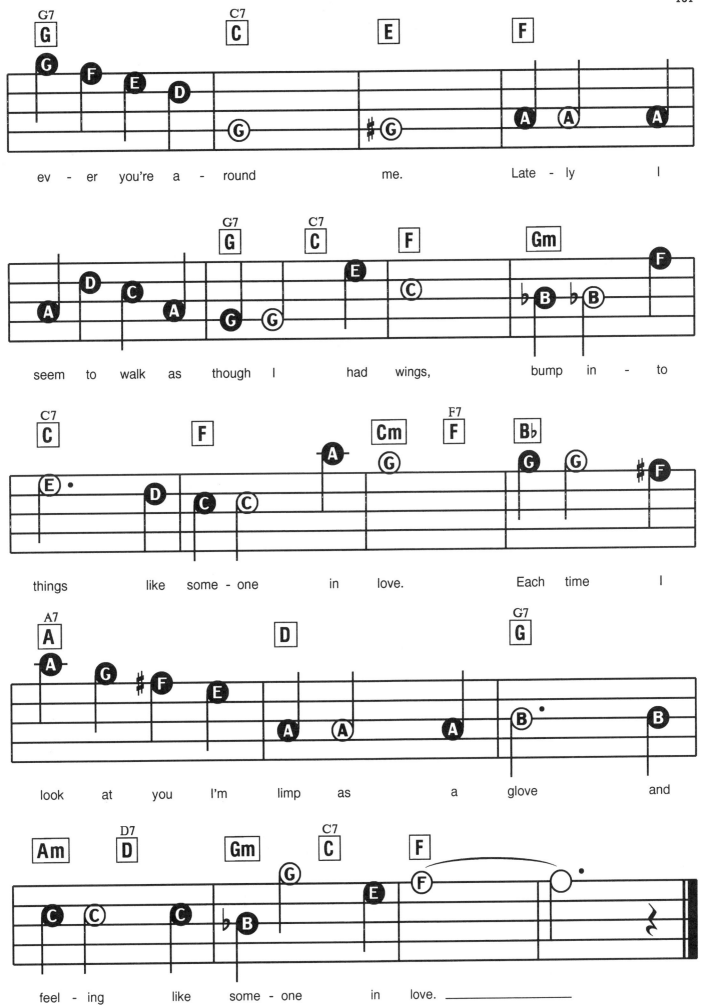

Little White Lies

Registration 2
Rhythm: Fox Trot or Swing

Words and Music by
Walter Donaldson

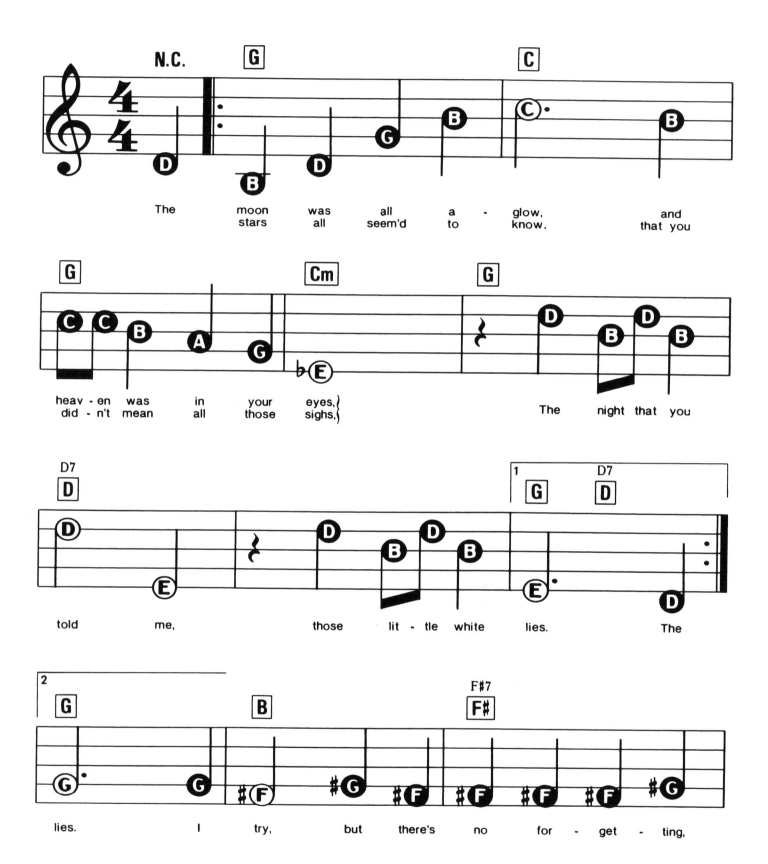

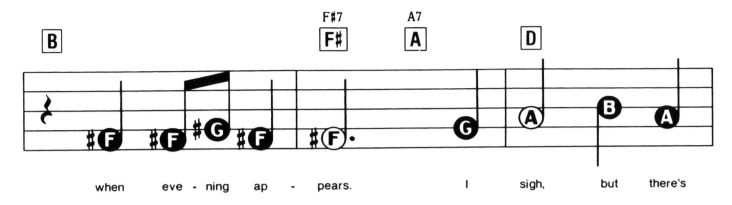

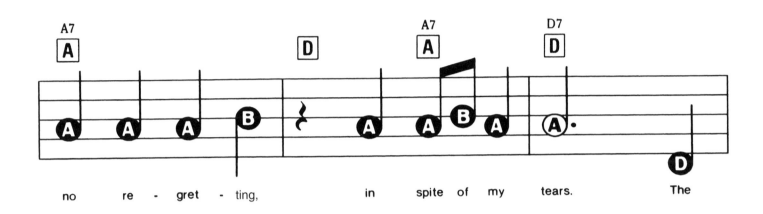

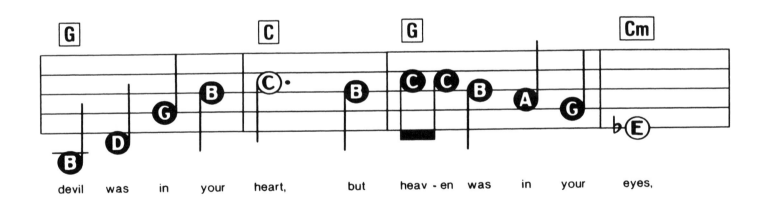

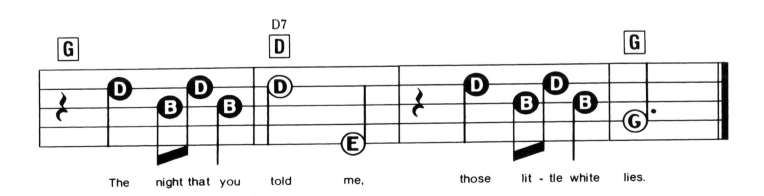

Lover
from the Paramount Picture LOVE ME TONIGHT

Registration 6
Rhythm: Waltz

Words by Lorenz Hart
Music by Richard Rodgers

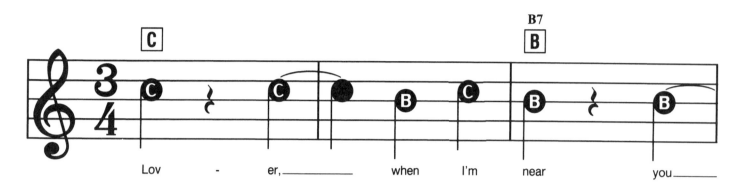

Lov - er,_____ when I'm near you_____

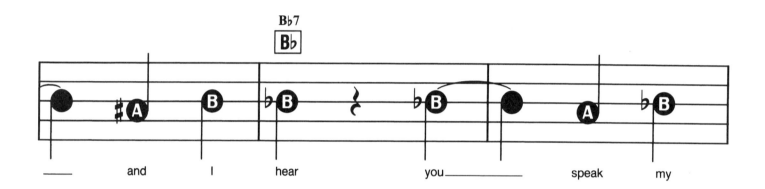

_____ and I hear you_____ speak my

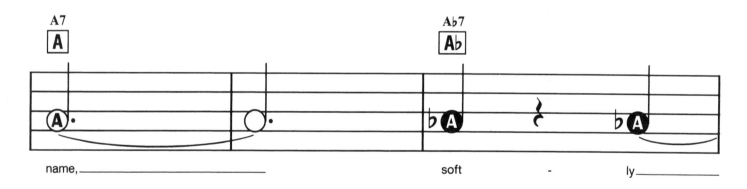

name,_____ soft - ly_____

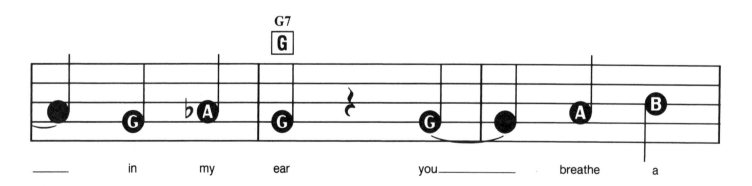

_____ in my ear you_____ breathe a

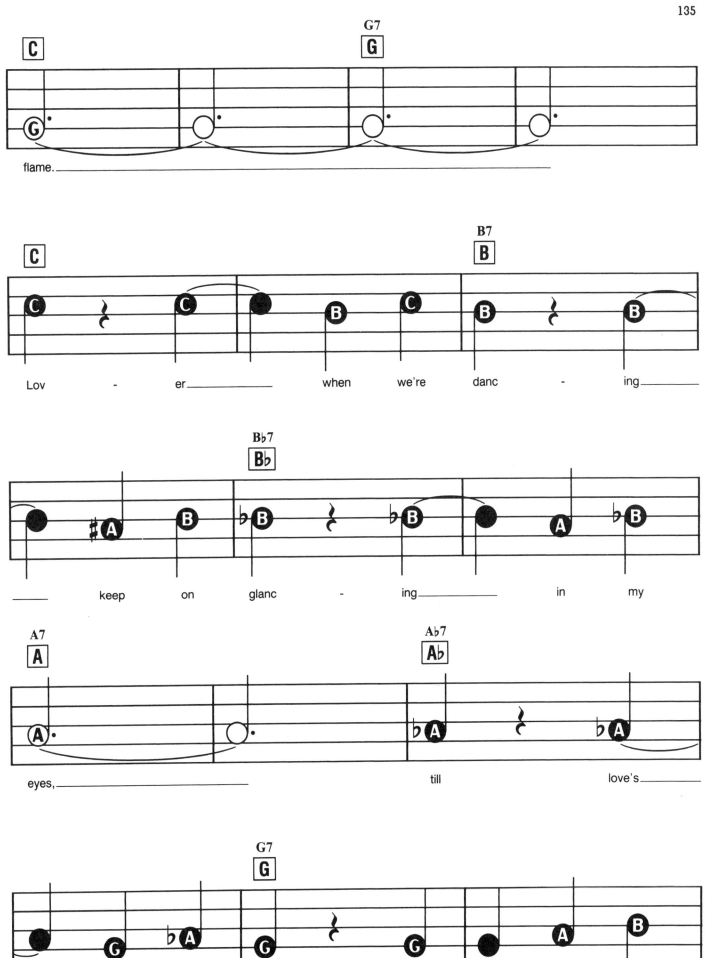

flame.

Lov - er when we're danc - ing keep on glanc - ing in my eyes, till love's own en - tranc - ing mu - sic

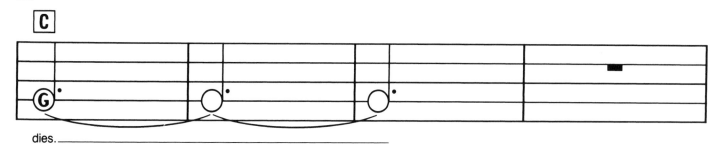

C

dies.

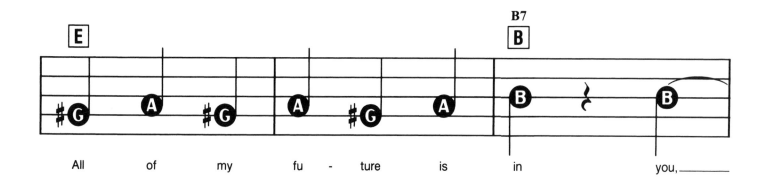

E   B7 / B

All of my fu - ture is in you,

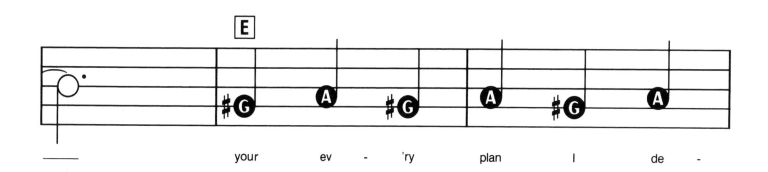

E

your ev - 'ry plan I de -

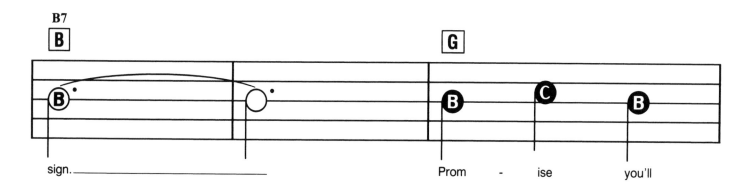

B7 / B   G

sign.   Prom - ise you'll

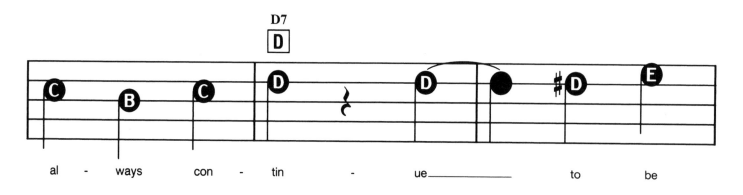

D7 / D

al - ways con - tin - ue to be

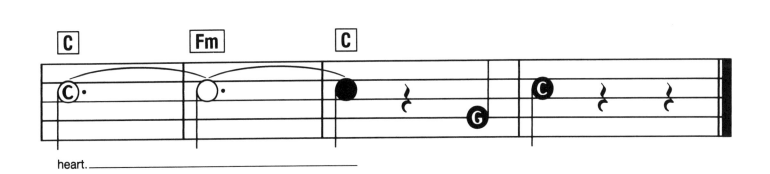

Memories Are Made of This

Registration 1
Rhythm: Swing

Words and Music by Richard Dehr,
Frank Miller and Terry Gilkyson

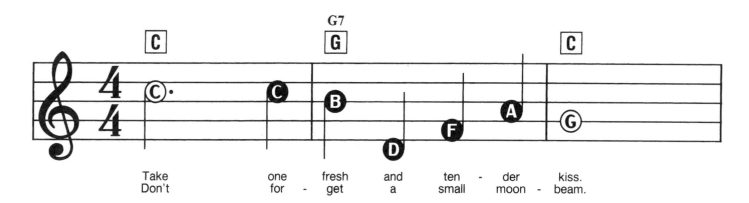

Take one fresh and a ten - der kiss.
Don't for - get a small moon - beam.

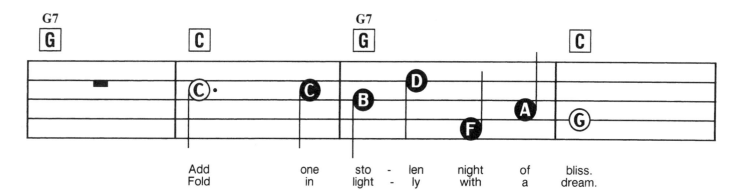

Add one sto - len night of bliss.
Fold in light - ly with a dream.

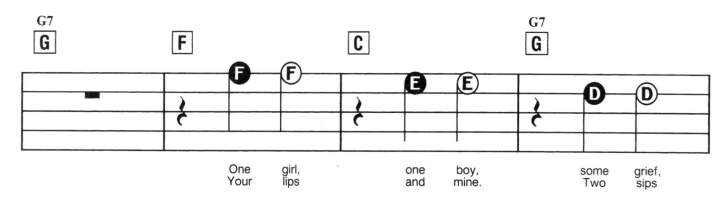

One girl, one boy, some grief,
Your lips and mine. Two sips

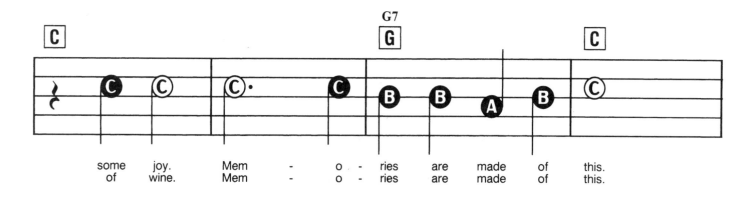

some joy. Mem - o - ries are made of this.
of wine. Mem - o - ries are made of this.

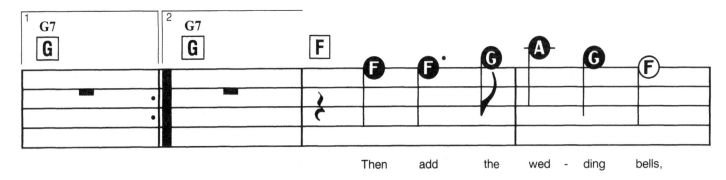

Then add the wed - ding bells,

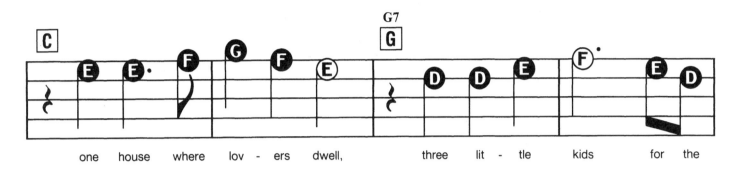

one house where lov - ers dwell, three lit - tle kids for the

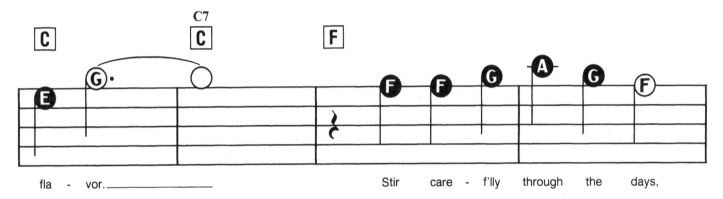

fla - vor._____ Stir care - f'lly through the days,

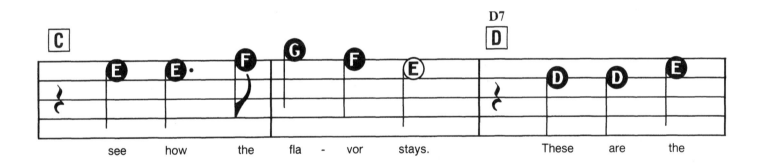

see how the fla - vor stays. These are the

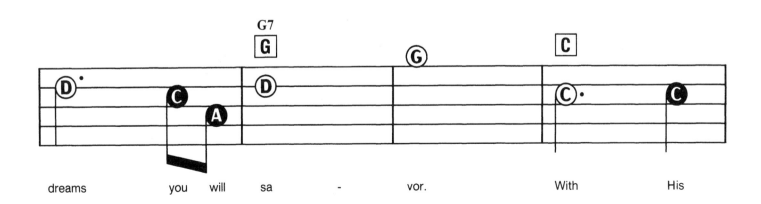

dreams you will sa - vor. With His

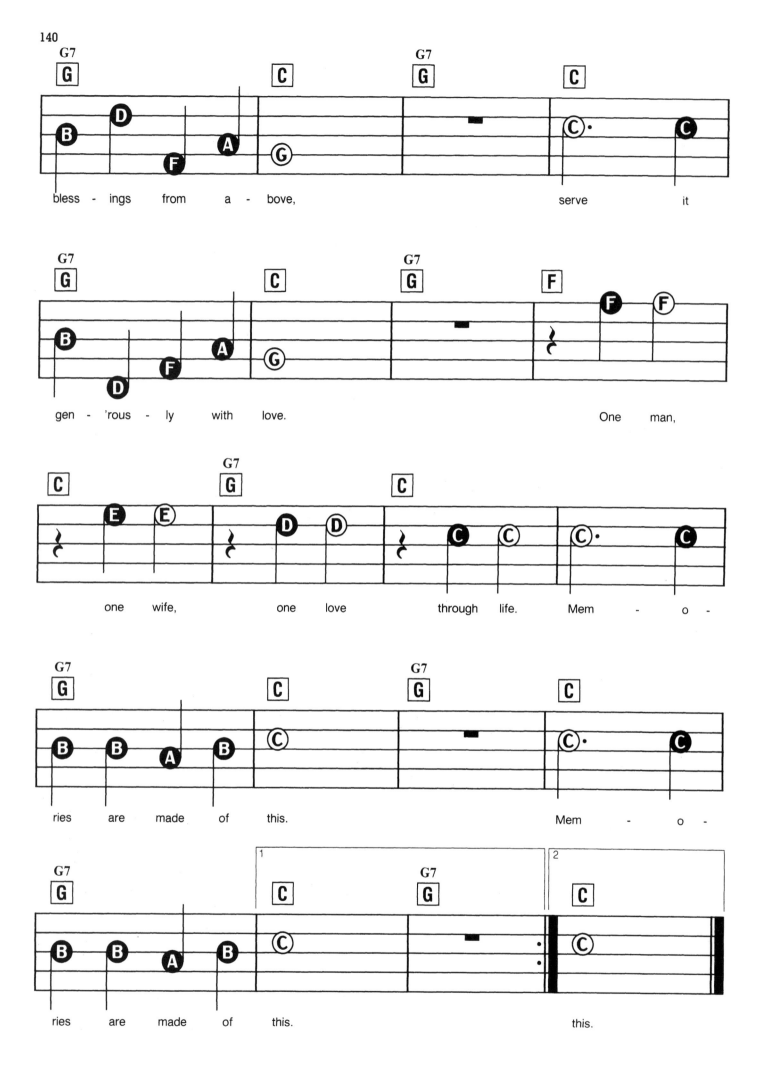

Lullaby of Birdland

Registration 2
Rhythm: Swing

Words by George David Weiss
Music by George Shearing

Lul - la - by of Bird - land, that's what I
Have you ev - er heard two tur - tle doves

al - ways hear
bill and coo when you sigh.
when they love?

Nev - er in my word land
That's the kind of mag - ic
could there be
mu - sic we
ways to re -
make with our

veal,
in a phrase, how I feel!

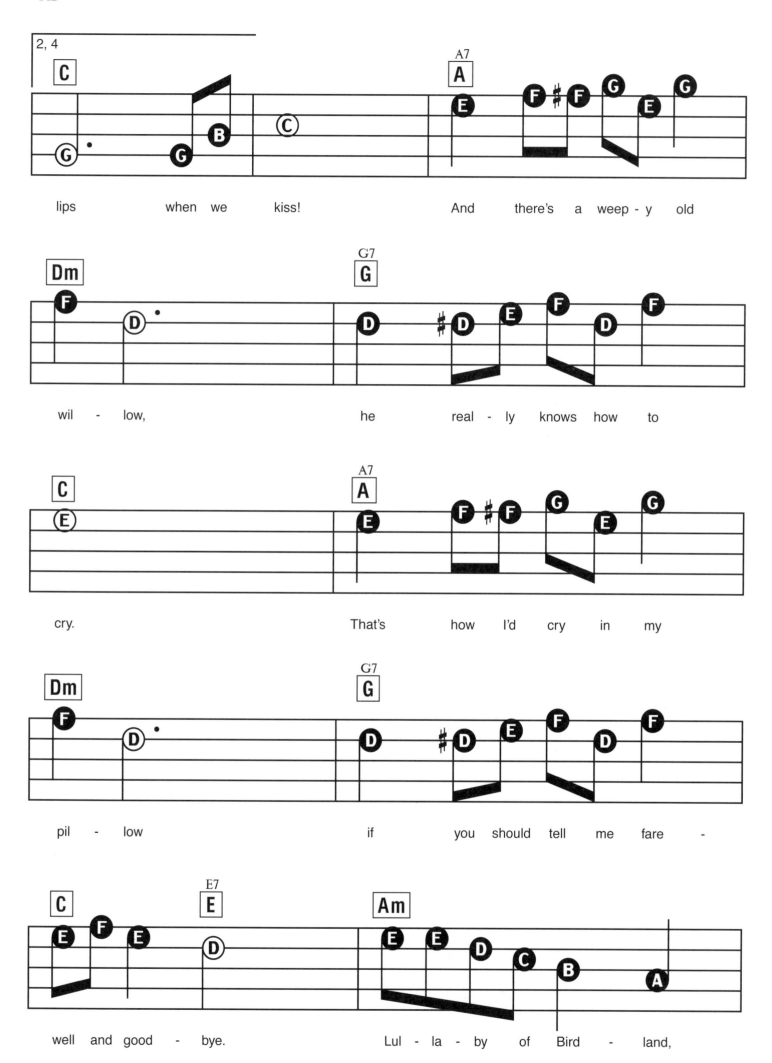

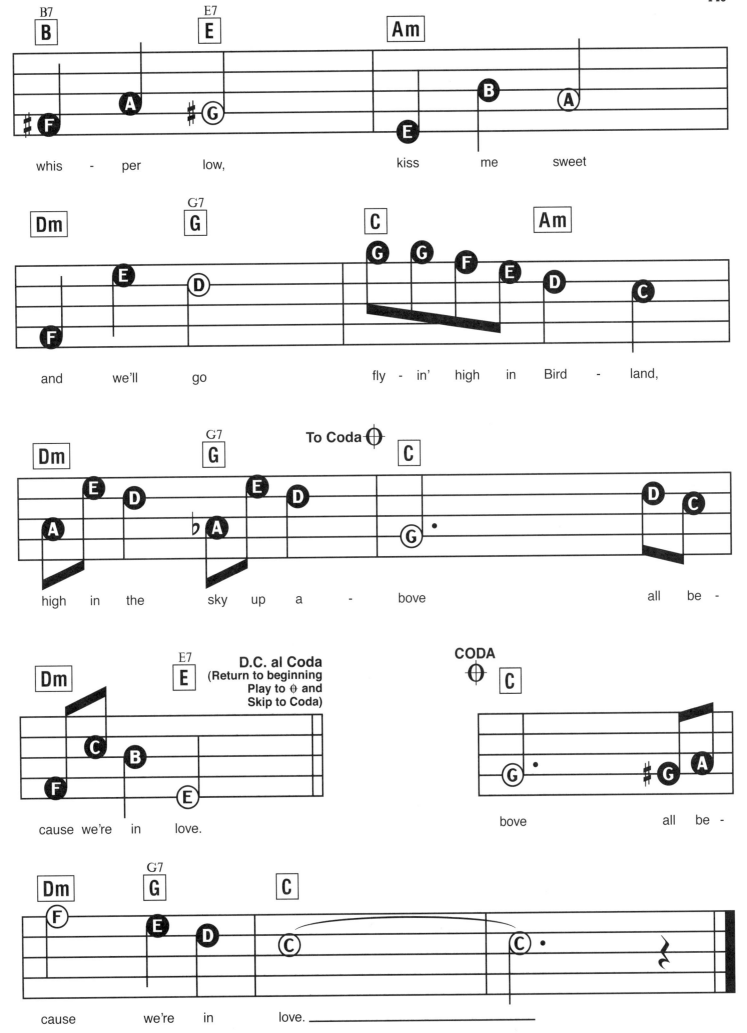

Manhattan
from the Broadway Musical THE GARRICK GAIETIES

Registration 7
Rhythm: Fox Trot

Words by Lorenz Hart
Music by Richard Rodgers

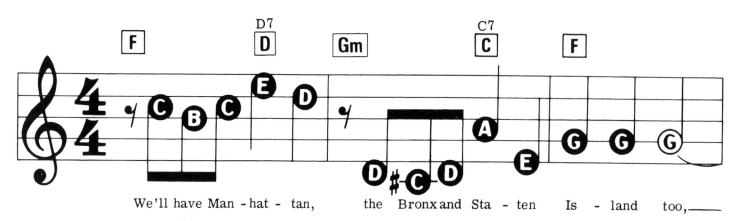

We'll have Man - hat - tan, the Bronx and Sta - ten Is - land too,_____

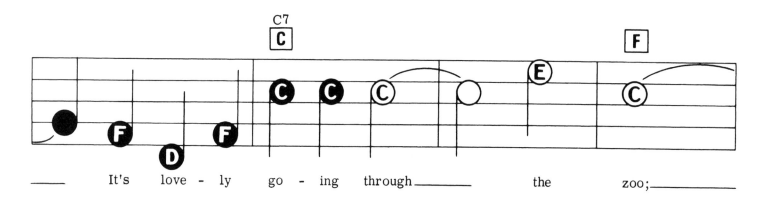

_____ It's love - ly go - ing through _____ the zoo;_____

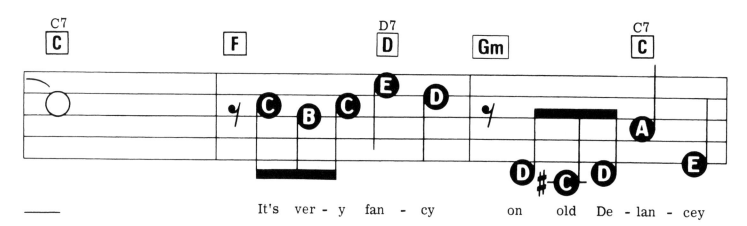

_____ It's ver - y fan - cy on old De - lan - cey

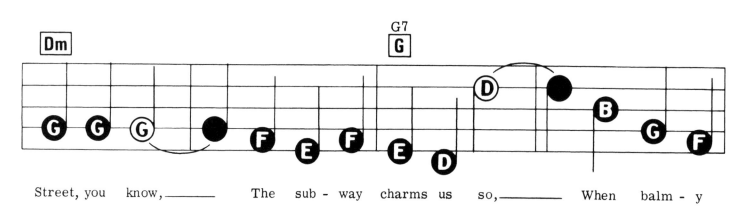

Street, you know,_____ The sub - way charms us so,_____ When balm - y

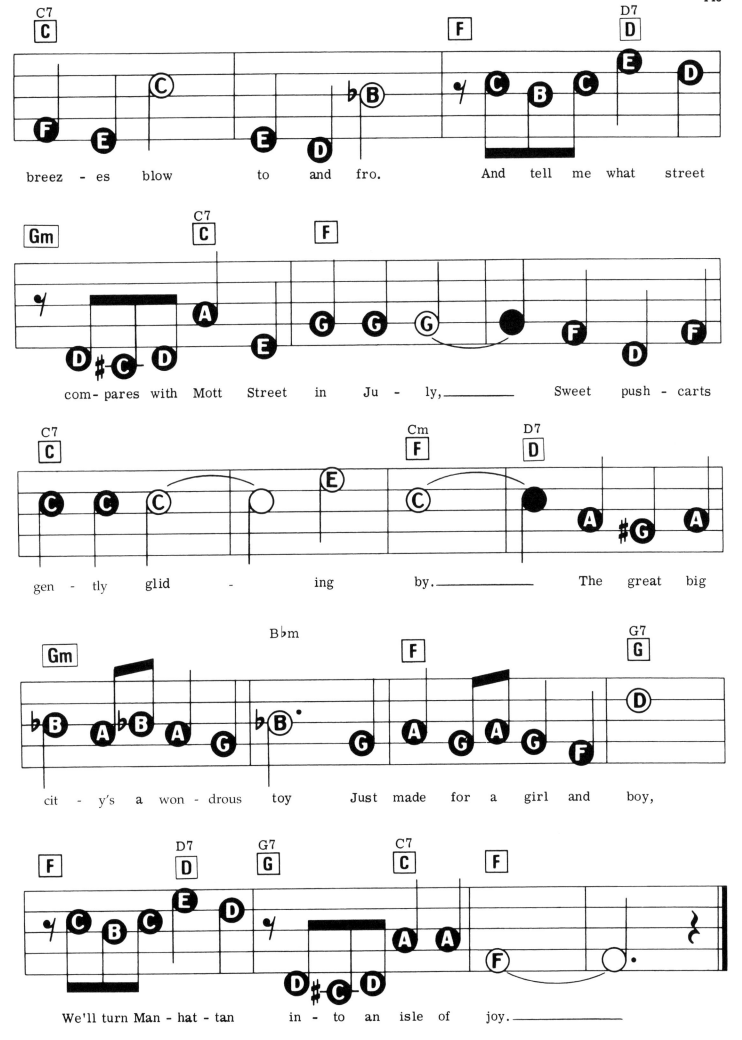

Midnight Sun

Registration 2
Rhythm: Fox Trot or Ballad

Words and Music by Lionel Hampton,
Sonny Burke and Johnny Mercer

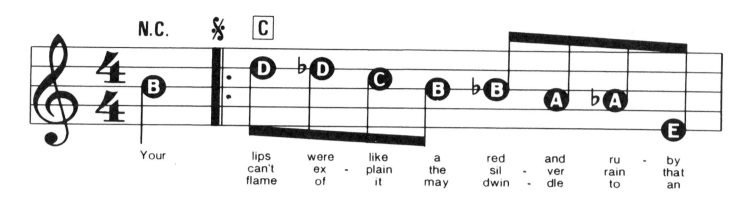

Your

lips were like a red and ru - by
can't ex - plain the sil - ver rain by that
flame of it may dwin - dle to an

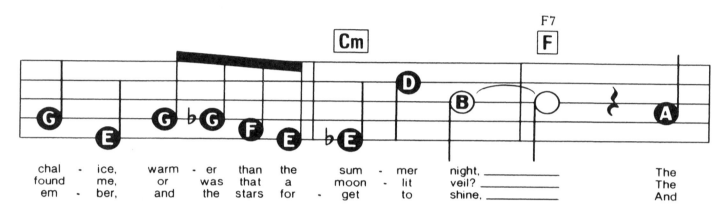

chal - ice, warm - er than the sum - mer night, _____ The
found me, or was that a moon - lit veil? _____ The
em - ber, and the stars for - get to shine, _____ And

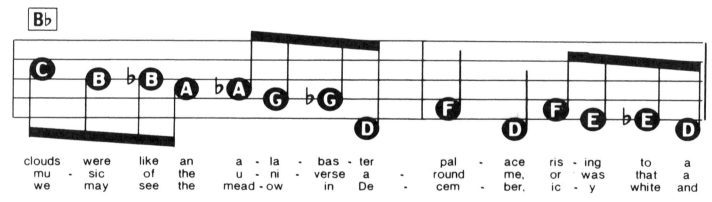

clouds were like an a - la - bas - ter pal - ace ris - ing to a
mu - sic of the u - ni - verse a - round me, or was that a
we may see the mead - ow in De - cem - ber, ic - y white and

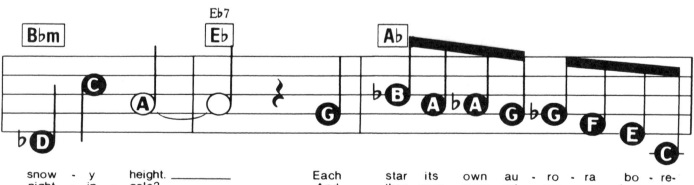

snow - y height. _____ Each star its own au - ro - ra bo - re-
night - in - gale? _____ And then your arms mi - rac - u - lous - ly
crys - tal - line. _____ But, oh, my dar - ling al - ways I'll re-

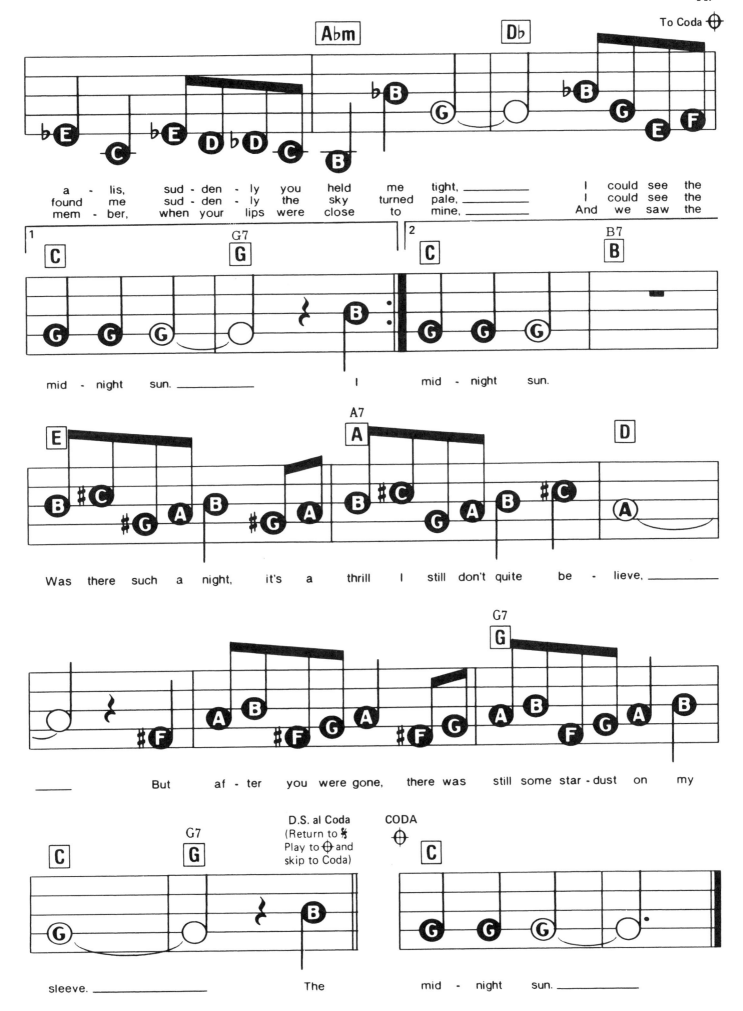

Mr. Wonderful
from the Musical MR. WONDERFUL

Registration 9
Rhythm: Swing

Words and Music by Jerry Bock,
Larry Holofcener and George Weiss

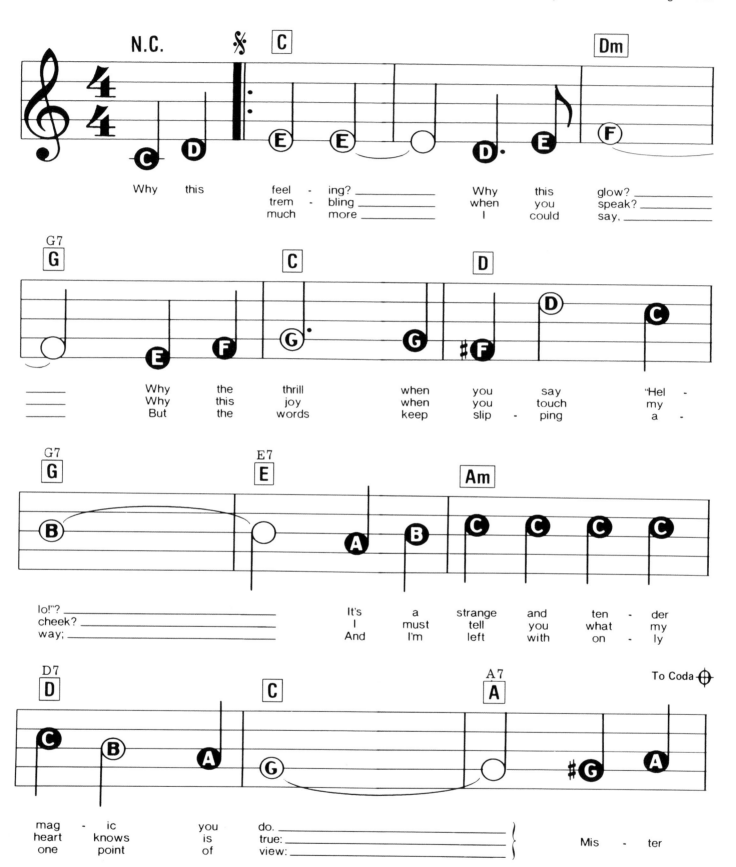

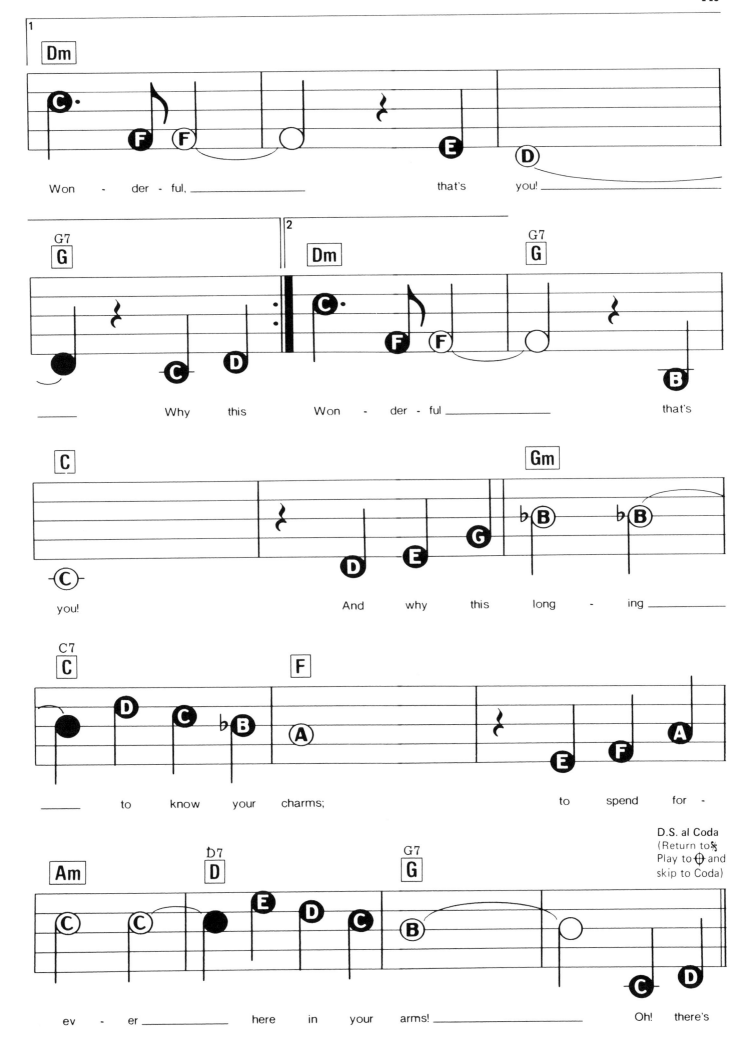

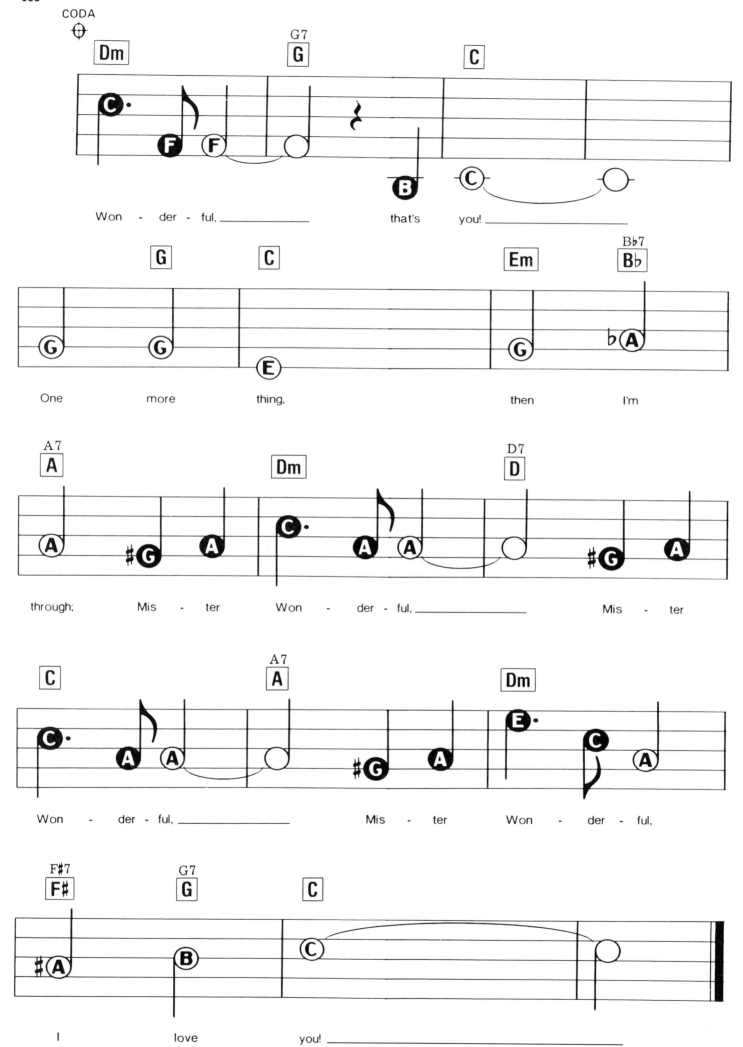

The Most Beautiful Girl in the World
from JUMBO

Registration 10
Rhythm: Waltz

Words by Lorenz Hart
Music by Richard Rodgers

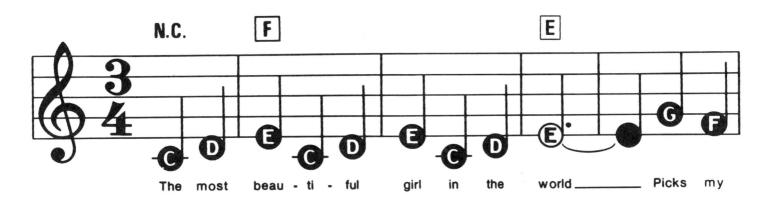

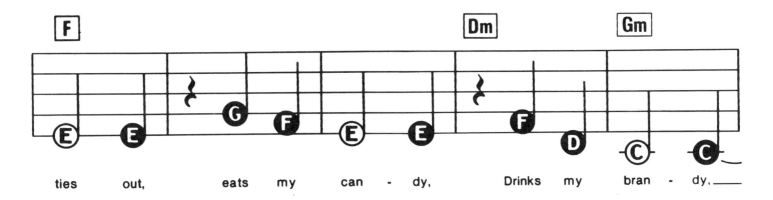

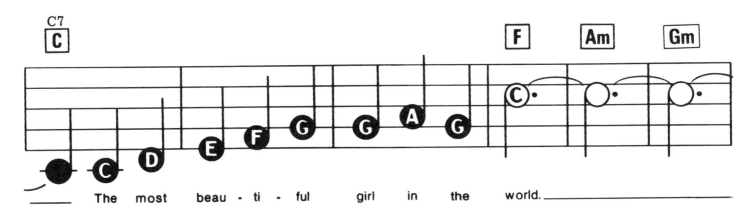

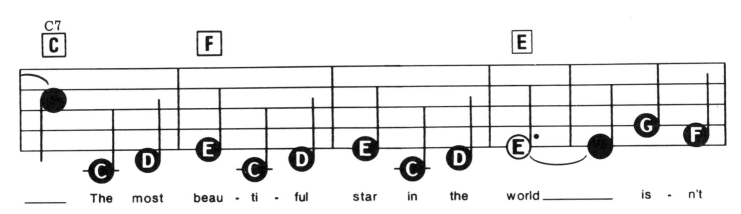

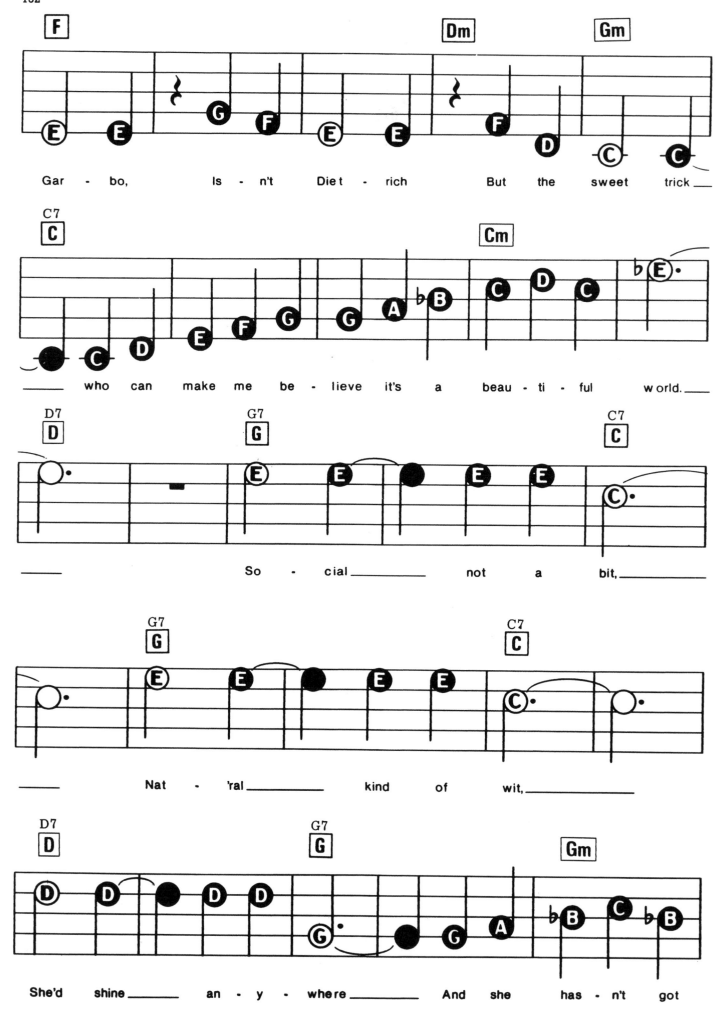

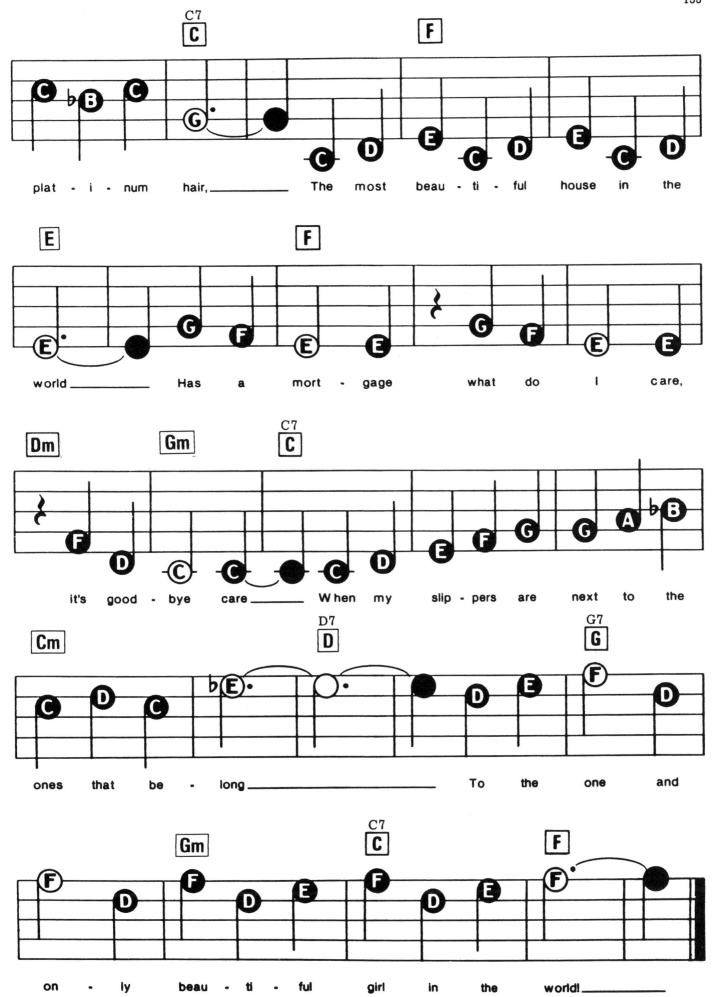

Moonlight in Vermont

Registration 2
Rhythm: Fox Trot or Swing

Words by John Blackburn
Music by Karl Suessdorf

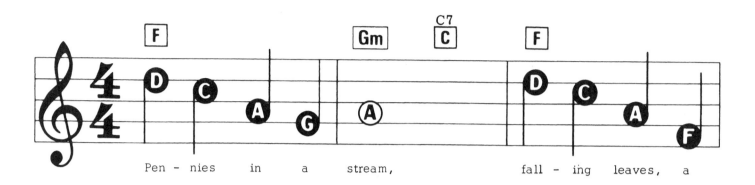

Pen - nies in a stream, fall - ing leaves, a

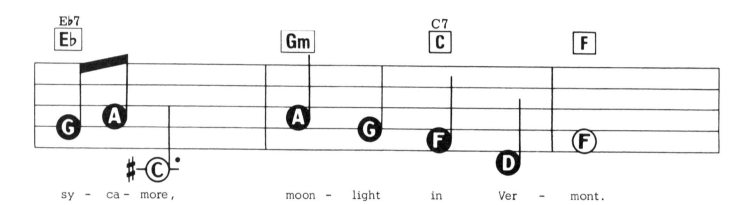

sy - ca - more, moon - light in Ver - mont.

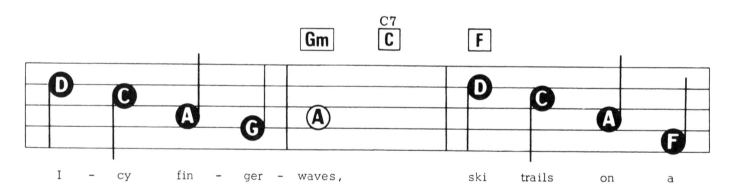

I - cy fin - ger - waves, ski trails on a

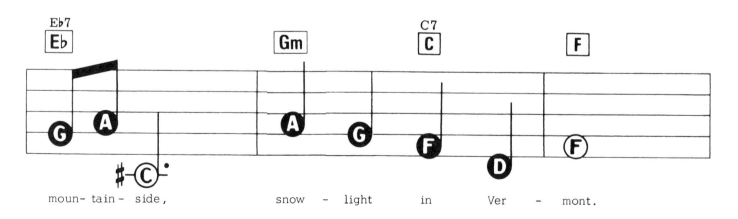

moun - tain - side, snow - light in Ver - mont.

155

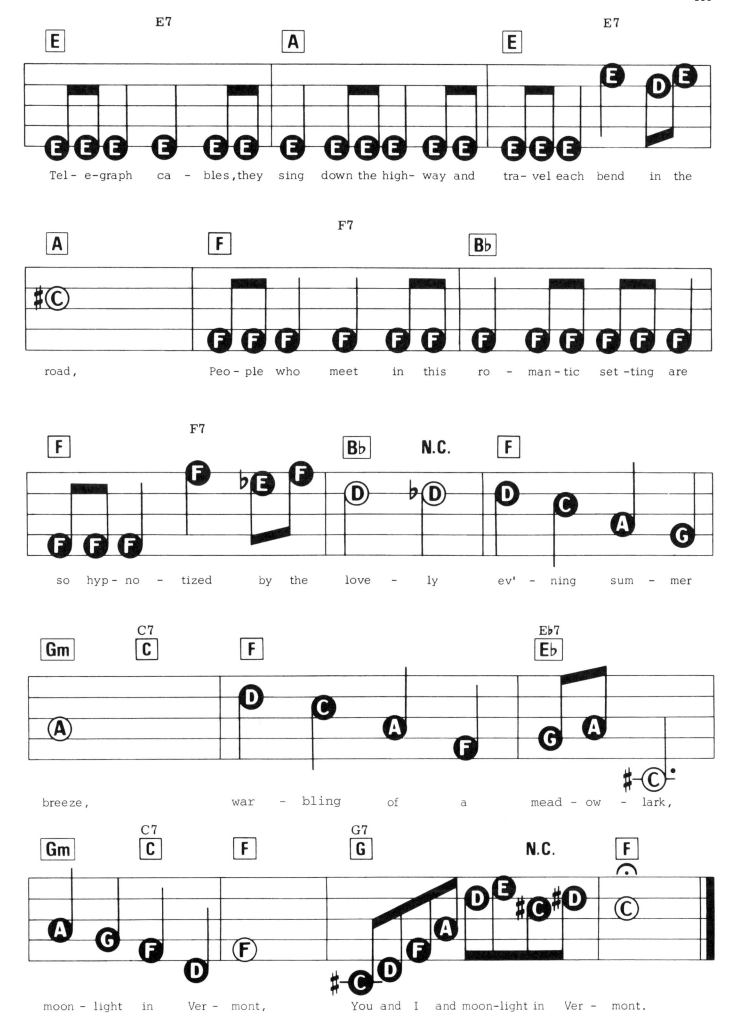

My Heart Belongs to Daddy

from LEAVE IT TO ME

Registration 7
Rhythm: Swing or Jazz

Words and Music by
Cole Porter

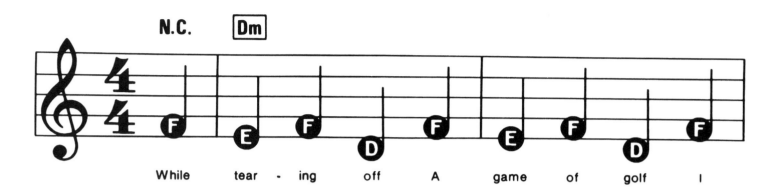

While tear - ing off A game of golf I

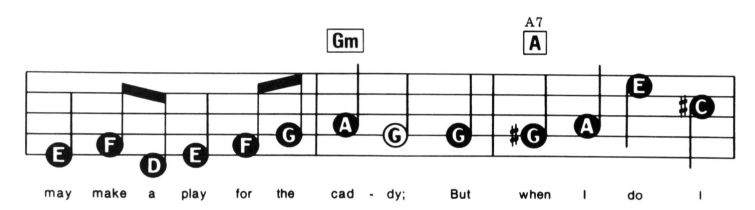

may make a play for the cad - dy; But when I do I

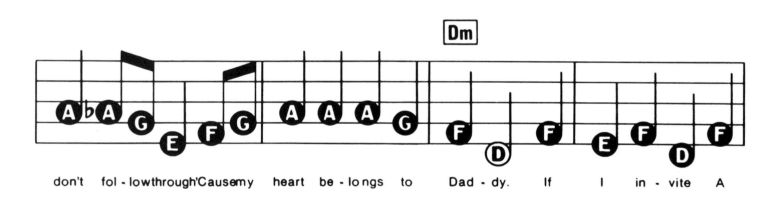

don't fol - lowthrough'Causemy heart be - lo ngs to Dad - dy. If I in - vite A

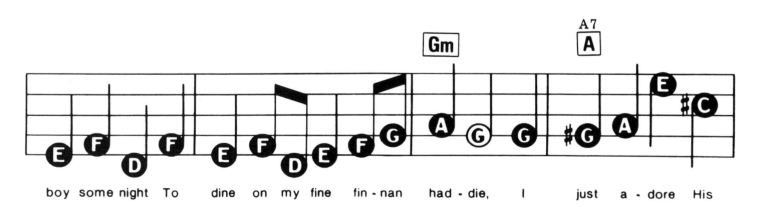

boy some night To dine on my fine fin - nan had - die, I just a - dore His

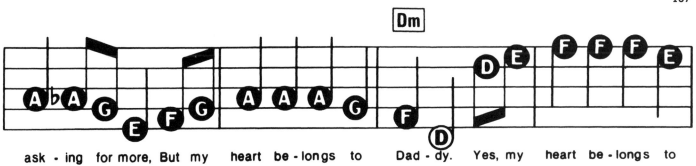

ask - ing for more, But my heart be - longs to Dad - dy. Yes, my heart be - longs to

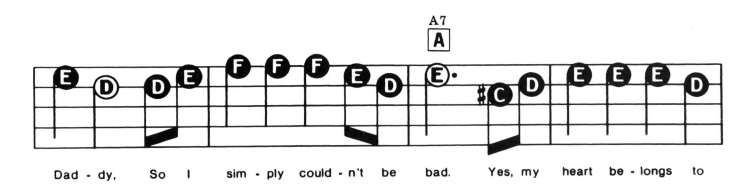

Dad - dy, So I sim - ply could - n't be bad. Yes, my heart be - longs to

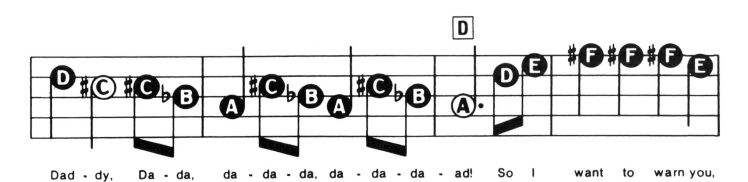

Dad - dy, Da - da, da - da - da, da - da - da - ad! So I want to warn you,

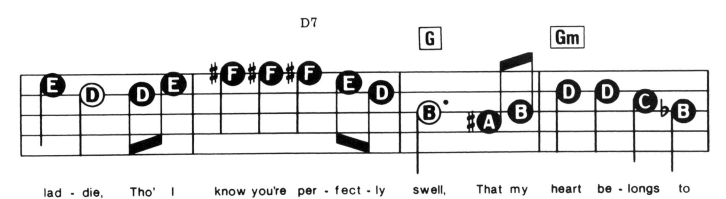

lad - die, Tho' I know you're per - fect - ly swell, That my heart be - longs to

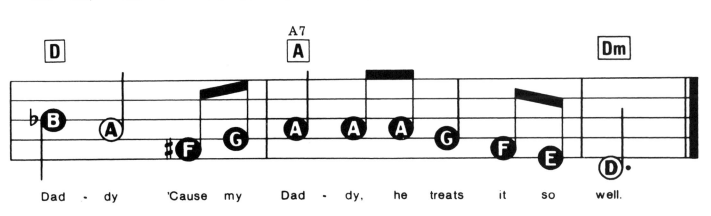

Dad - dy 'Cause my Dad - dy, he treats it so well.

My Ship
from the Musical Production LADY IN THE DARK

Registration 9
Rhythm: Fox Trot or Swing

Words by Ira Gershwin
Music by Kurt Weill

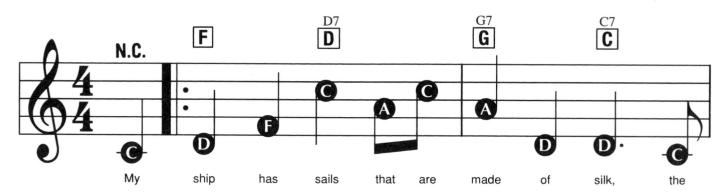

My ship has sails that are made of silk, the

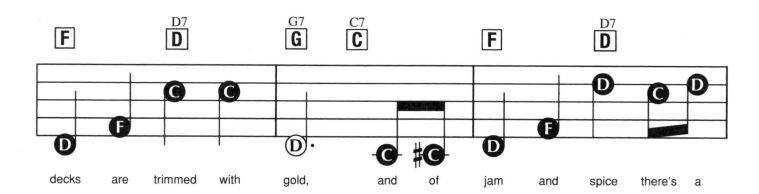

decks are trimmed with gold, and of jam and spice there's a

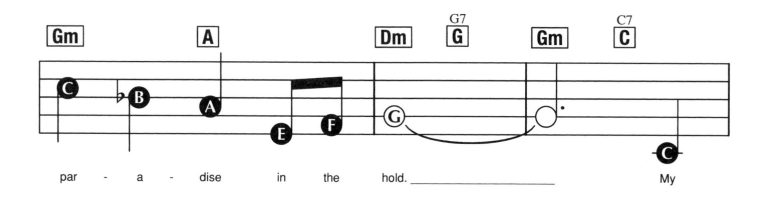

par - a - dise in the hold. _____ My

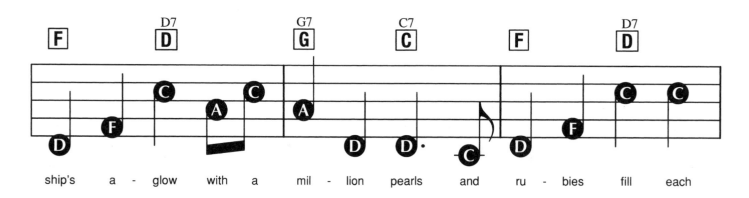

ship's a - glow with a mil - lion pearls and ru - bies fill each

159

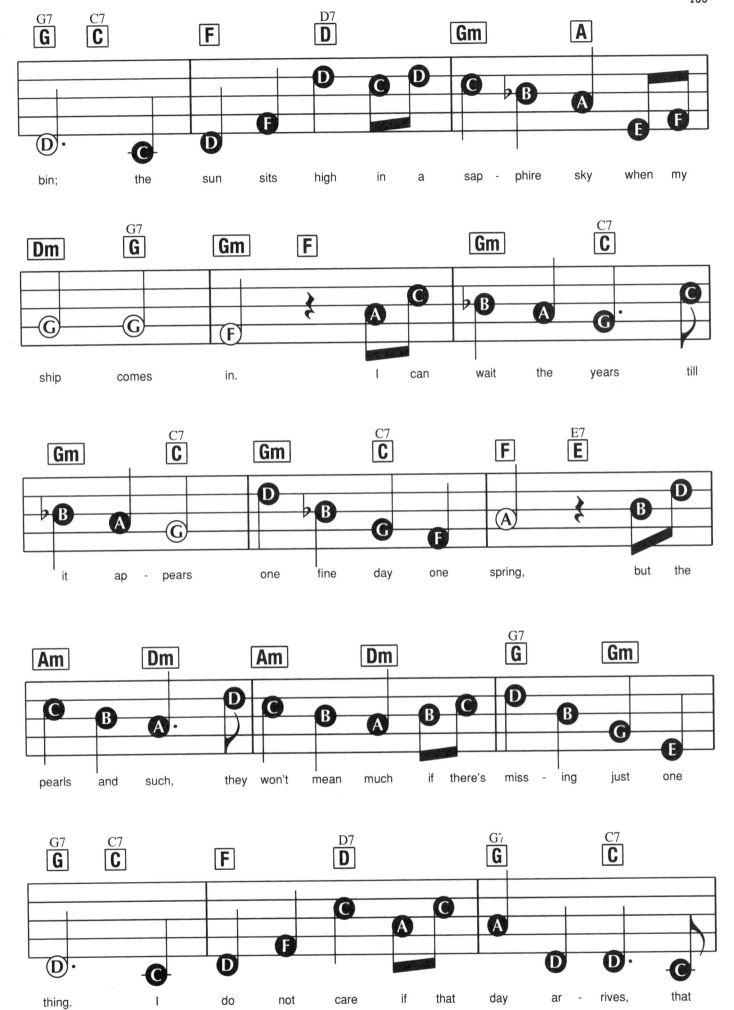

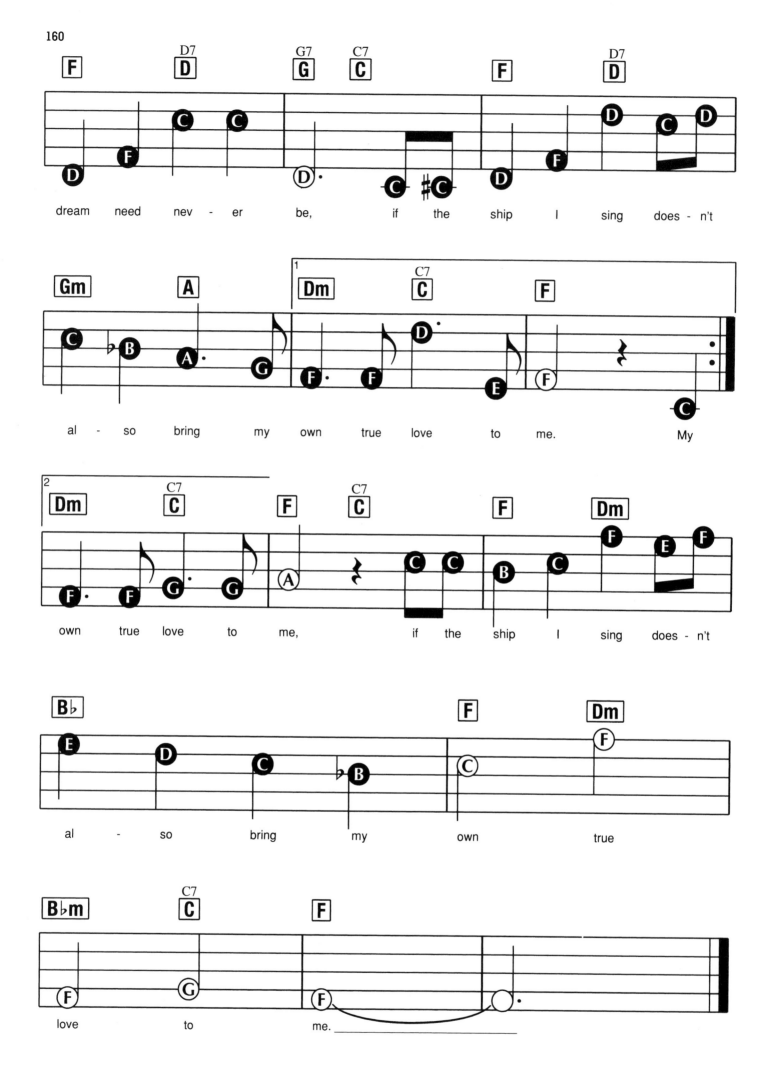

People
from FUNNY GIRL

Registration 1
Rhythm: Ballad

Words by Bob Merrill
Music by Jule Styne

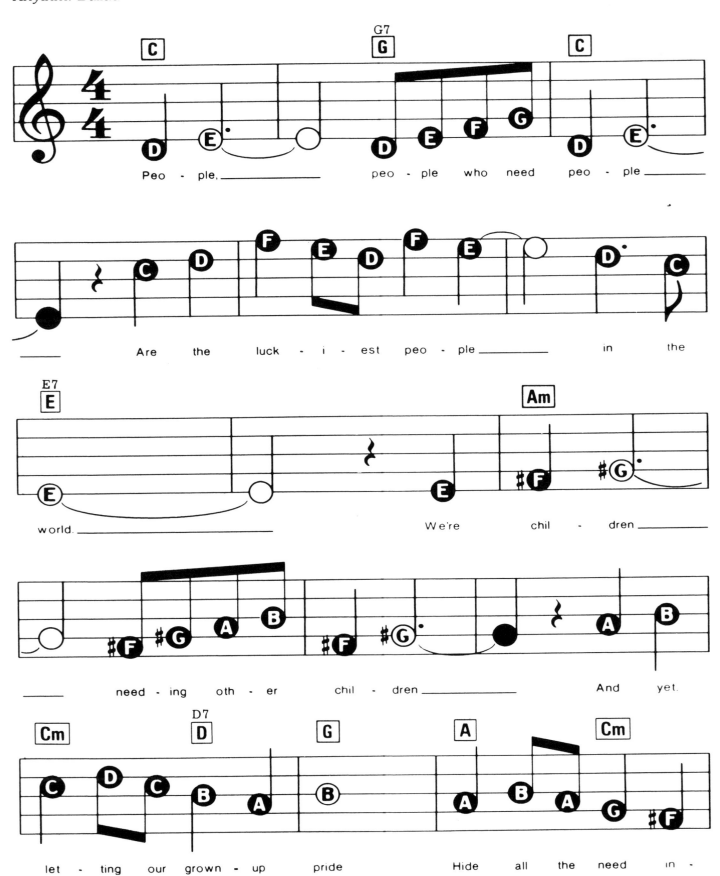

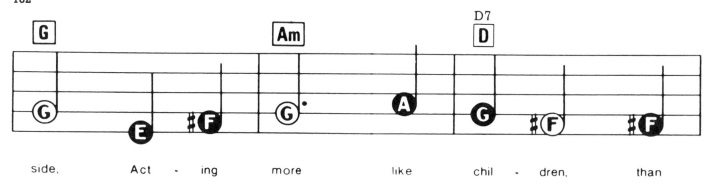

side,   Act - ing   more   like   chil - dren,   than

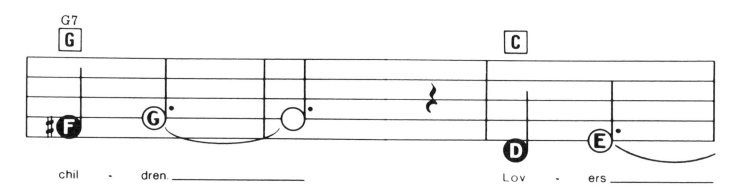

chil - dren. _____   Lov - ers _____

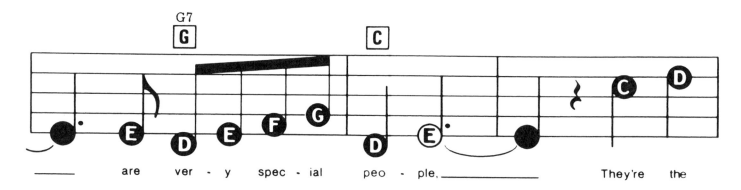

_____   are   ver - y   spec - ial   peo - ple, _____   They're   the

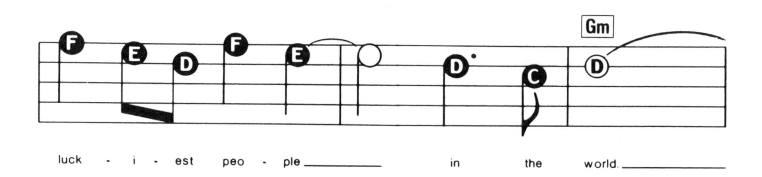

luck - i - est   peo - ple _____   in   the   world. _____

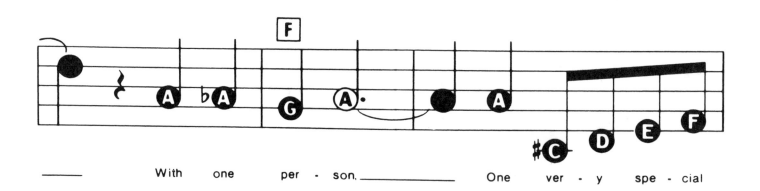

_____   With   one   per - son. _____   One   ver - y   spe - cial

163

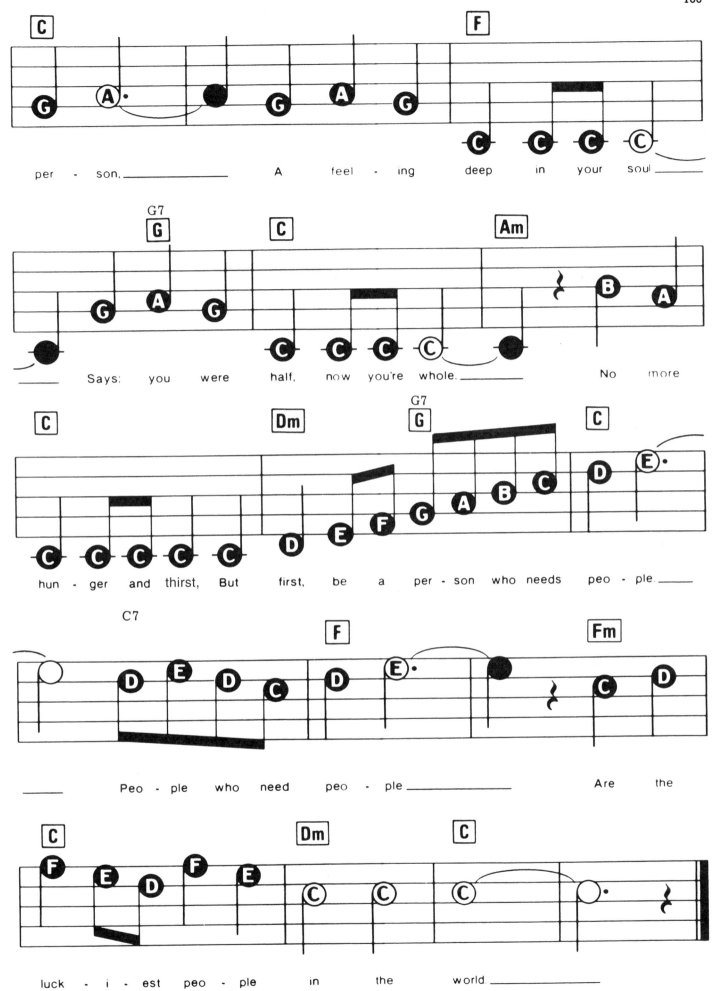

The Party's Over

from BELLS ARE RINGING

Registration 9
Rhythm: Fox Trot or Ballad

Words by Betty Comden and Adolph Green
Music by Jule Styne

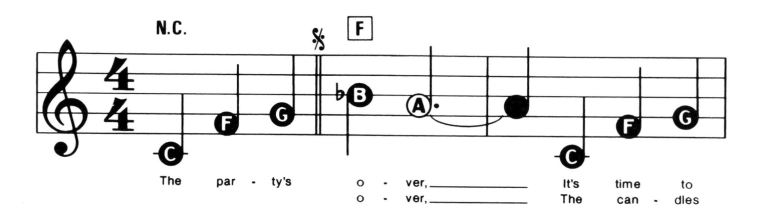

The par - ty's o - ver, _____ It's time to
o - ver, _____ The can - dles

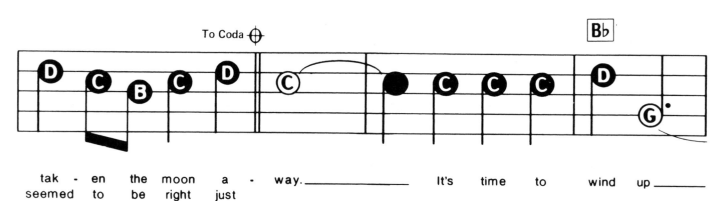

call it a day. _____ They've burst your pret - ty bal - loon and
flick - er and dim. _____ You danced and dreamed through the night, It

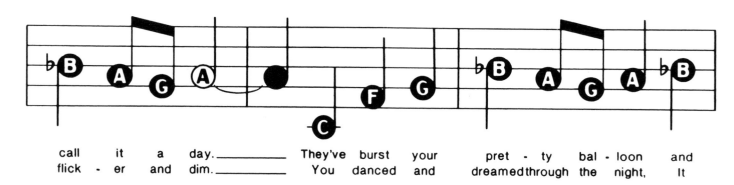

tak - en the moon a - way. _____ It's time to wind up _____
seemed to be right just

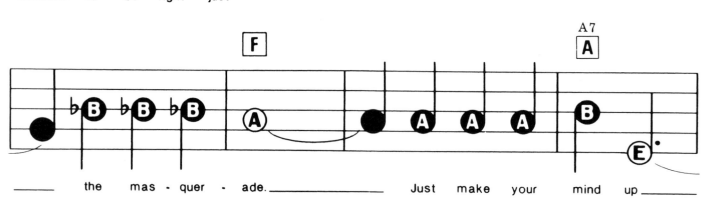

_____ the mas - quer - ade. _____ Just make your mind up _____

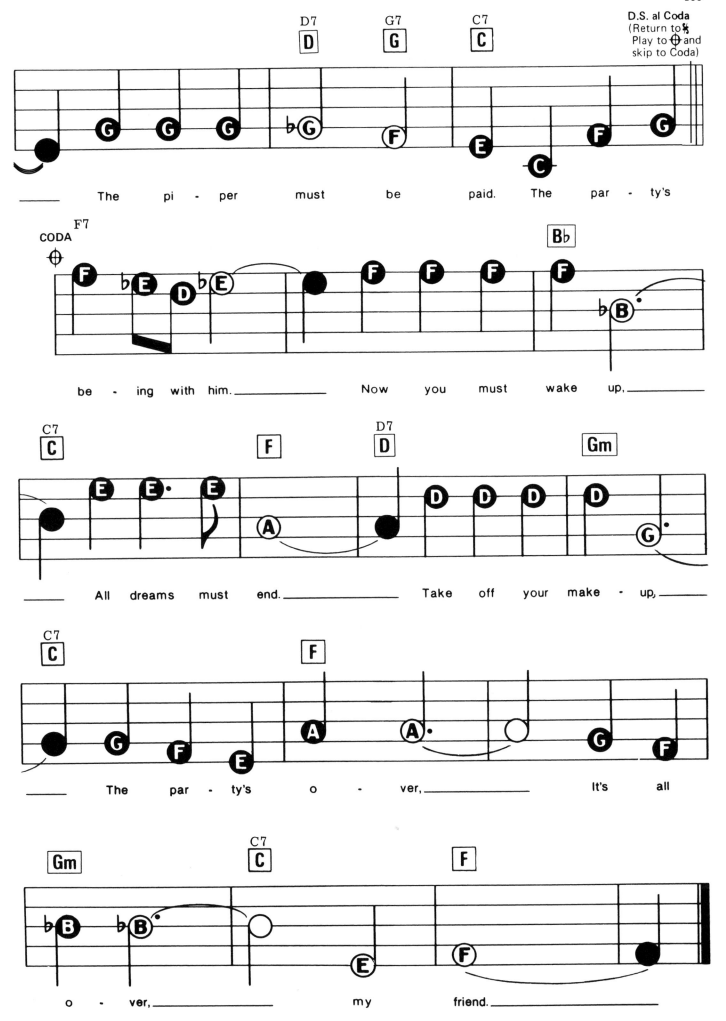

Put On a Happy Face
from BYE BYE BIRDIE

Registration 5
Rhythm: Swing

Lyric by Lee Adams
Music by Charles Strouse

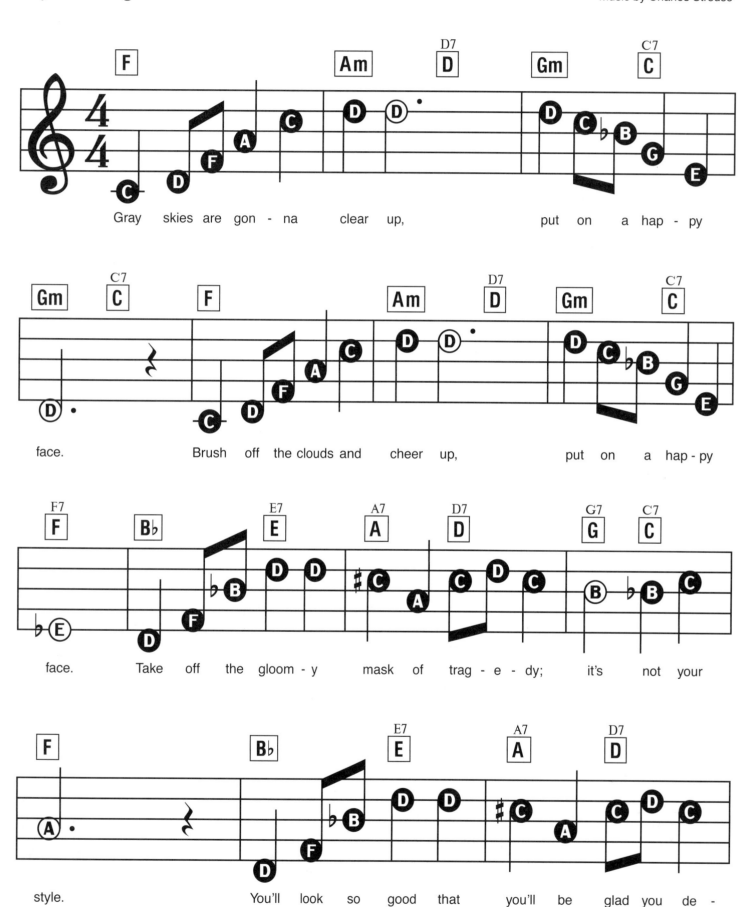

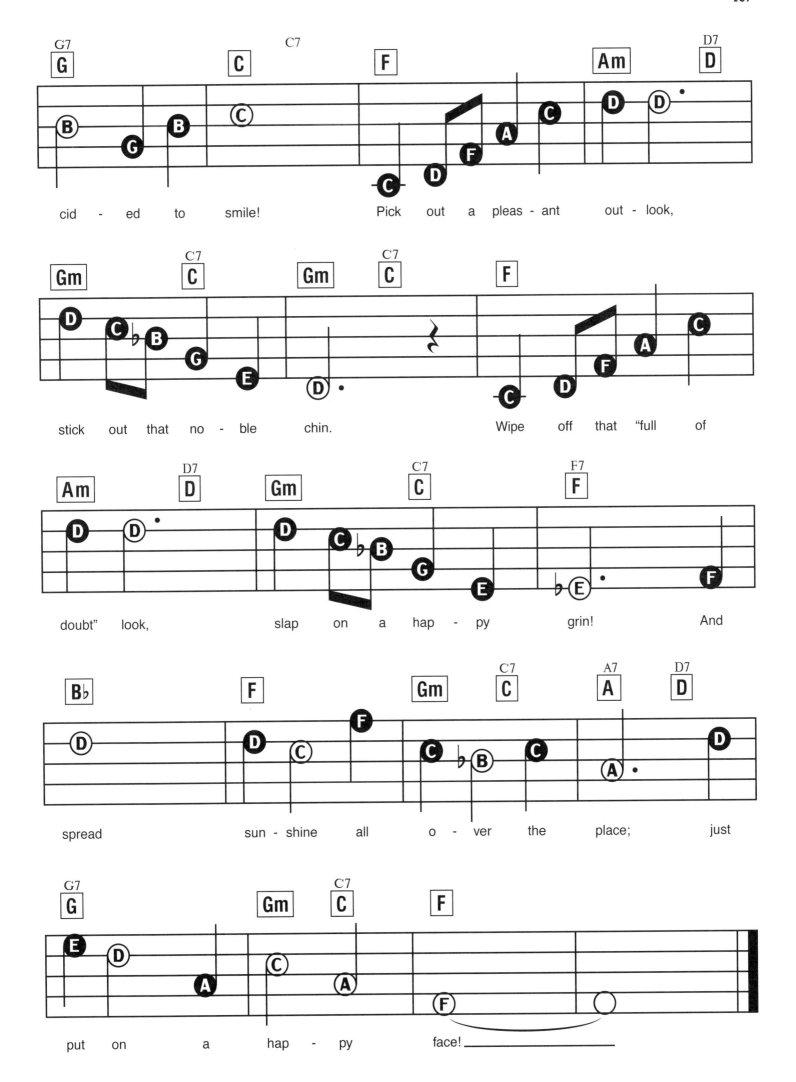

Ramblin' Rose

Registration: 2
Rhythm: Fox Trot

Words and Music by Noel Sherman
and Joe Sherman

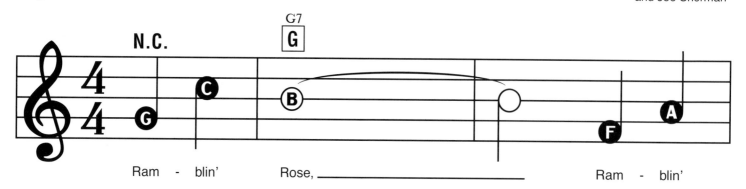

Ram - blin' Rose, _____ Ram - blin'

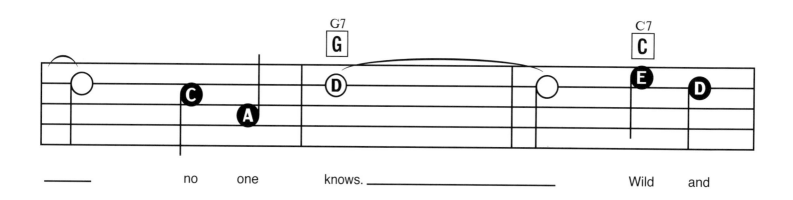

Rose, _____ why you ram - ble _____

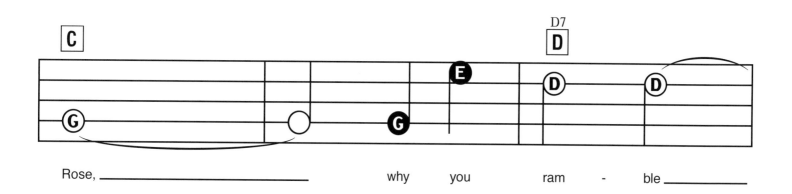

_____ no one knows. _____ Wild and

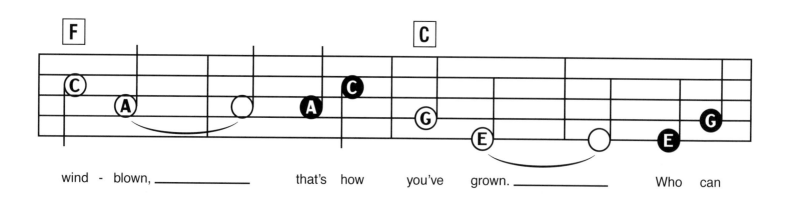

wind - blown, _____ that's how you've grown. _____ Who can

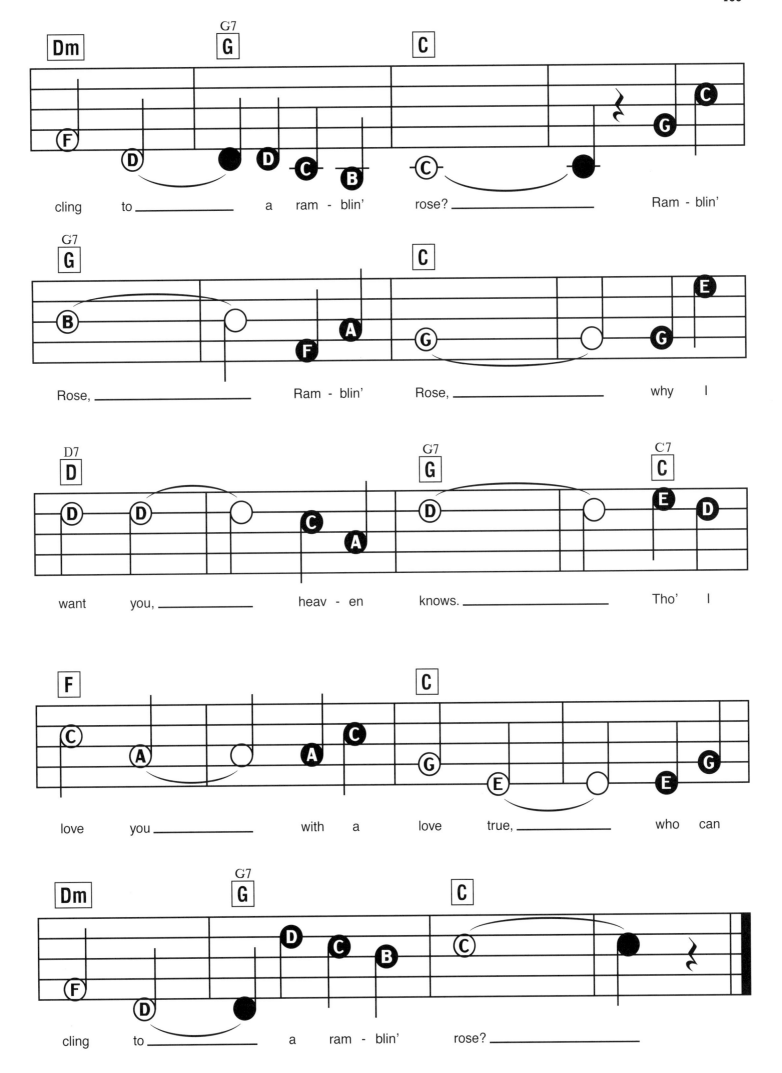

Rock-a-Bye Your Baby
with a Dixie Melody
from SINBAD

Registration 9
Rhythm: Fox Trot or Swing

Words by Sam M. Lewis and Joe Young
Music by Jean Schwartz

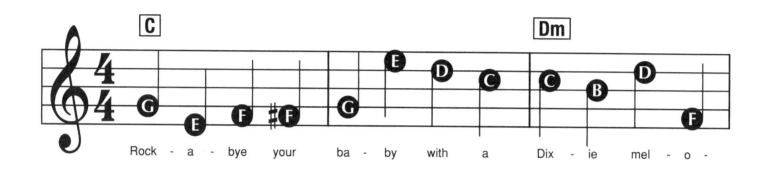

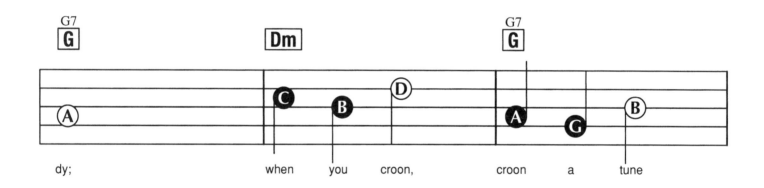

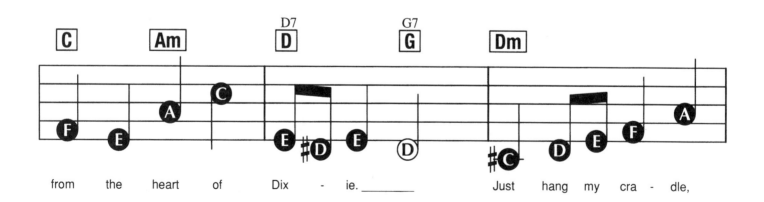

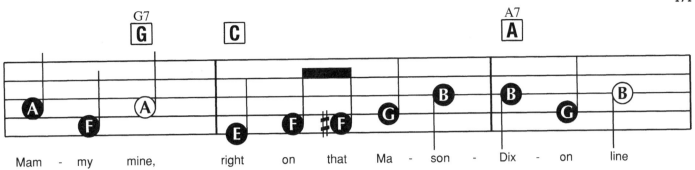

Mam - my mine, right on that Ma - son - Dix - on line

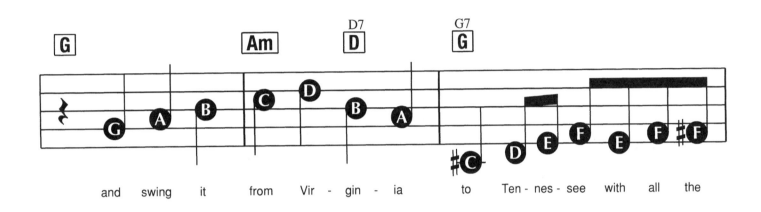

and swing it from Vir - gin - ia to Ten - nes - see with all the

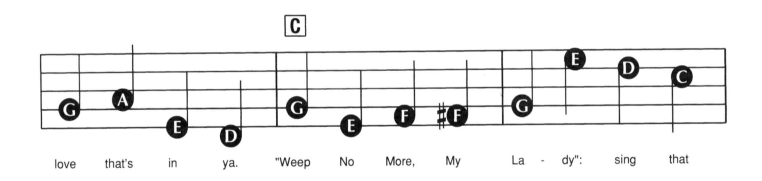

love that's in ya. "Weep No More, My La - dy": sing that

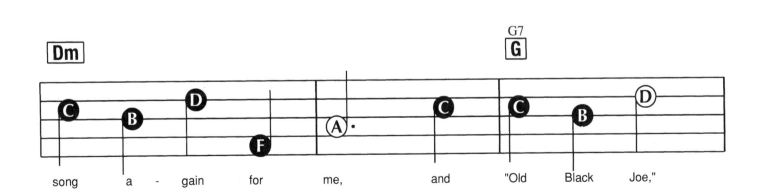

song a - gain for me, and "Old Black Joe,"

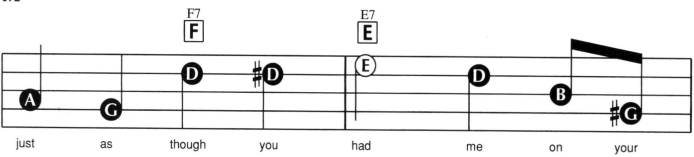

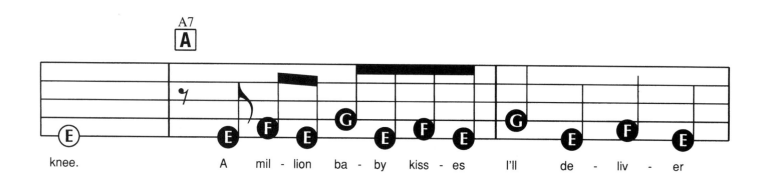

just as though you had me on your

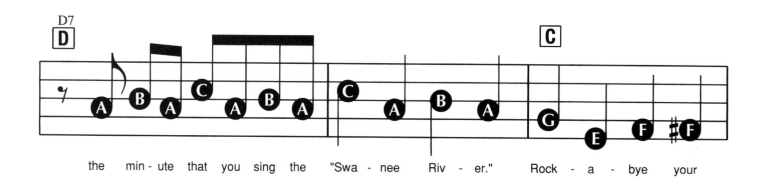

knee. A mil - lion ba - by kiss - es I'll de - liv - er

the min - ute that you sing the "Swa - nee Riv - er." Rock - a - bye your

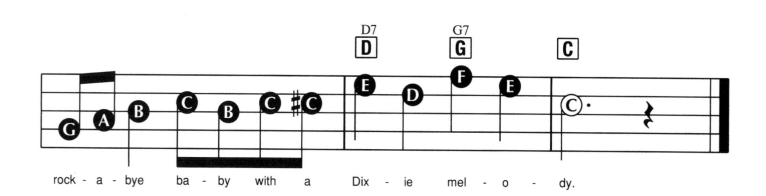

rock - a - bye ba - by with a Dix - ie mel - o - dy.

Route 66

Registration 7
Rhythm: Swing

By Bobby Troup

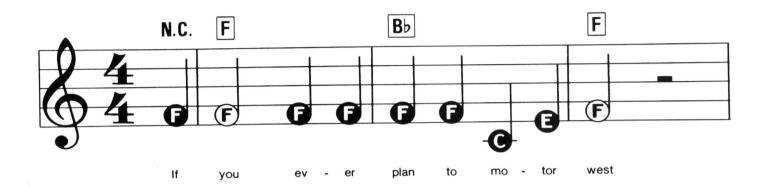

If you ev - er plan to mo - tor west

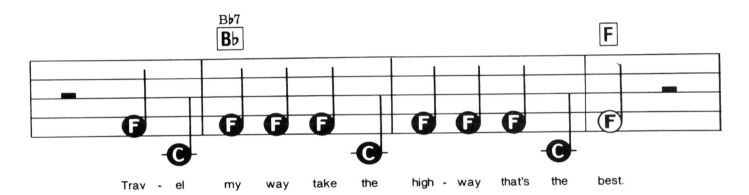

Trav - el my way take the high - way that's the best.

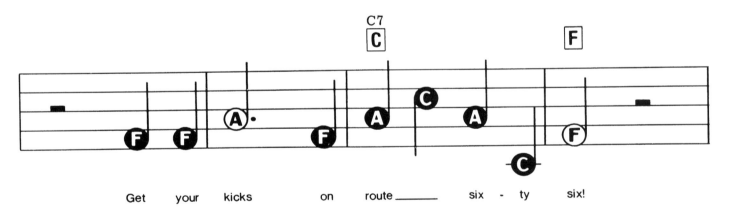

Get your kicks on route _____ six - ty six!

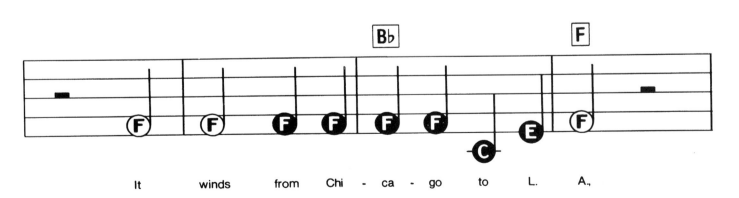

It winds from Chi - ca - go to L. A.,

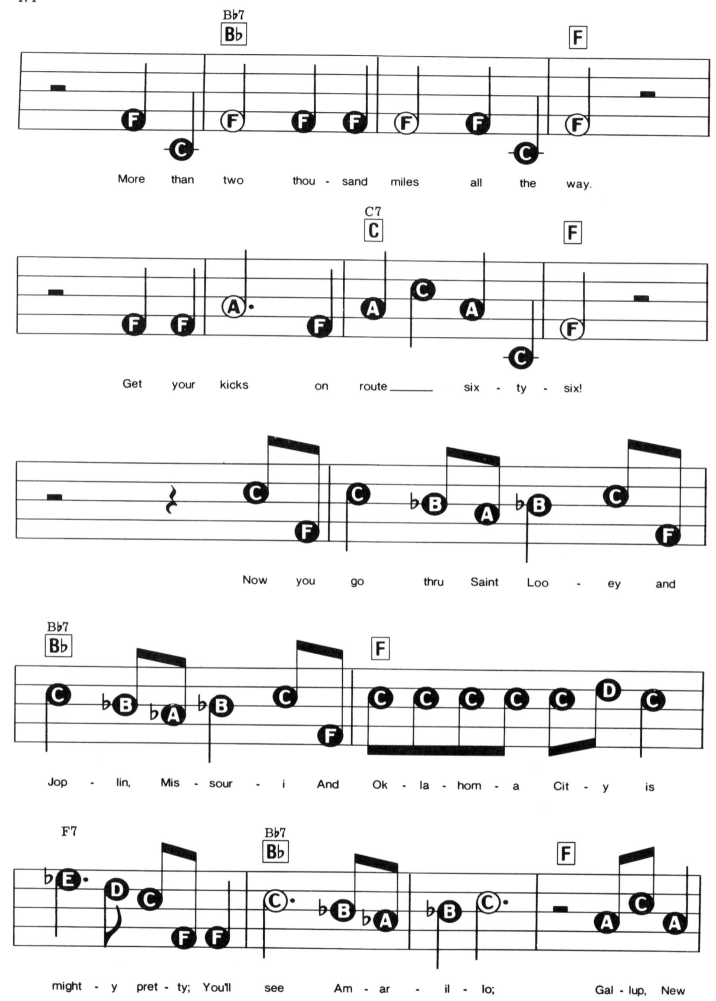

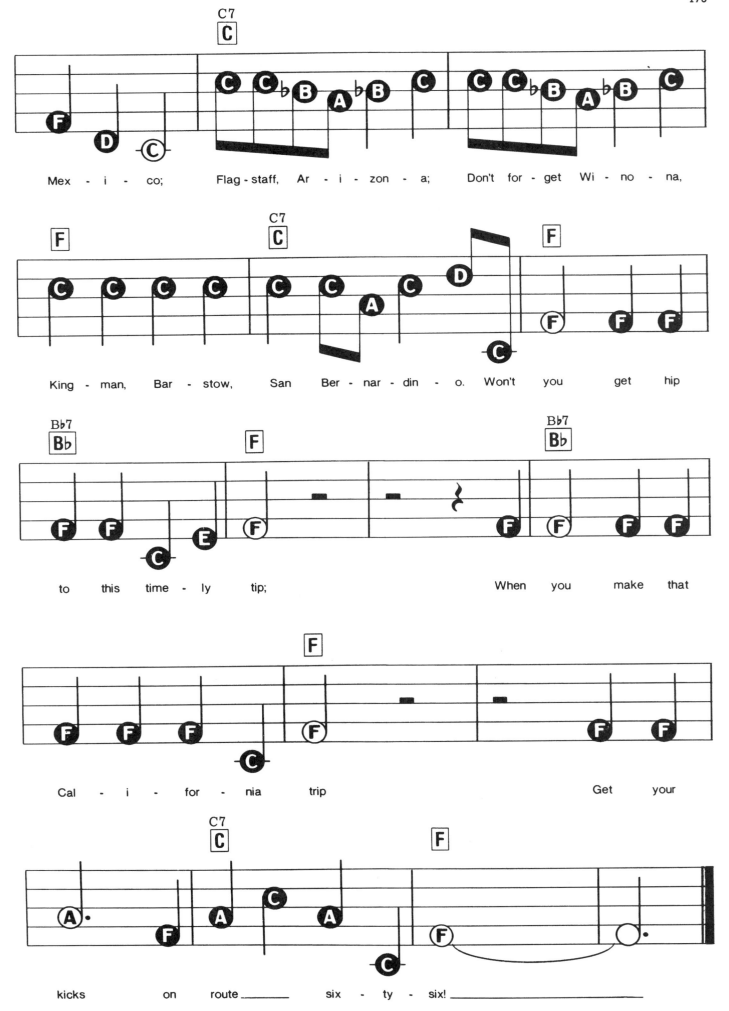

Second Hand Rose

Registration 8
Rhythm: Fox Trot

Words by Grant Clarke
Music by James F. Hanley

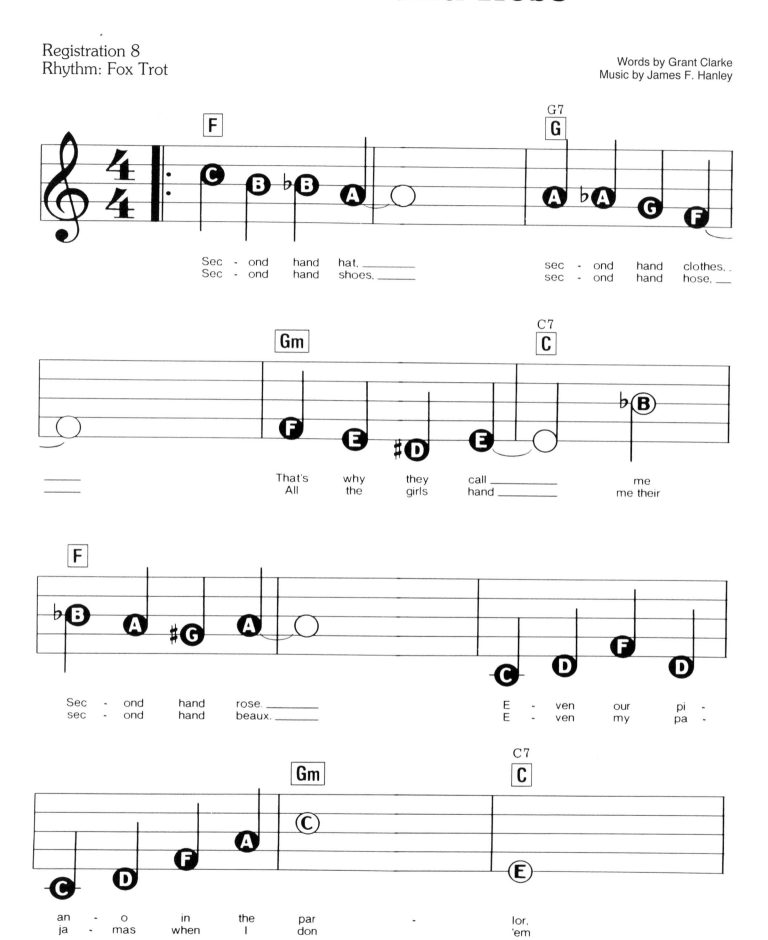

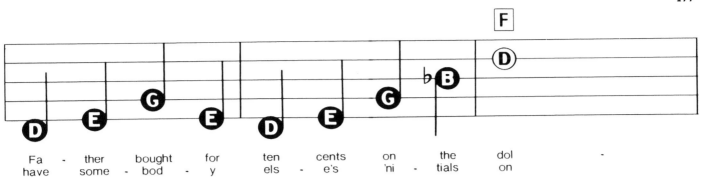

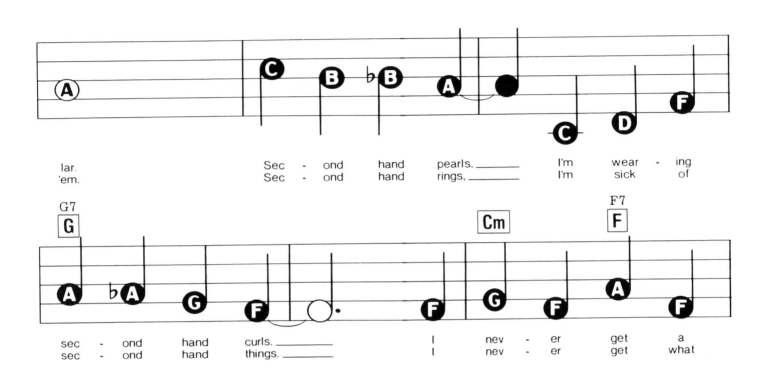

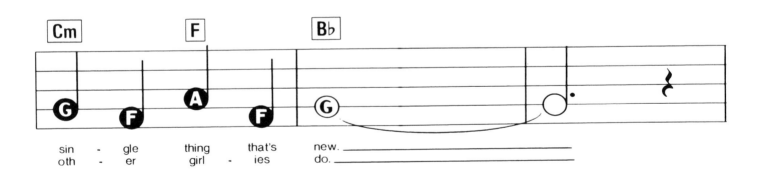

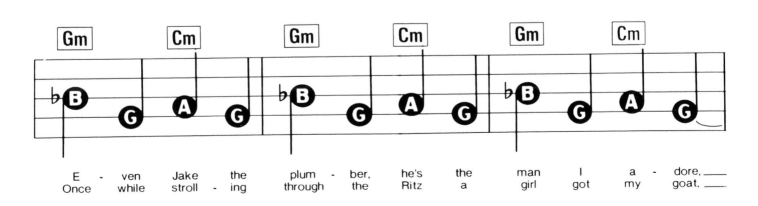

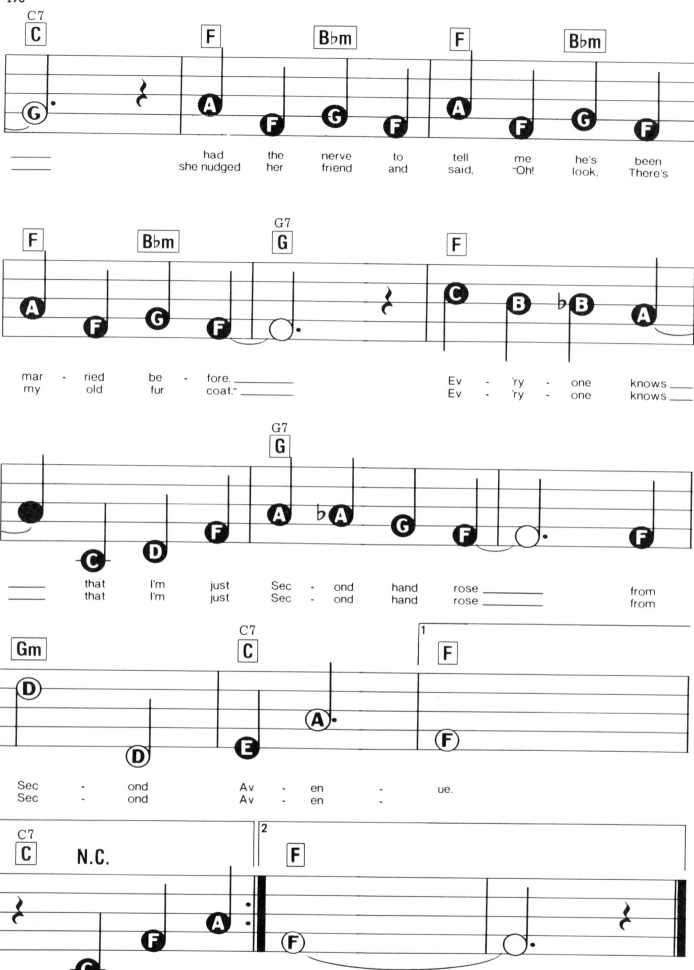

Shoo Fly Pie
and Apple Pan Dowdy

Registration 2
Rhythm: Swing

Words by Sammy Gallop
Music by Guy Wood

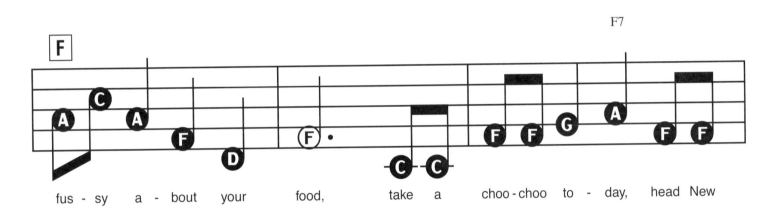

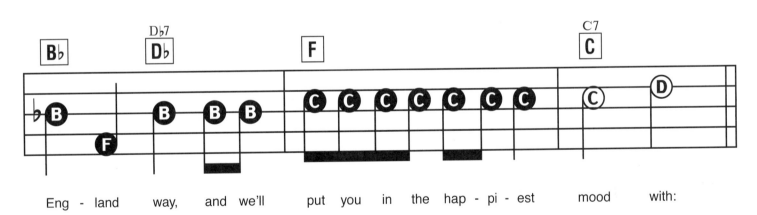

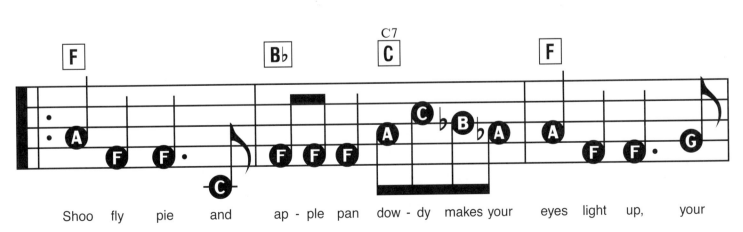

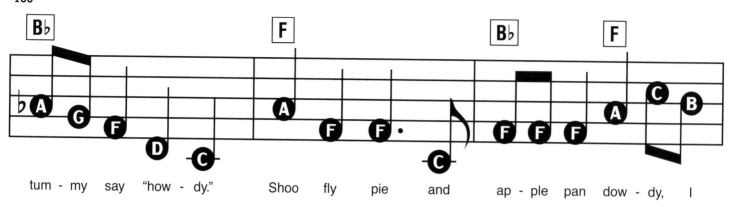

tum - my say "how - dy." Shoo fly pie and ap - ple pan dow - dy, I

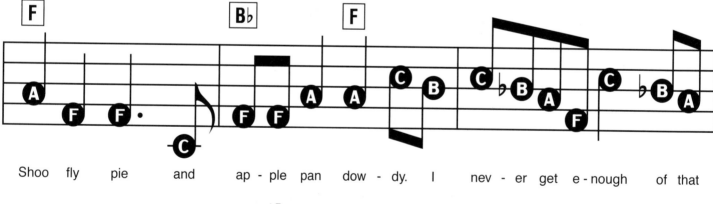

nev - er get e - nough of that won - der - ful stuff. Shoo fly pie and

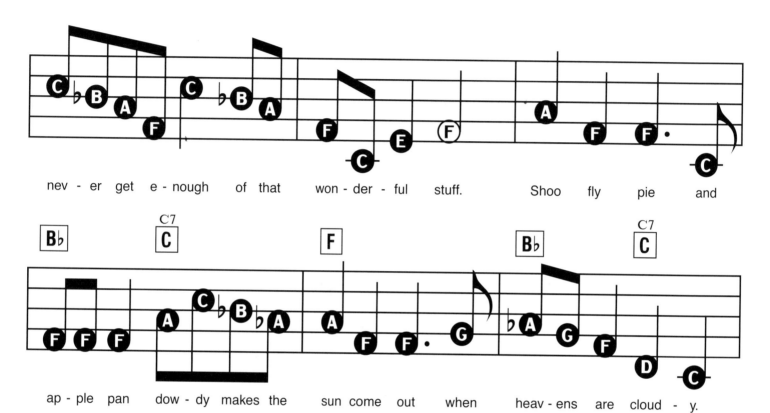

ap - ple pan dow - dy makes the sun come out when heav - ens are cloud - y.

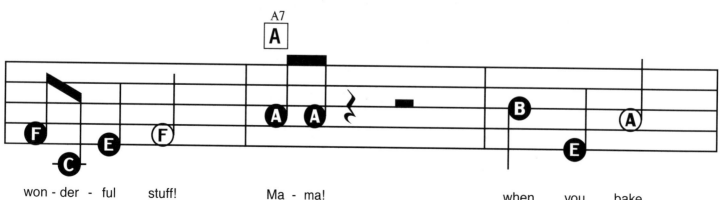

Shoo fly pie and ap - ple pan dow - dy. I nev - er get e - nough of that

won - der - ful stuff! Ma - ma! when you bake.

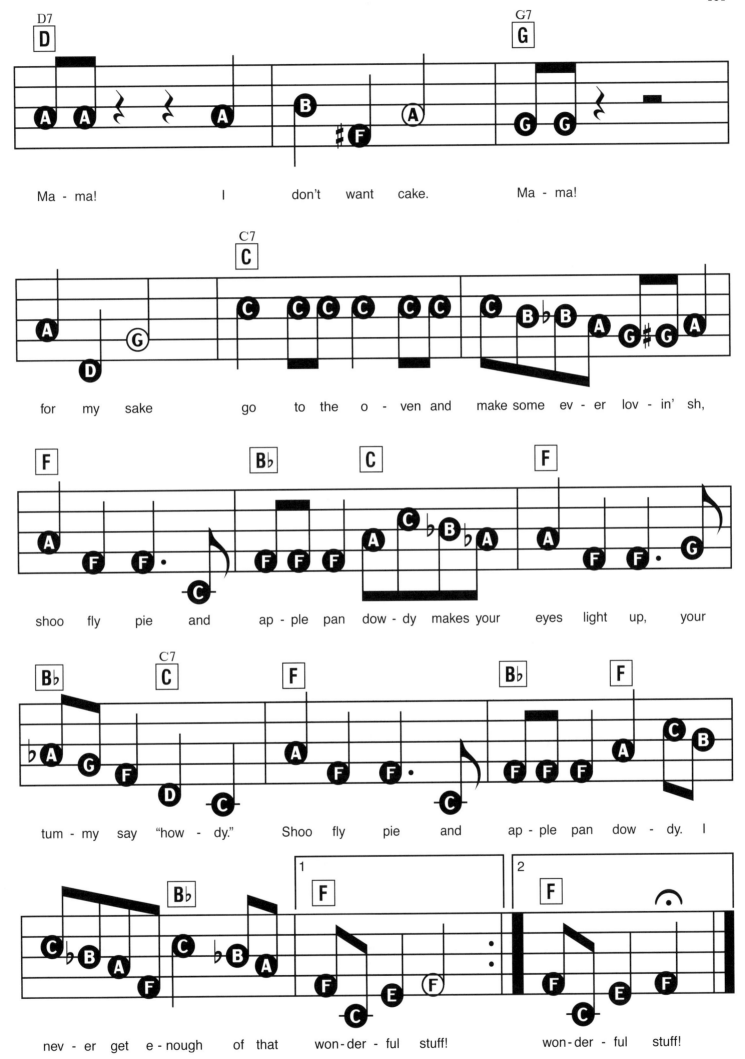

Sentimental Journey

Registration 2
Rhythm: Fox Trot or Swing

Words and Music by Bud Green,
Les Brown and Ben Homer

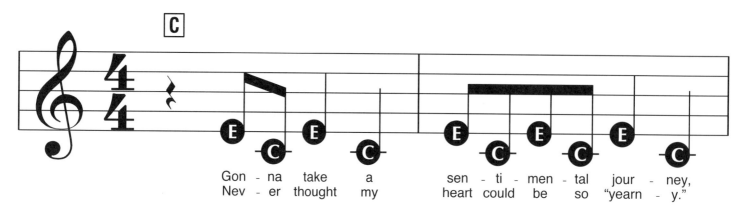

Gon - na take a sen - ti - men - tal jour - ney,
Nev - er thought my heart could be so "yearn - y."

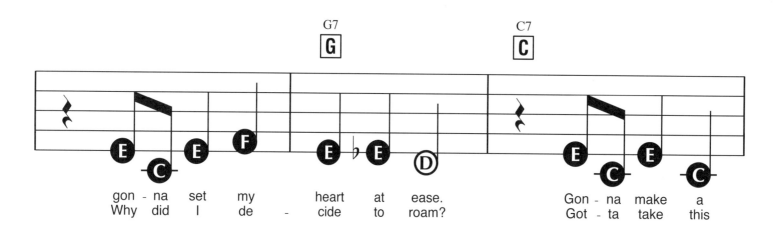

gon - na set my heart at ease. Gon - na make a
Why did I de - cide to roam? Got - ta take this

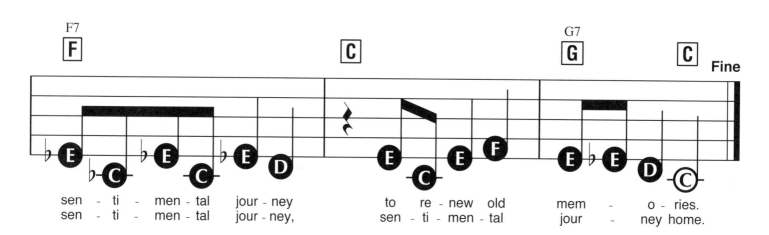

sen - ti - men - tal jour - ney to re - new old mem - o - ries.
sen - ti - men - tal jour - ney, sen - ti - men - tal jour - ney home.

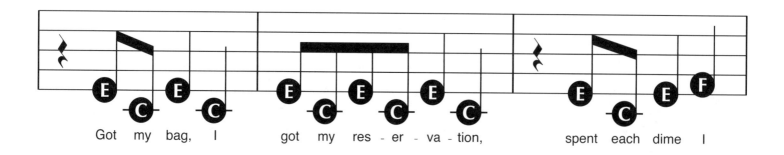

Got my bag, I got my res - er - va - tion, spent each dime I

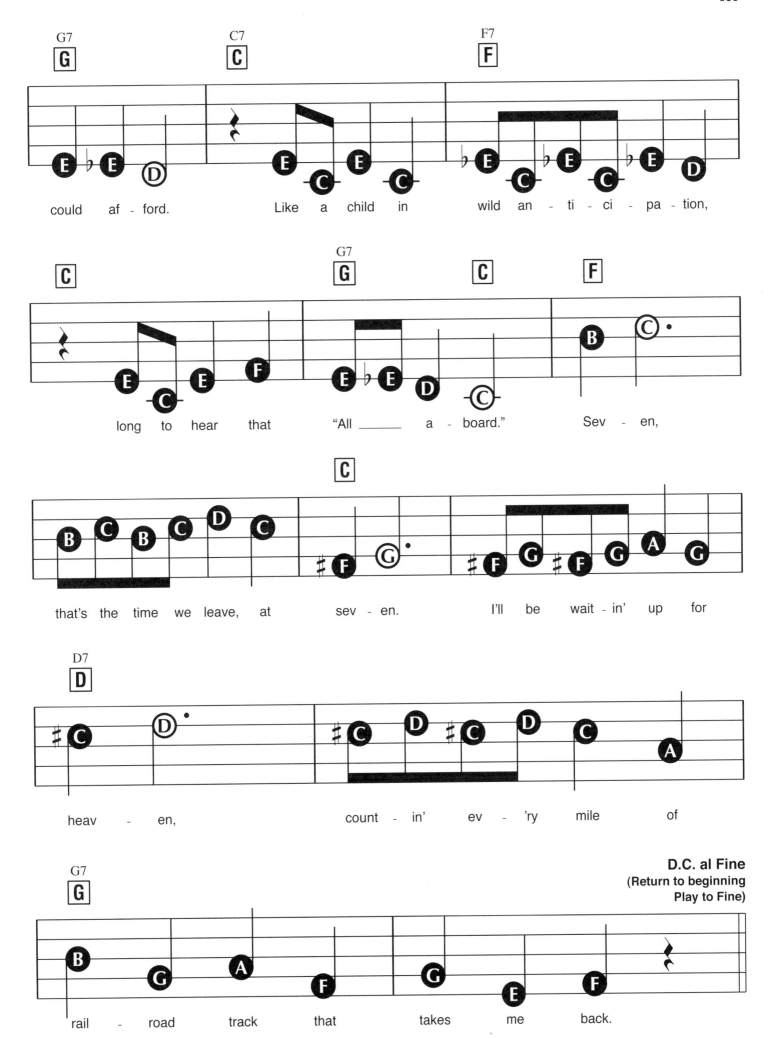

D.C. al Fine
(Return to beginning
Play to Fine)

Smile
Theme from MODERN TIMES

Registration 9
Rhythm: Ballad or Fox Trot

Words by John Turner and Geoffrey Parsons
Music by Charles Chaplin

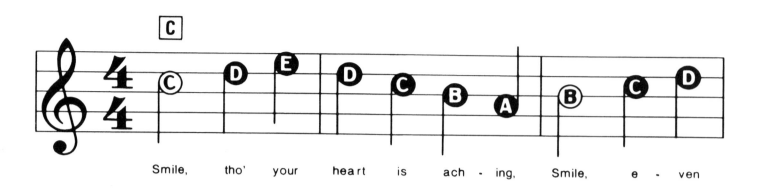

Smile, tho' your heart is ach - ing, Smile, e - ven

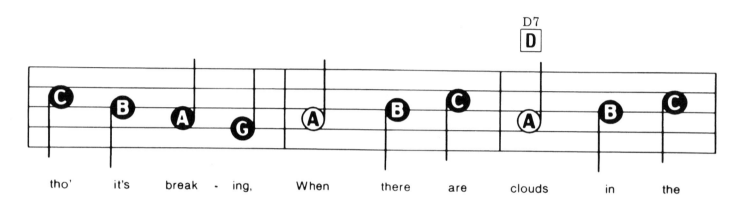

tho' it's break - ing, When there are clouds in the

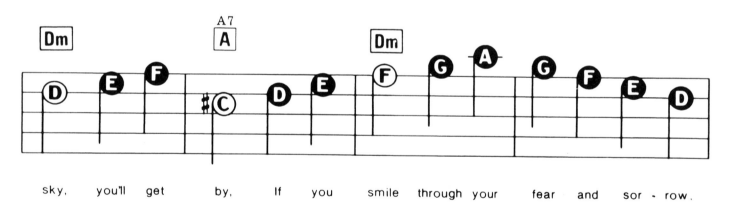

sky, you'll get by, If you smile through your fear and sor - row.

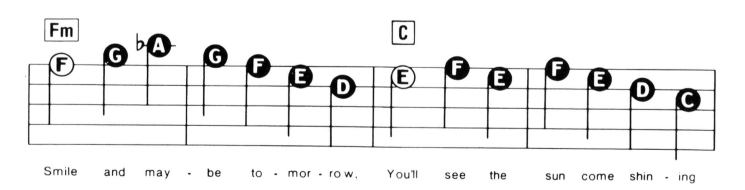

Smile and may - be to - mor - row, You'll see the sun come shin - ing

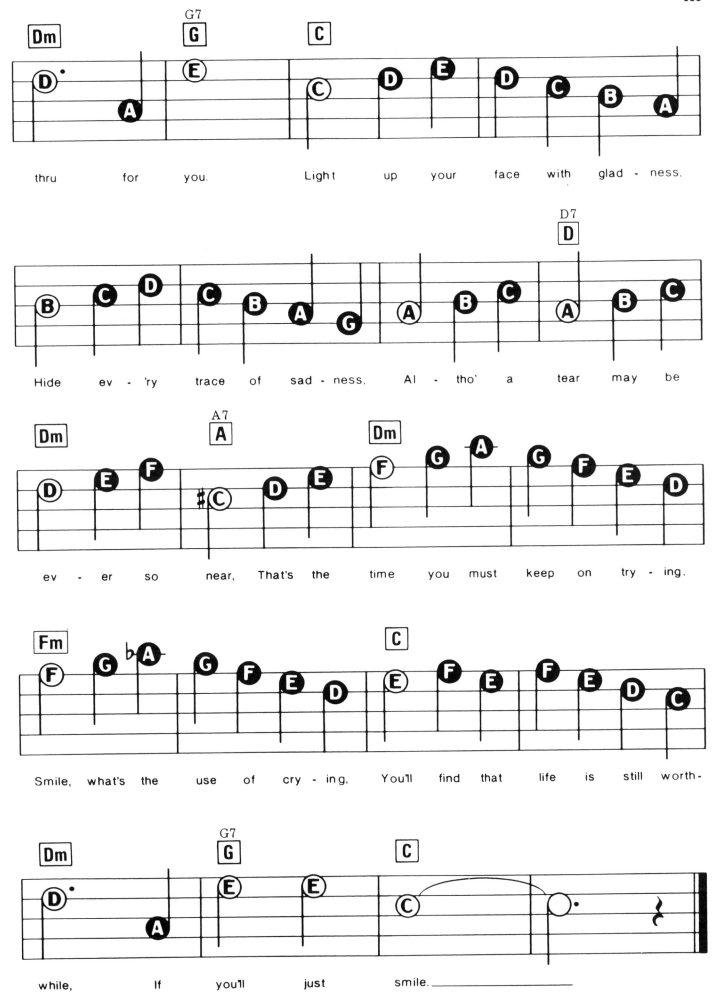

Smoke Gets in Your Eyes
from ROBERTA

Registration 10
Rhythm: Ballad or Swing

Words by Otto Harbach
Music by Jerome Kern

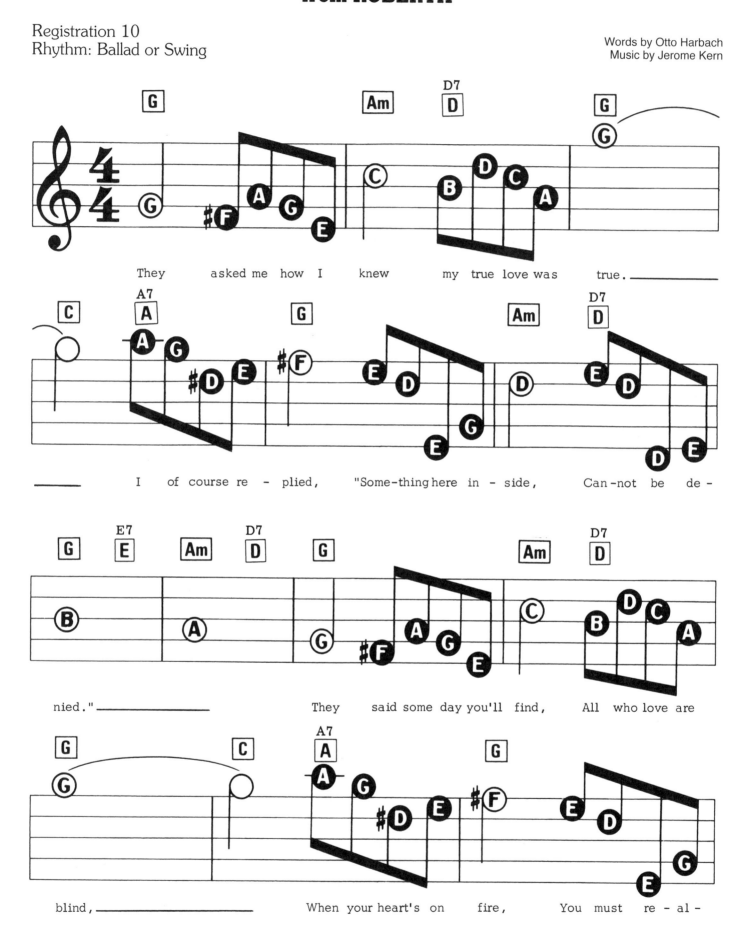

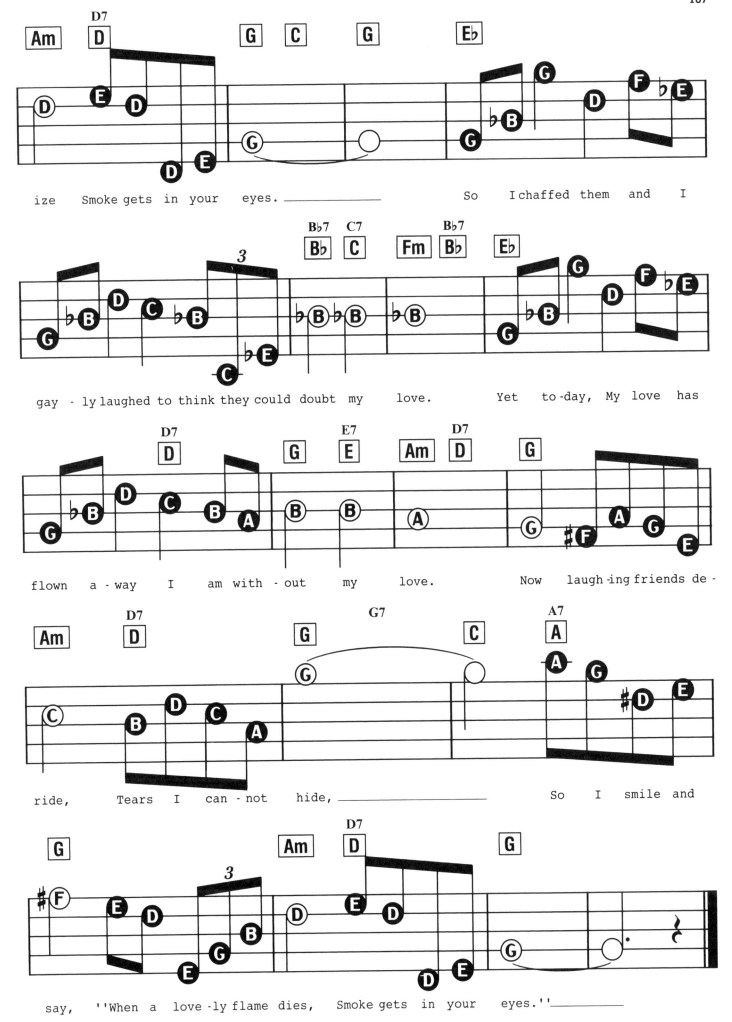

The Song Is Ended
(But the Melody Lingers On)

Registration 10
Rhythm: Waltz

Words and Music by
Irving Berlin

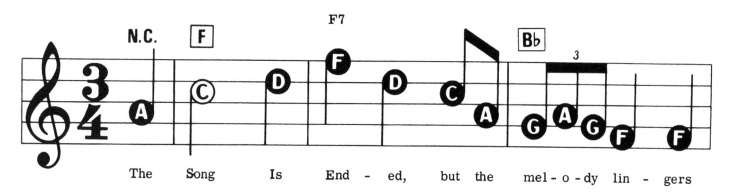

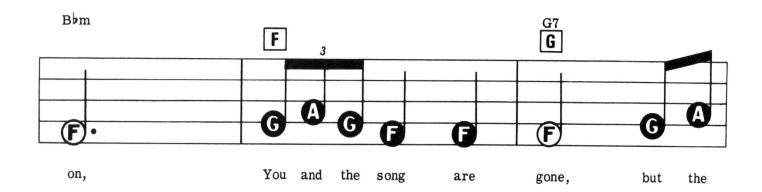

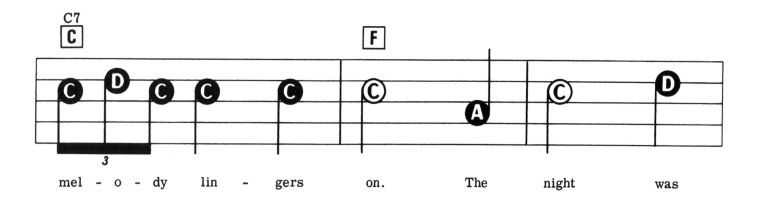

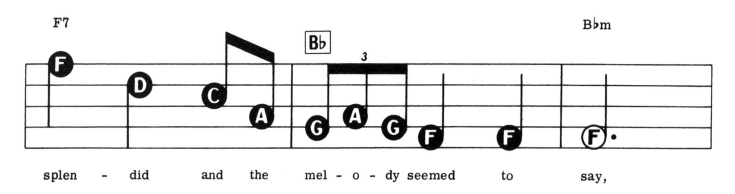

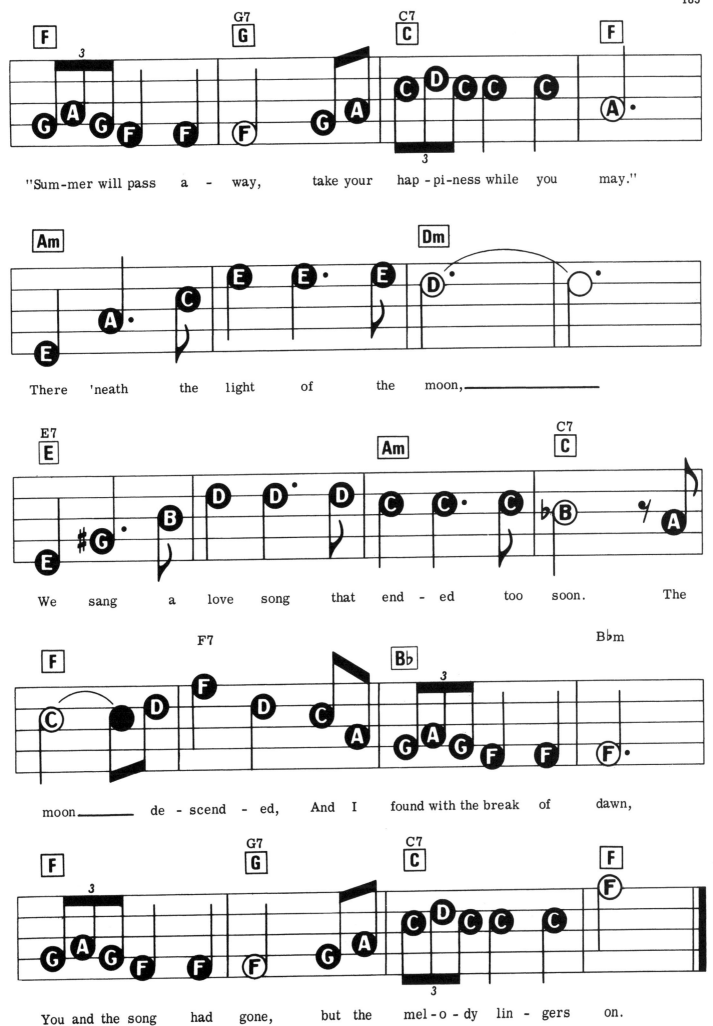

Speak Low
from the Musical Production ONE TOUCH OF VENUS

Registration 2
Rhythm: Bossa Nova or Latin

Words by Ogden Nash
Music by Kurt Weill

Speak

low _____ when you speak, love. _____
low, _____ dar - ling, speak low. _____
late, _____ dar - ling, we're late. _____

_____ Our sum - mer day with - ers a - way too
_____ Love is a spark lost in the dark too
The cur - tain de - scends, ev - 'ry - thing ends too

soon, too soon. Speak low _____ when you speak,
soon, too soon. I feel _____ wher - ev - er I
soon, too soon. I wait, _____

love. _____ Our _____ mo - ment is swift, like _____ ships a -
go _____ That to - mor - row is near, to - mor - row is

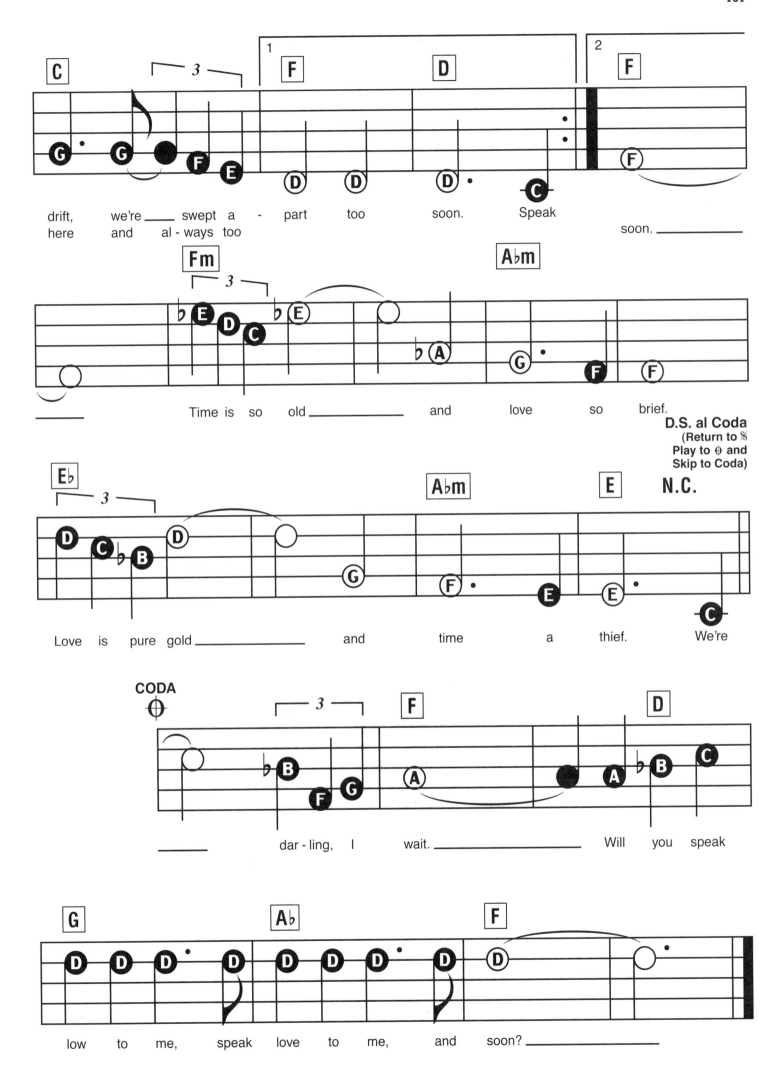

A Sunday Kind of Love

Registration 2
Rhythm: Swing or Jazz

Words and Music by Louis Prima, Anita Nye Leonard,
Stanley Rhodes and Barbara Belle

I want a Sun-day kind of love,___ a love to last past

Sat-ur-day night,___ I'd like to know it's more than love at first sight.___

I want a Sun-day kind of love._____ I want a love that's on the square.___

Can't seem to find some-bod-y to care.___ I'm on a lone-ly road that

leads me no-where.___ I need a Sun-day kind of love._____ I

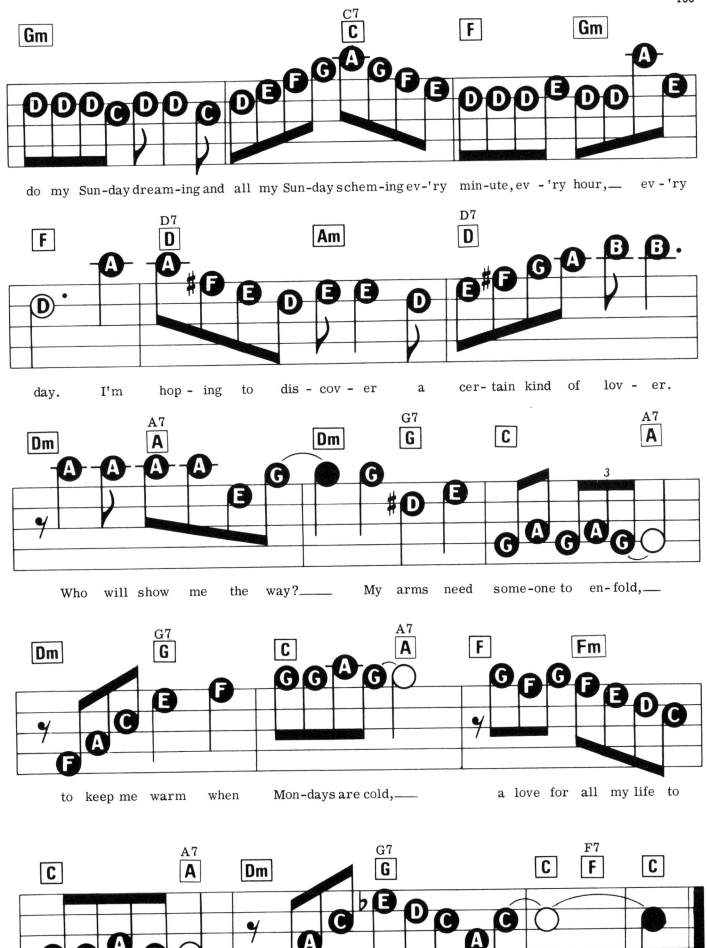

193

(Love Is)
The Tender Trap

Registration 3
Rhythm: Fox Trot or Swing

Words by Sammy Cahn
Music by James Van Heusen

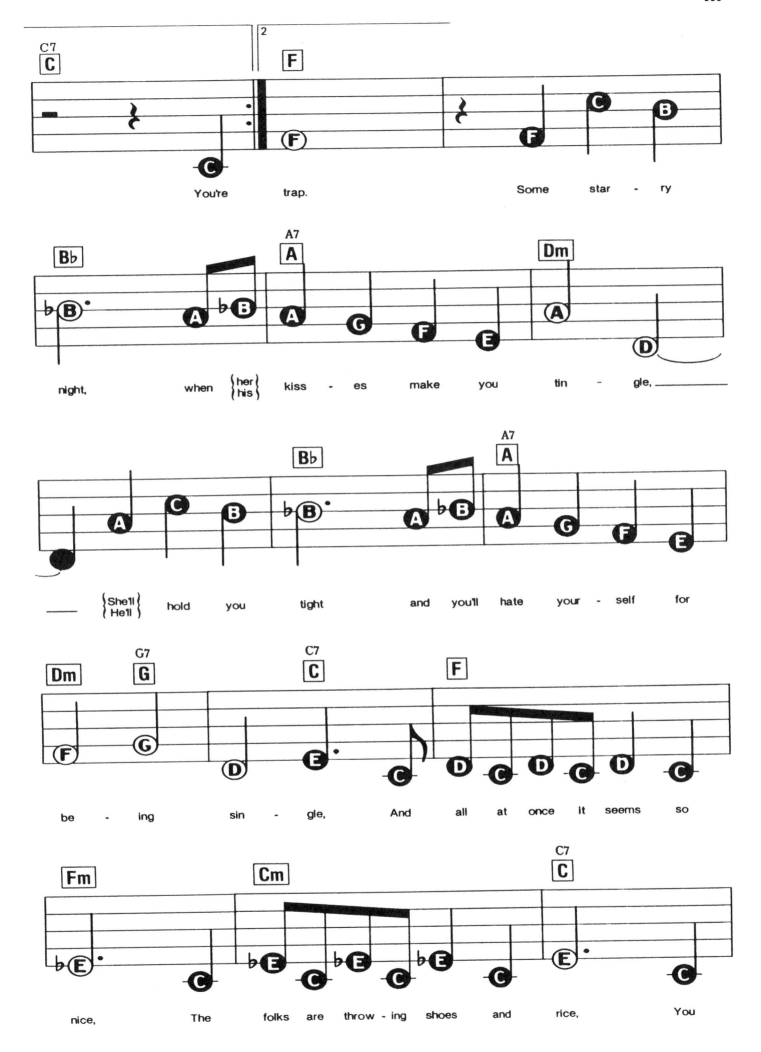

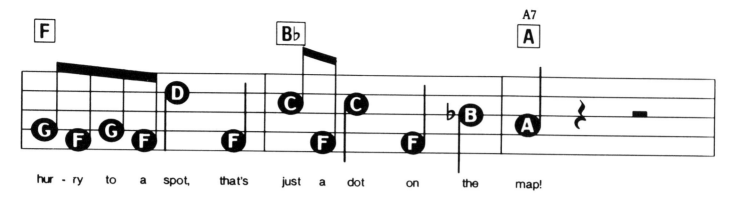

hur - ry to a spot, that's just a dot on the map!

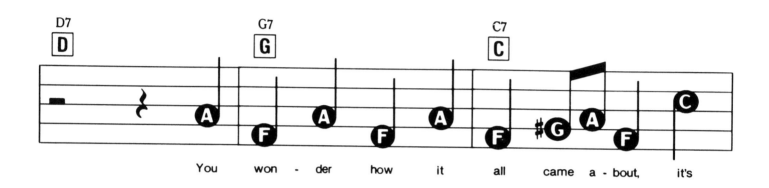

You won - der how it all came a - bout, it's

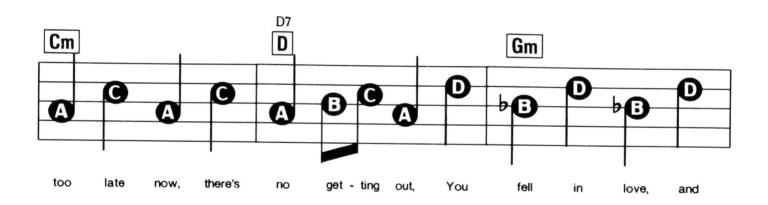

too late now, there's no get - ting out, You fell in love, and

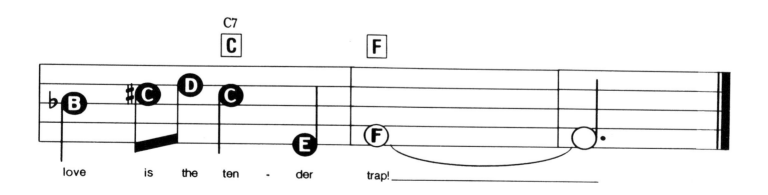

love is the ten - der trap!

Sunrise, Sunset
from the Musical FIDDLER ON THE ROOF

Registration 1
Rhythm: Waltz

Words by Sheldon Harnick
Music by Jerry Bock

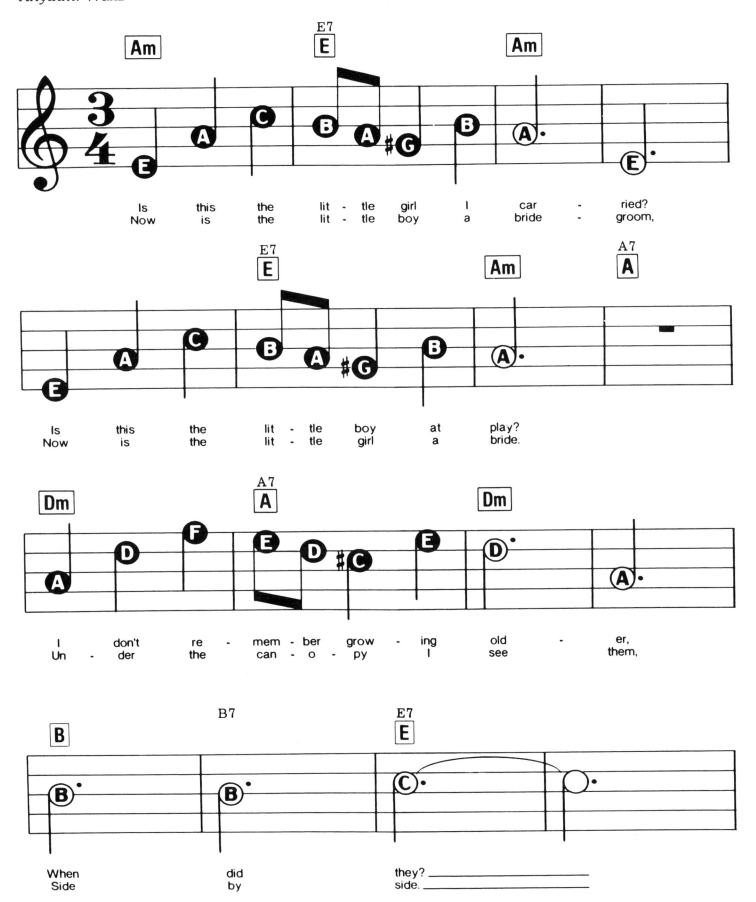

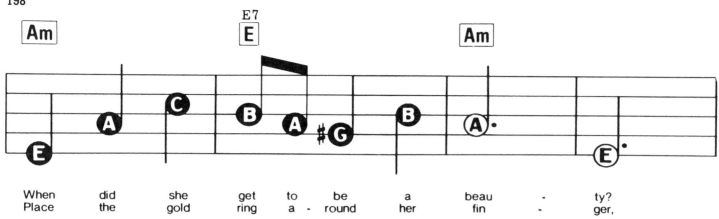

When did she get to be a beau - ty?
Place the gold ring a - round her fin - ger,

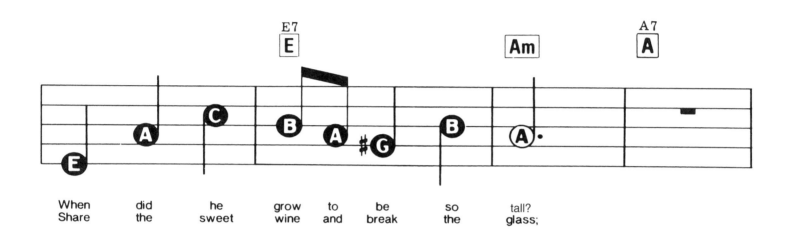

When did he grow to be so tall?
Share the sweet wine and break the glass;

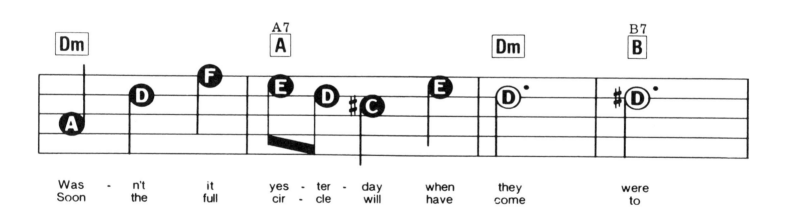

Was - n't it yes - ter - day when they were
Soon the full cir - cle will have come to

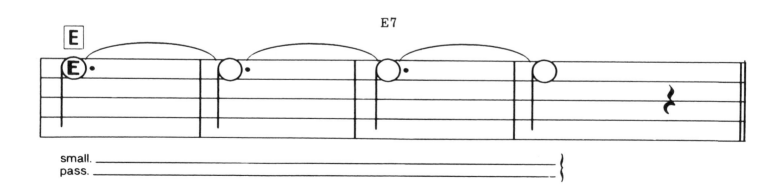

small.
pass.

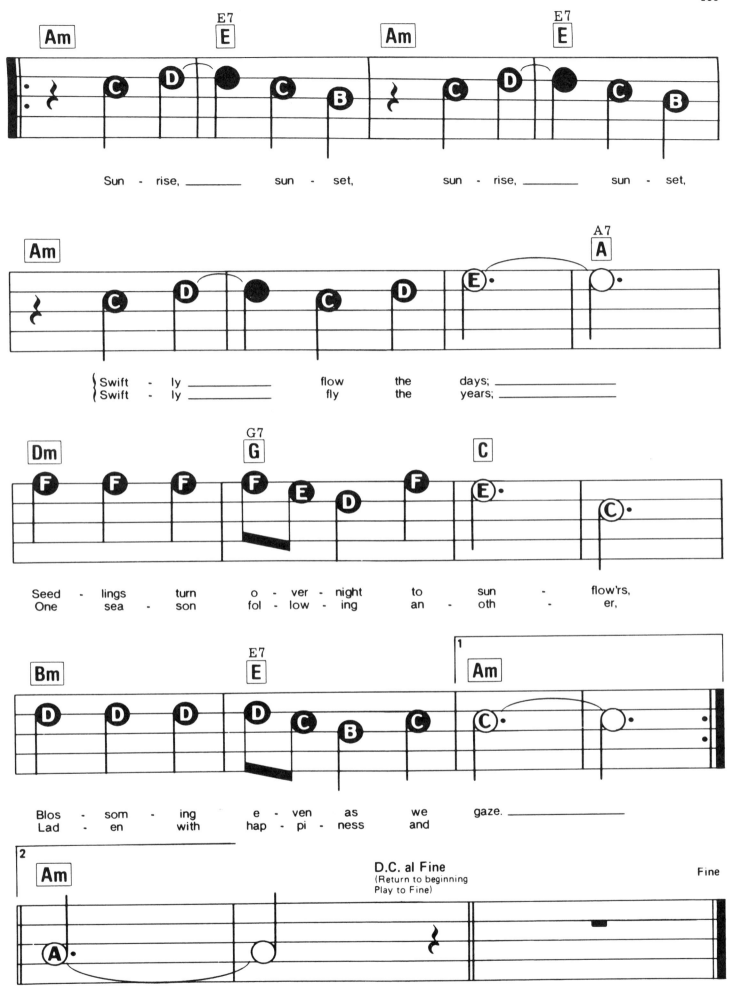

Sun - rise, _____ sun - set, sun - rise, _____ sun - set,

Swift - ly _____ flow the days; _____
Swift - ly _____ fly the years; _____

Seed - lings turn o - ver - night to sun - flow'rs,
One sea - son fol - low - ing an - oth - er,

Blos - som - ing e - ven as we gaze. _____
Lad - en with hap - pi - ness and

D.C. al Fine
(Return to beginning
Play to Fine)

Fine

tears. _____

Swinging on a Star
from GOING MY WAY

Registration 2
Rhythm: Swing

Words by Johnny Burke
Music by Jimmy Van Heusen

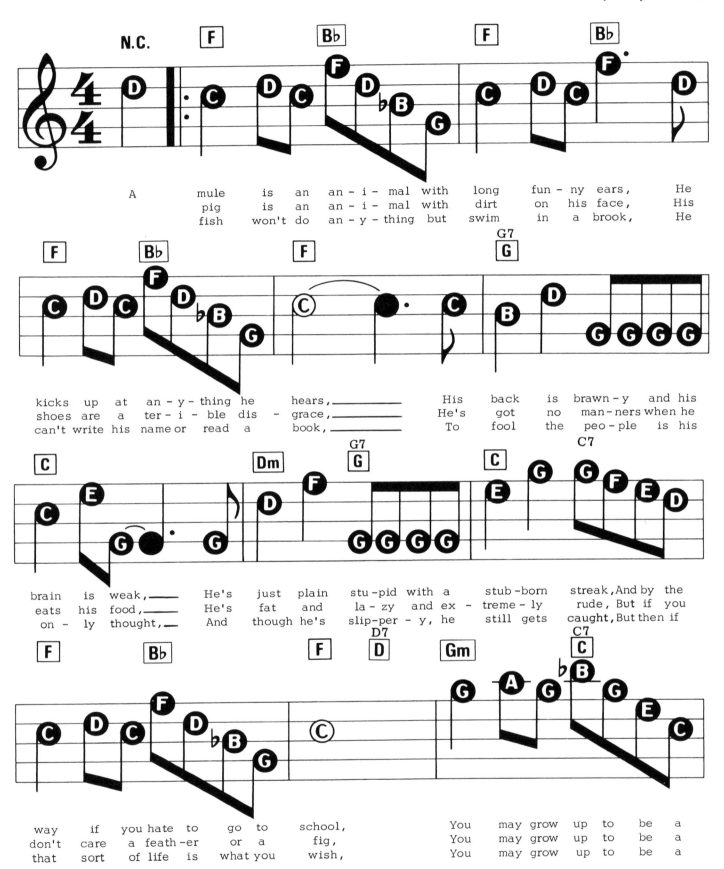

A mule is an an-i-mal with long fun-ny ears, He
pig is an an-i-mal with dirt on his face, His
fish won't do an-y-thing but swim in a brook, He

kicks up at an-y-thing he hears,_____ His back is brawn-y and his
shoes are a ter-i-ble dis-grace,_____ He's got no man-ners when he
can't write his name or read a book,_____ To fool the peo-ple is his

brain is weak,____ He's just plain stu-pid with a stub-born streak, And by the
eats his food,____ He's fat and la-zy and ex-treme-ly rude, But if you
on-ly thought,___ And though he's slip-per-y, he still gets caught, But then if

way if you hate to go to school, You may grow up to be a
don't care a feath-er or a fig, You may grow up to be a
that sort of life is what you wish, You may grow up to be a

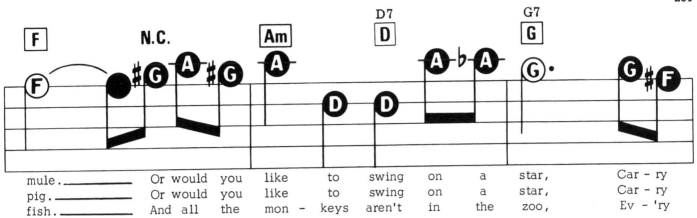

mule._____ Or would you like to swing on a star, Car – ry
pig._____ Or would you like to swing on a star, Car – ry
fish._____ And all the mon – keys aren't in the zoo, Ev – 'ry

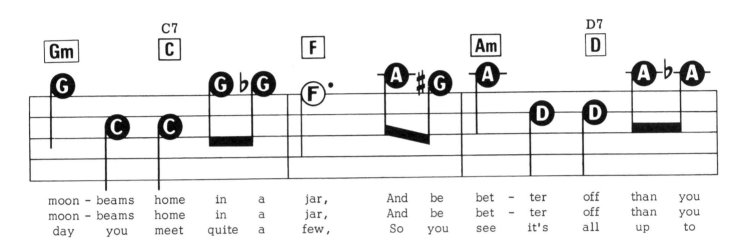

moon – beams home in a jar, And be bet – ter off than you
moon – beams home in a jar, And be bet – ter off than you
day you meet quite a few, So you see it's all up to

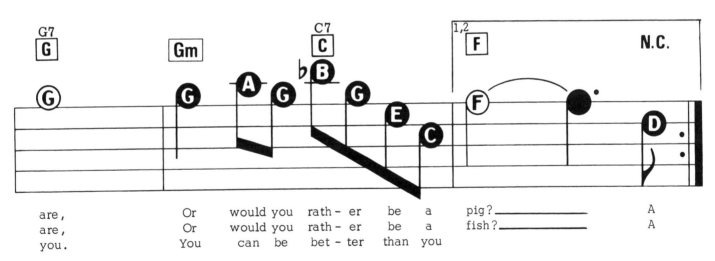

are, Or would you rath – er be a pig?_____ A
are, Or would you rath – er be a fish?_____ A
you. You can be bet – ter than you

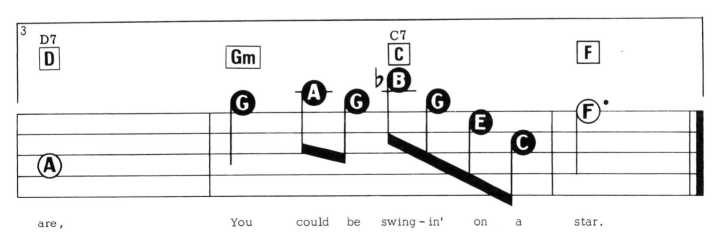

are, You could be swing – in' on a star.

Tenderly
from TORCH SONG

Registration 2
Rhythm: Waltz

Lyric by Jack Lawrence
Music by Walter Gross

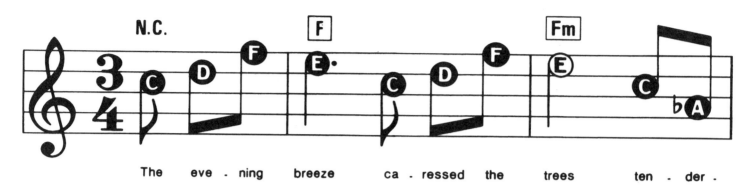

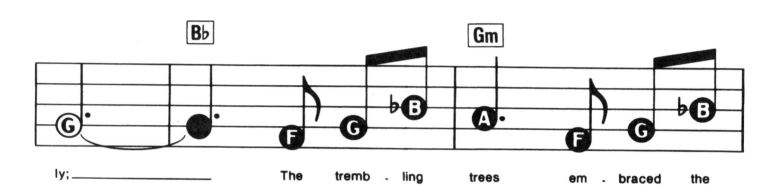

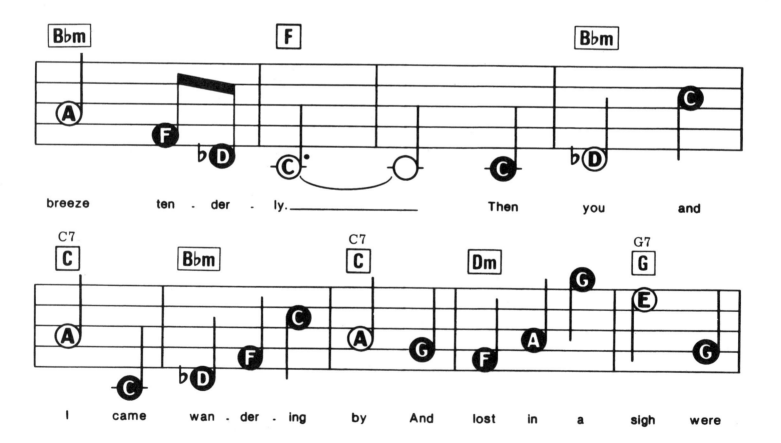

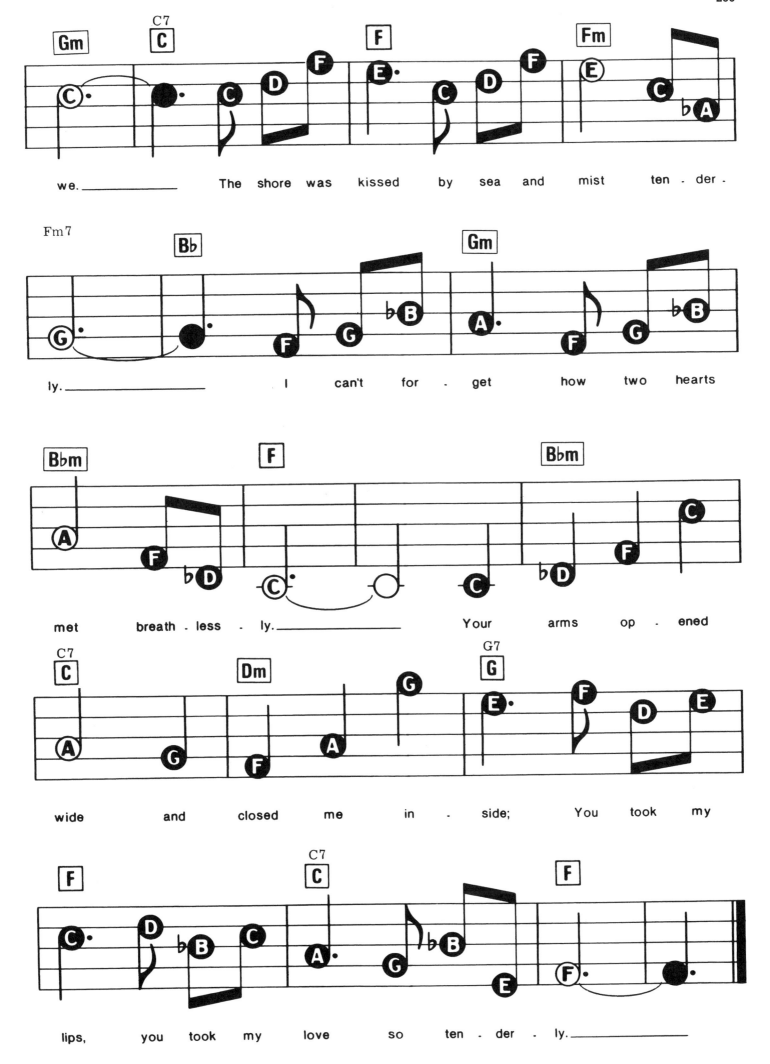

That Old Black Magic
from the Paramount Picture STAR SPANGLED RHYTHM

Registration 1
Rhythm: Fox Trot or Swing

Words by Johnny Mercer
Music by Harold Arlen

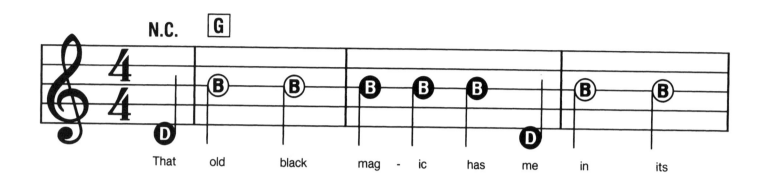

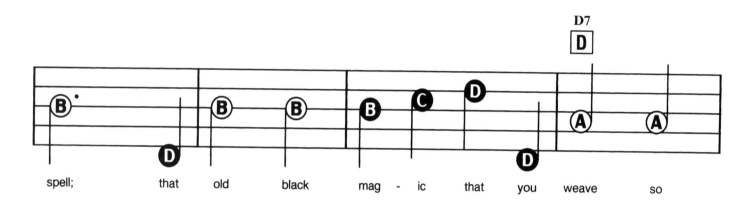

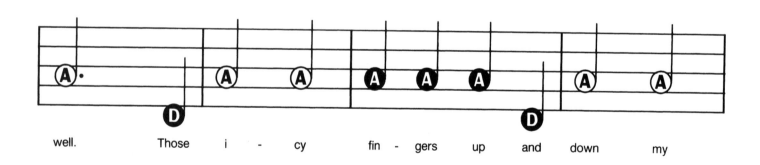

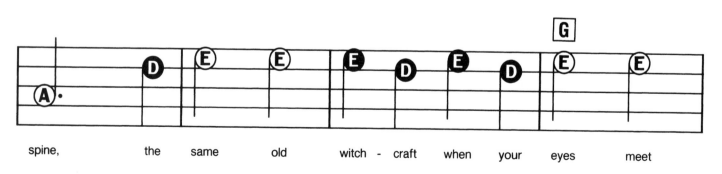

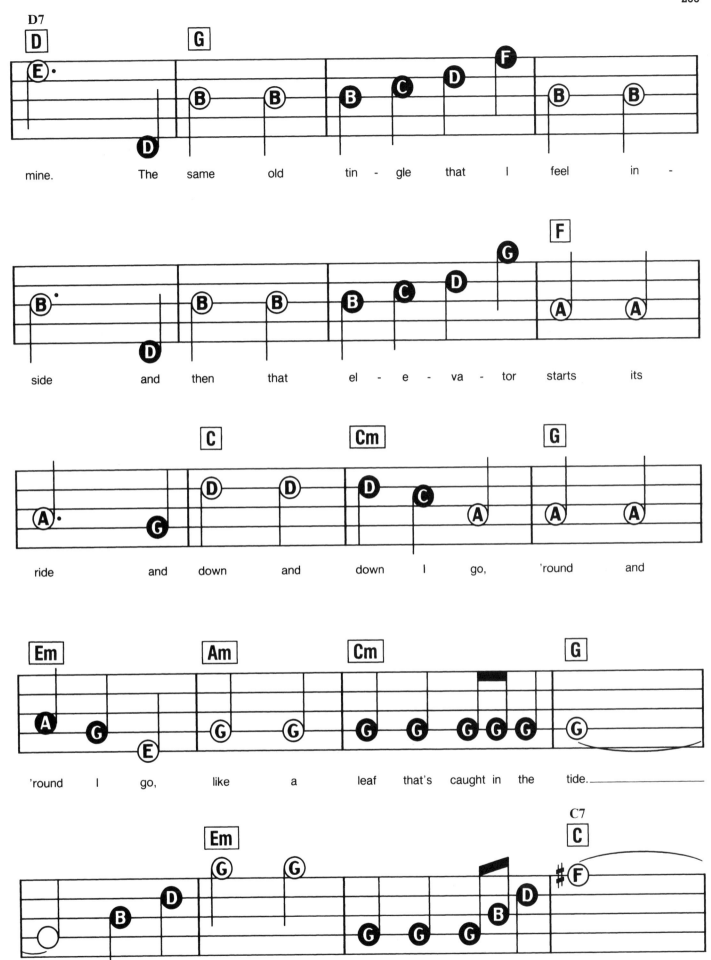

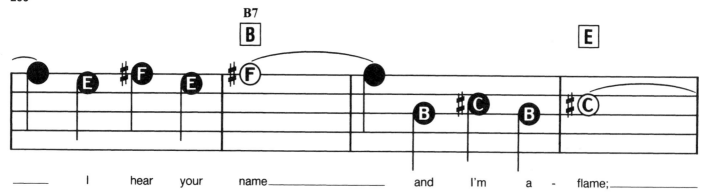

I hear your name_____ and I'm a - flame;_____

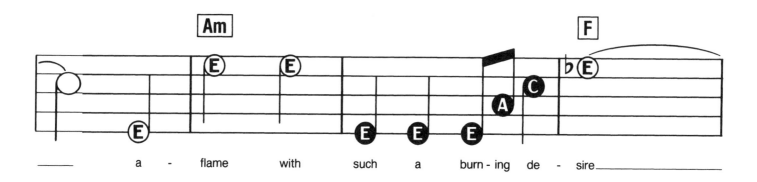

_____ a - flame with such a burn - ing de - sire_____

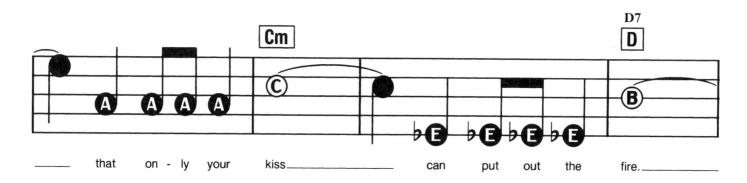

_____ that on - ly your kiss_____ can put out the fire._____

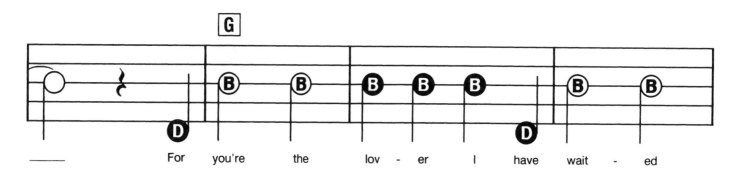

_____ For you're the lov - er I have wait - ed

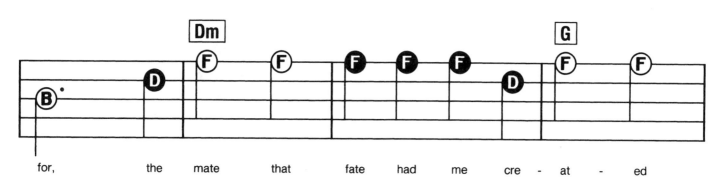

for, the mate that fate had me cre - at - ed

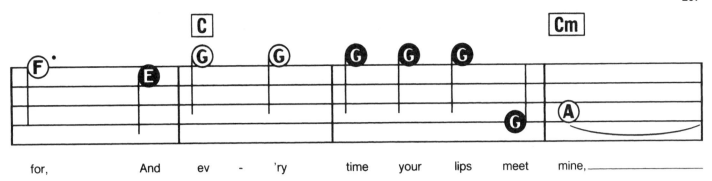

for, And ev - 'ry time your lips meet mine,_____

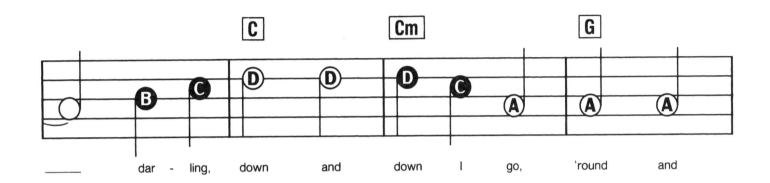

_____ dar - ling, down and down I go, 'round and

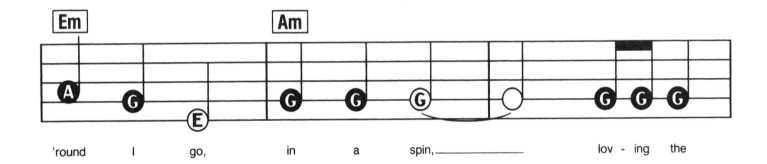

'round I go, in a spin,_____ lov - ing the

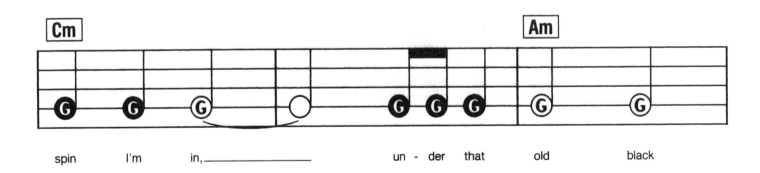

spin I'm in,_____ un - der that old black

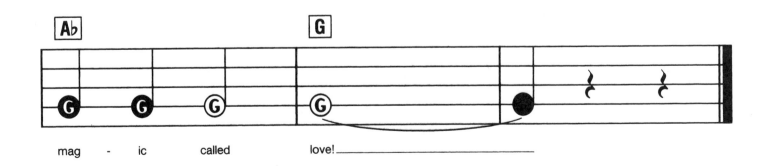

mag - ic called love!_____

That's Amoré
(That's Love)
from the Paramount Picture THE CADDY

Registration 3
Rhythm: Waltz

Words by Jack Brooks
Music by Harry Warren

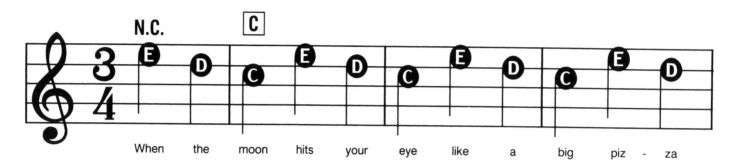

When the moon hits your eye like a big piz - za

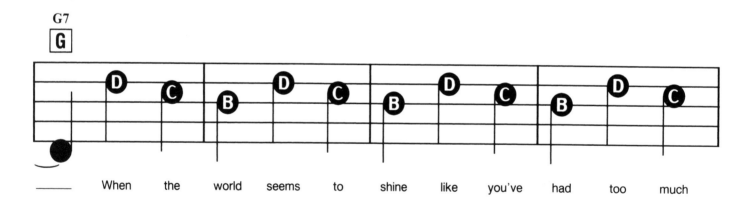

pie, that's a - mor - é. _____

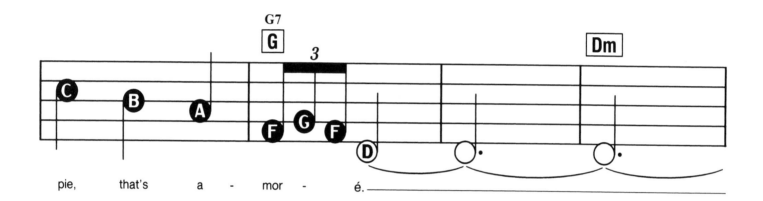

When the world seems to shine like you've had too much

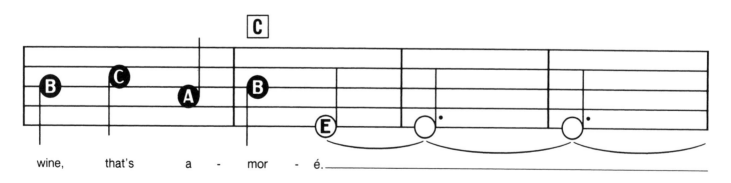

wine, that's a - mor - é. _____

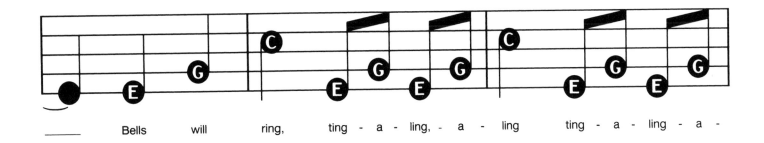

_____ Bells will ring, ting - a - ling, - a - ling ting - a - ling - a -

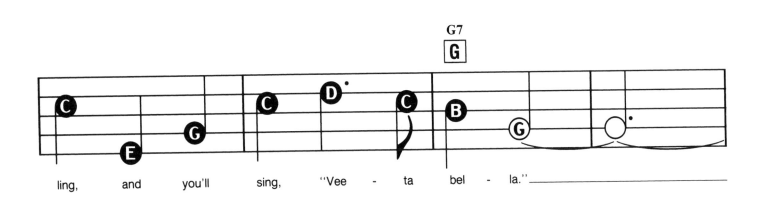

G7

ling, and you'll sing, "Vee - ta bel - la." _____

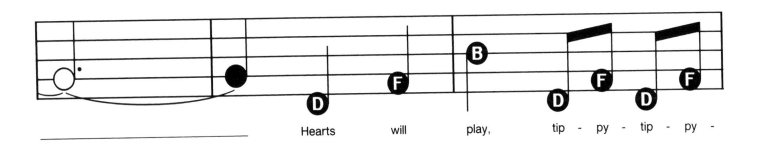

_____ Hearts will play, tip - py - tip - py -

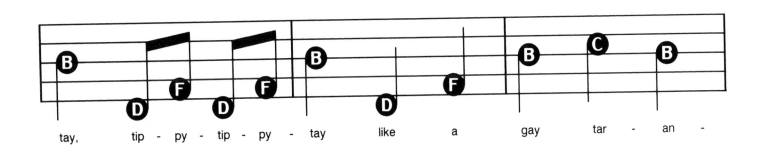

tay, tip - py - tip - py - tay like a gay tar - an -

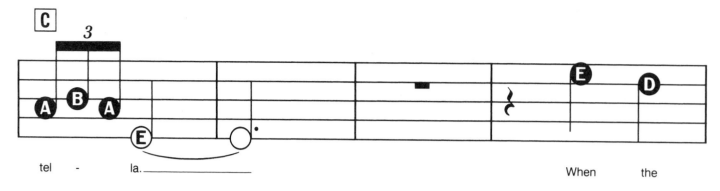

tel - la. _____ When the

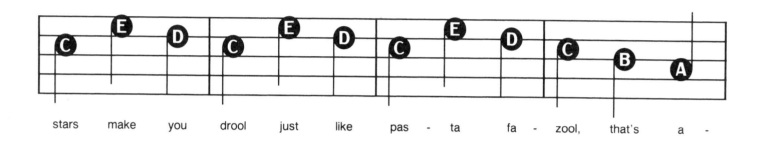

stars make you drool just like pas - ta fa - zool, that's a -

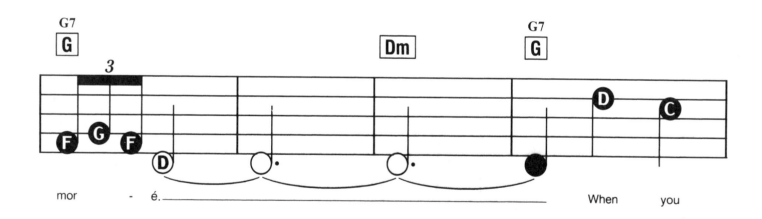

mor - é. _____ When you

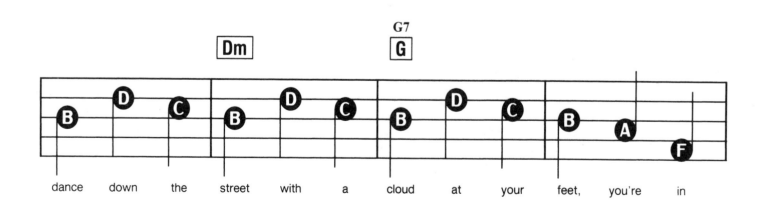

dance down the street with a cloud at your feet, you're in

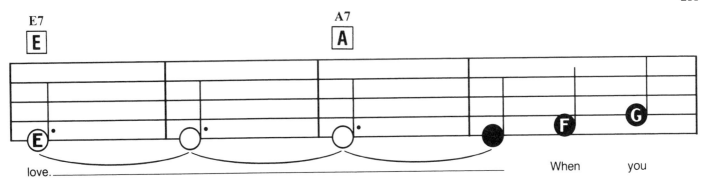

love._____ When you

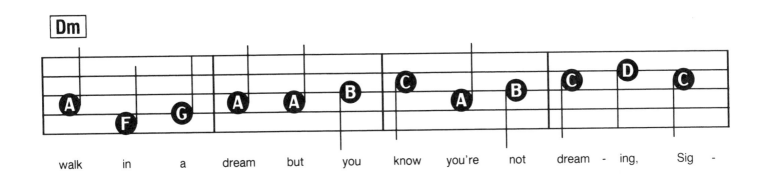

walk in a dream but you know you're not dream - ing, Sig -

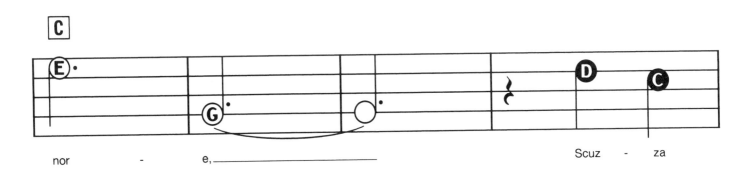

nor - e,_____ Scuz - za

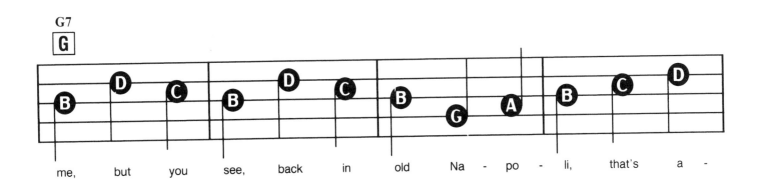

me, but you see, back in old Na - po - li, that's a -

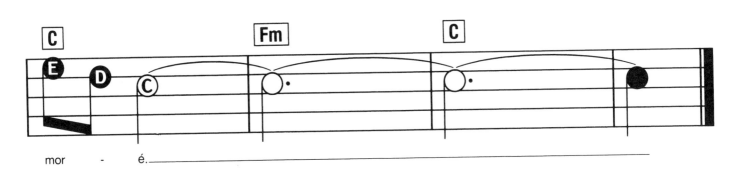

mor - é._____

That's Entertainment
from THE BAND WAGON

Registration 5
Rhythm: Fox Trot or Swing

Words by Howard Dietz
Music by Arthur Schwartz

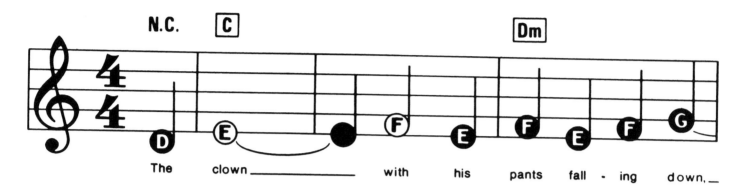

The clown _____ with his pants fall - ing down,_

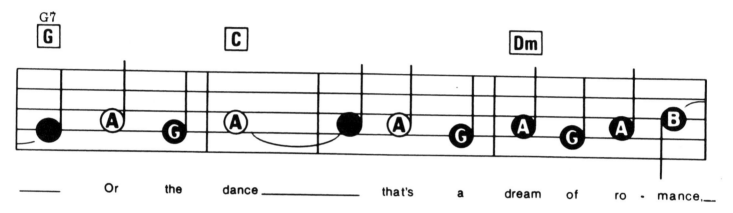

_____ Or the dance _____ that's a dream of ro - mance,_

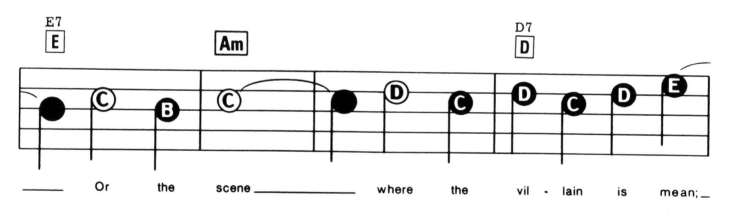

_____ Or the scene _____ where the vil - lain is mean;_

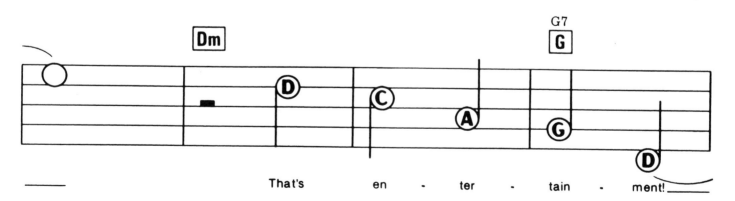

_____ That's en - ter - tain - ment!

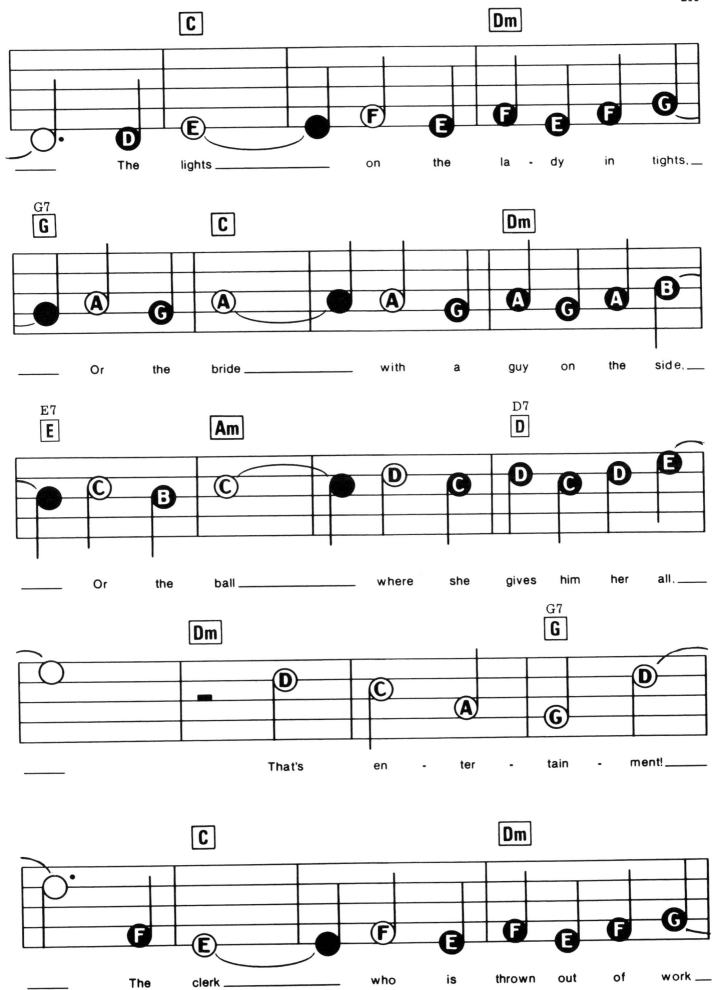

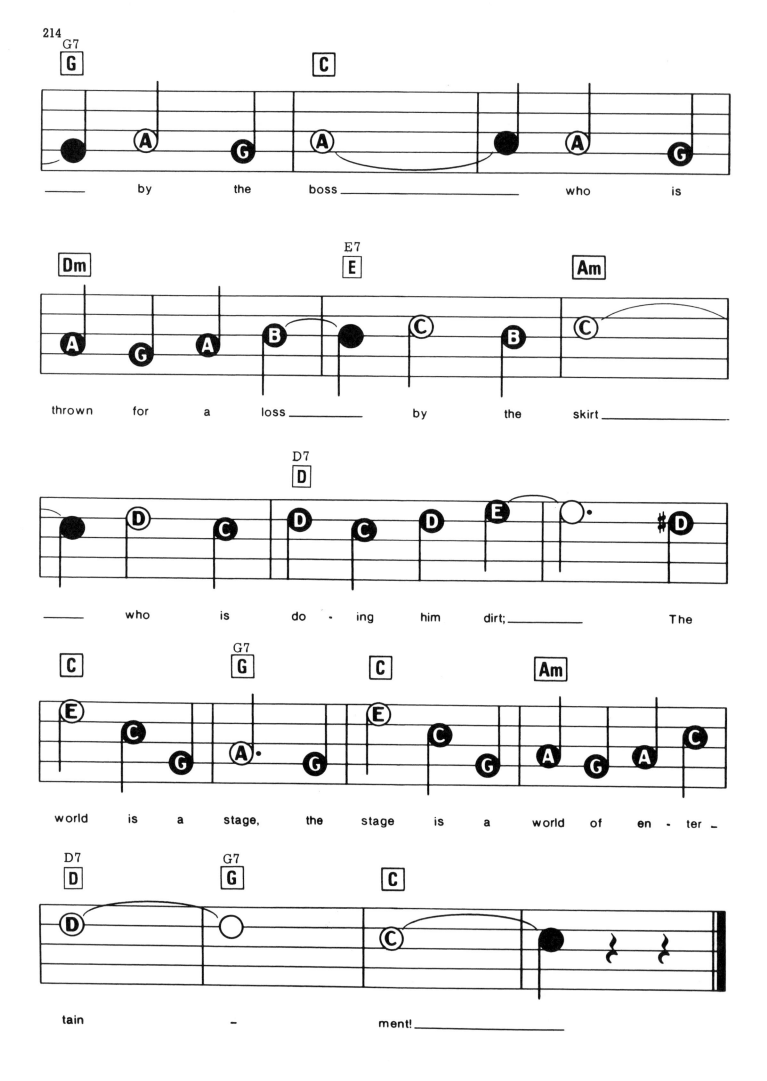

Wives and Lovers
(Hey, Little Girl)
from the Paramount Picture WIVES AND LOVERS

Registration 1
Rhythm: Waltz or Jazz Waltz

Words by Hal David
Music by Burt Bacharach

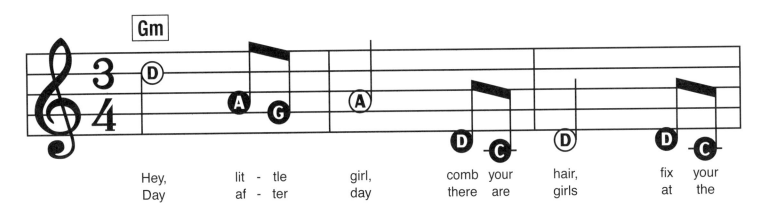

Hey, lit - tle girl, comb your hair, fix your
Day af - ter day there are girls at the

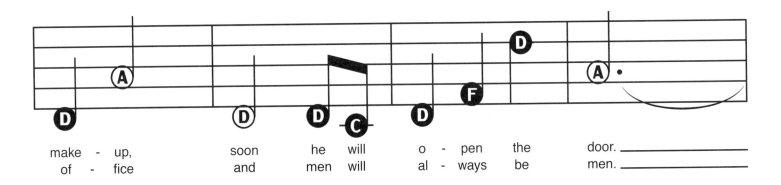

make - up, soon he will o - pen the door. _____
of - fice soon and men will al - ways be men. _____

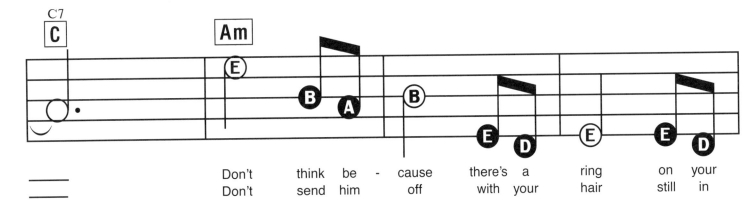

Don't think be - cause there's a ring on your
Don't send him off with your hair still in

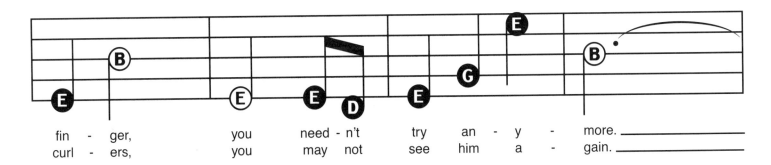

fin - ger, you need - n't try an - y - more. _____
curl - ers, you may not see him a - gain. _____

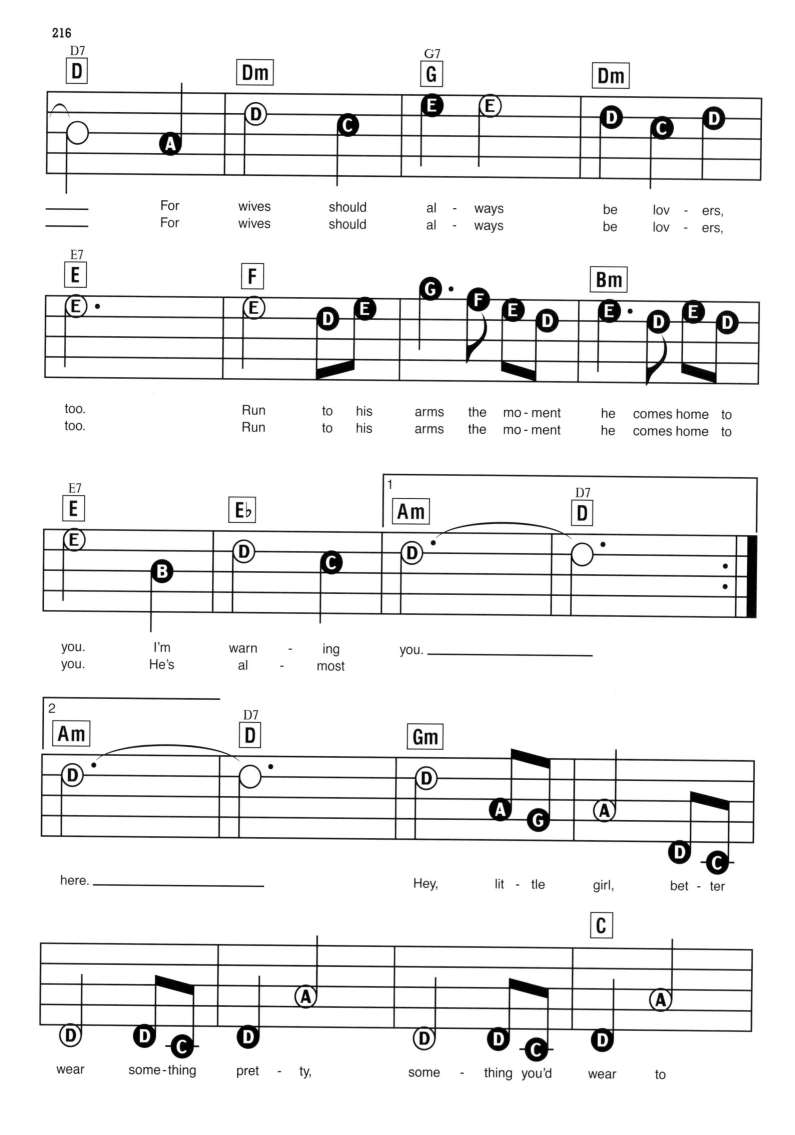

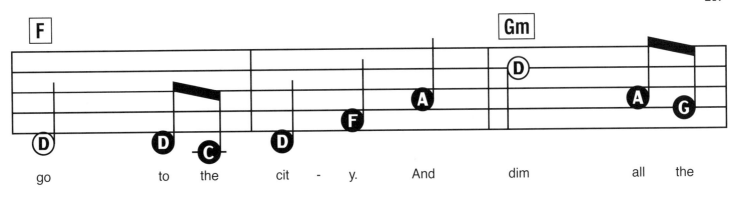

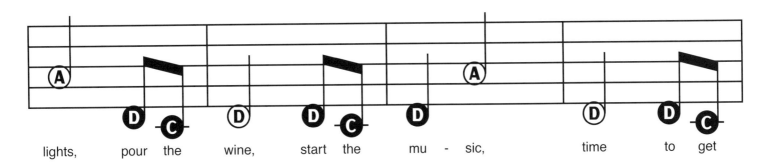

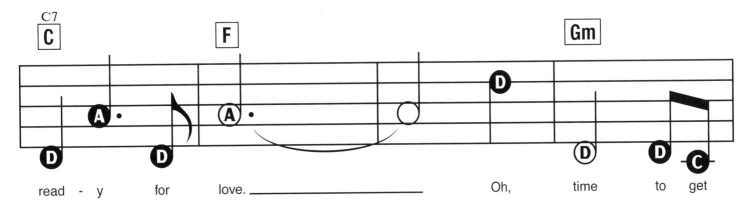

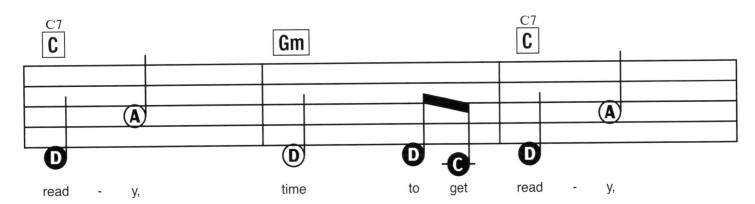

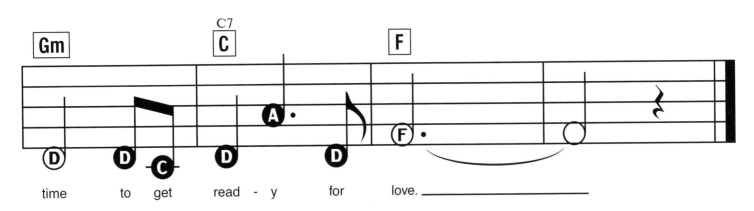

There Will Never Be Another You
from the Motion Picture ICELAND

Registration 1
Rhythm: Swing

Lyric by Mack Gordon
Music by Harry Warren

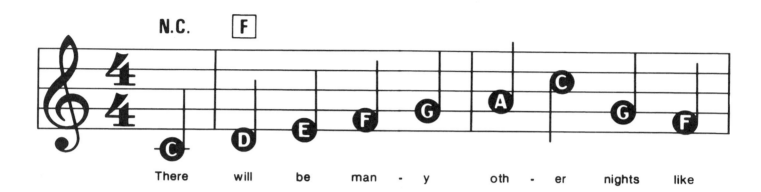

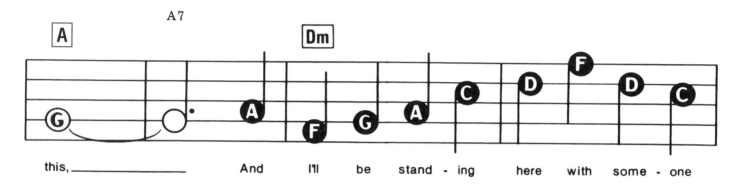

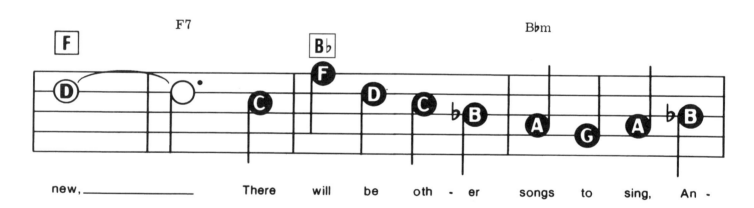

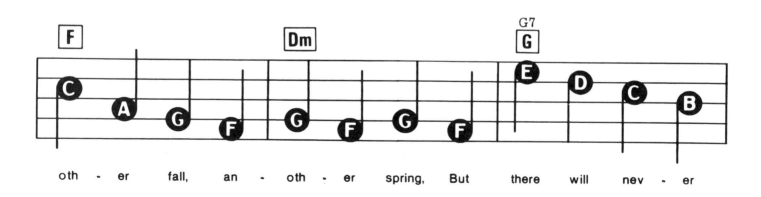

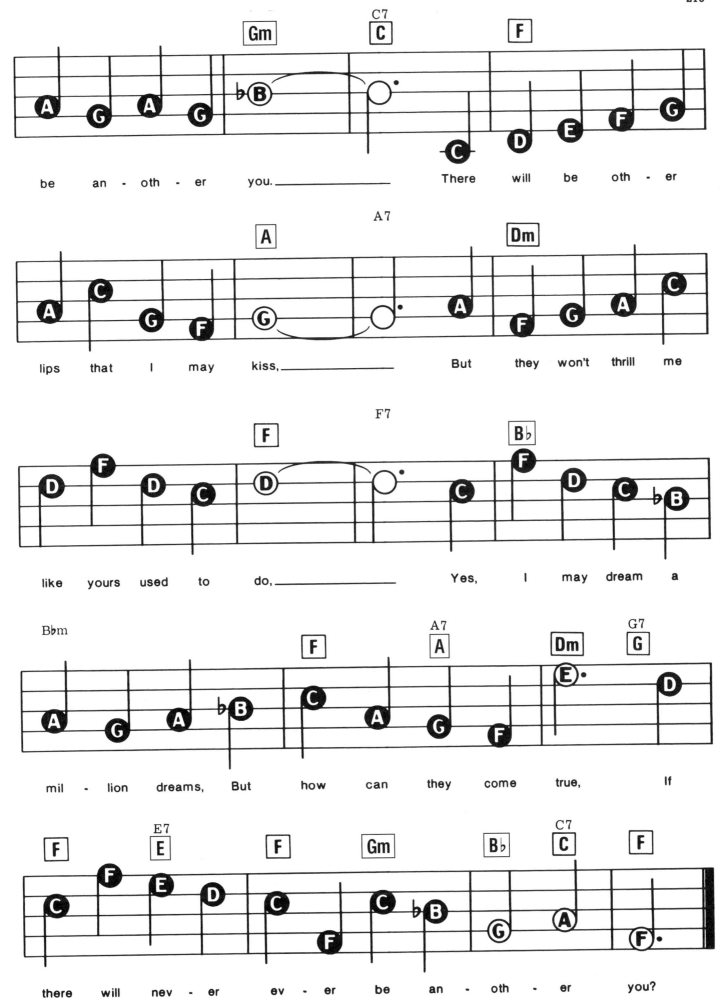

Till There Was You
from Meredith Willson's THE MUSIC MAN

Registration 2
Rhythm: Ballad

By Meredith Willson

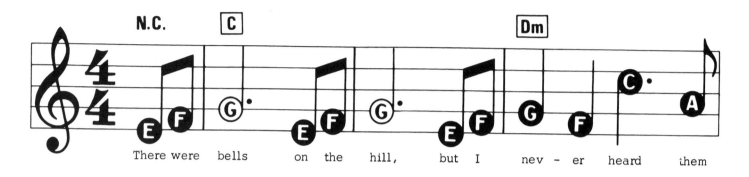

There were bells on the hill, but I nev - er heard them

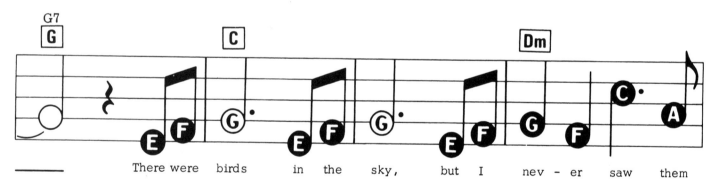

ring - ing, No, I nev - er heard them at all till there was you.____

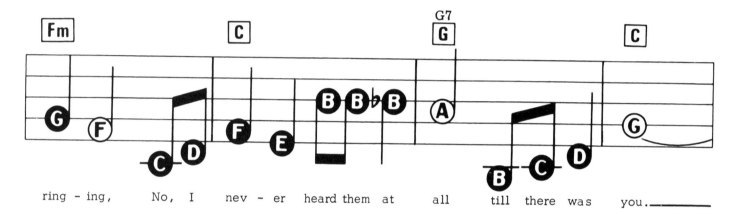

____ There were birds in the sky, but I nev - er saw them

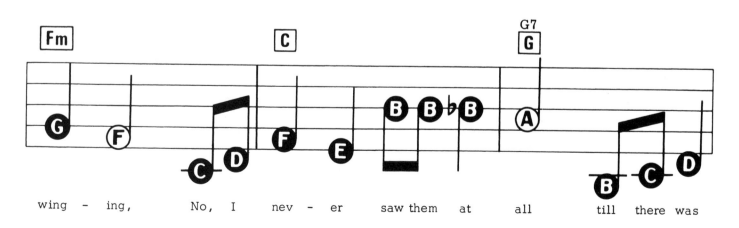

wing - ing, No, I nev - er saw them at all till there was

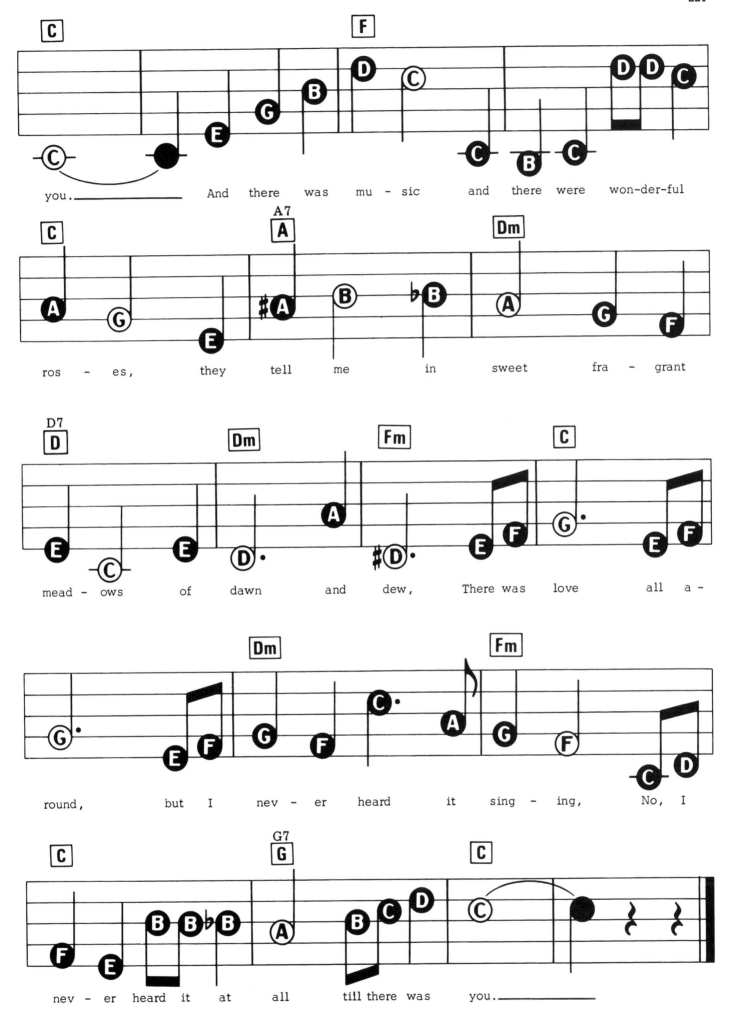

Too Young

Registration 1
Rhythm: Ballad

Words by Sylvia Dee
Music by Sid Lippman

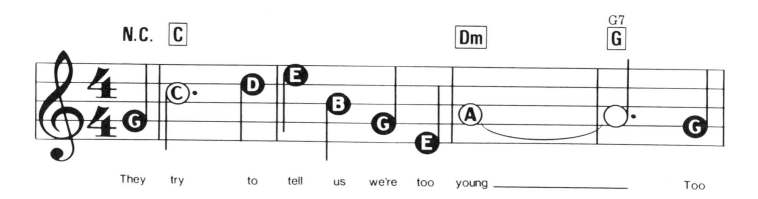

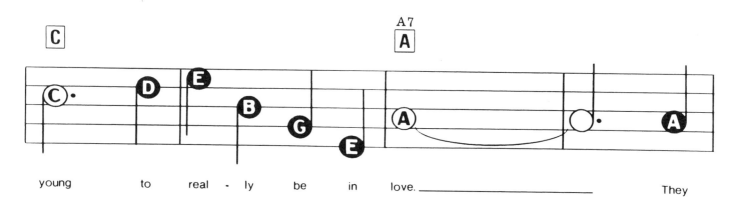

They try to tell us we're too young _____ Too

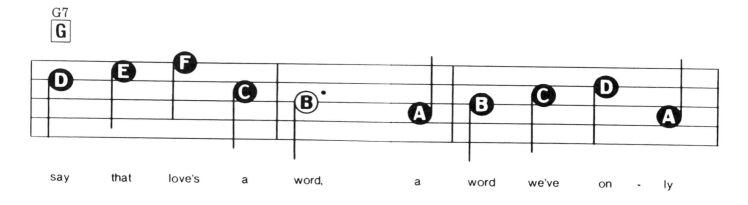

young to real - ly be in love. _____ They

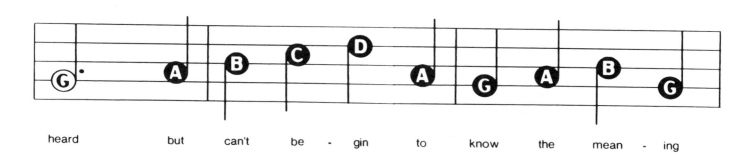

say that love's a word, a word we've on - ly

heard but can't be - gin to know the mean - ing

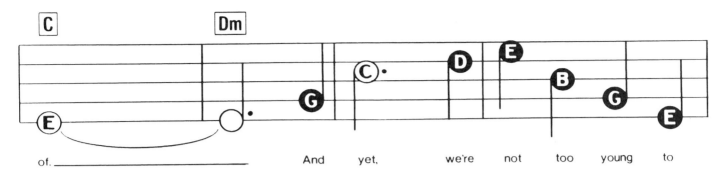

of. _____ And yet, we're not too young to

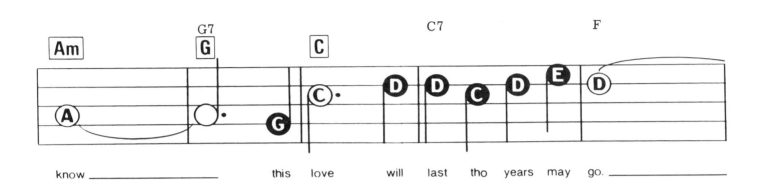

know _____ this love will last tho years may go. _____

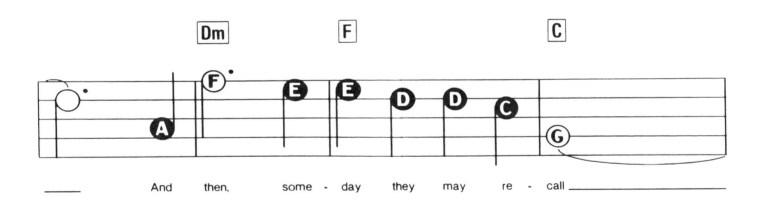

_____ And then, some - day they may re - call _____

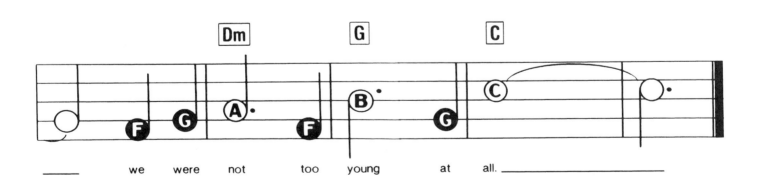

_____ we were not too young at all. _____

True Love
from HIGH SOCIETY

Registration 4
Rhythm: Waltz

Words and Music by
Cole Porter

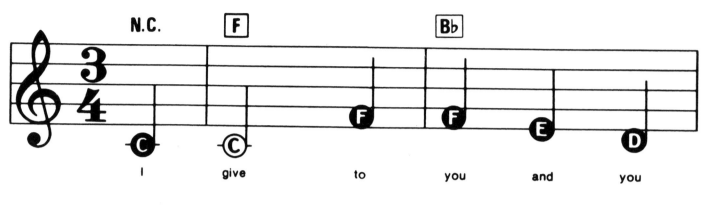

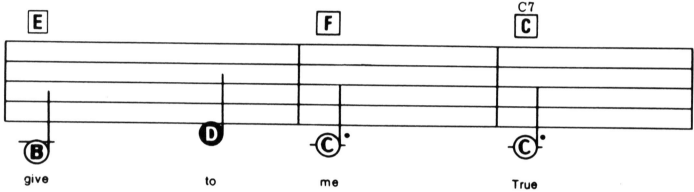

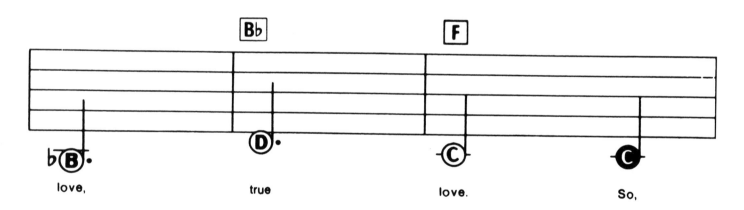

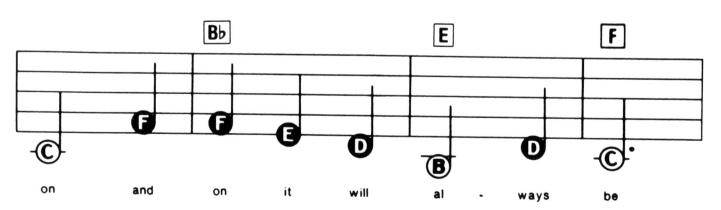

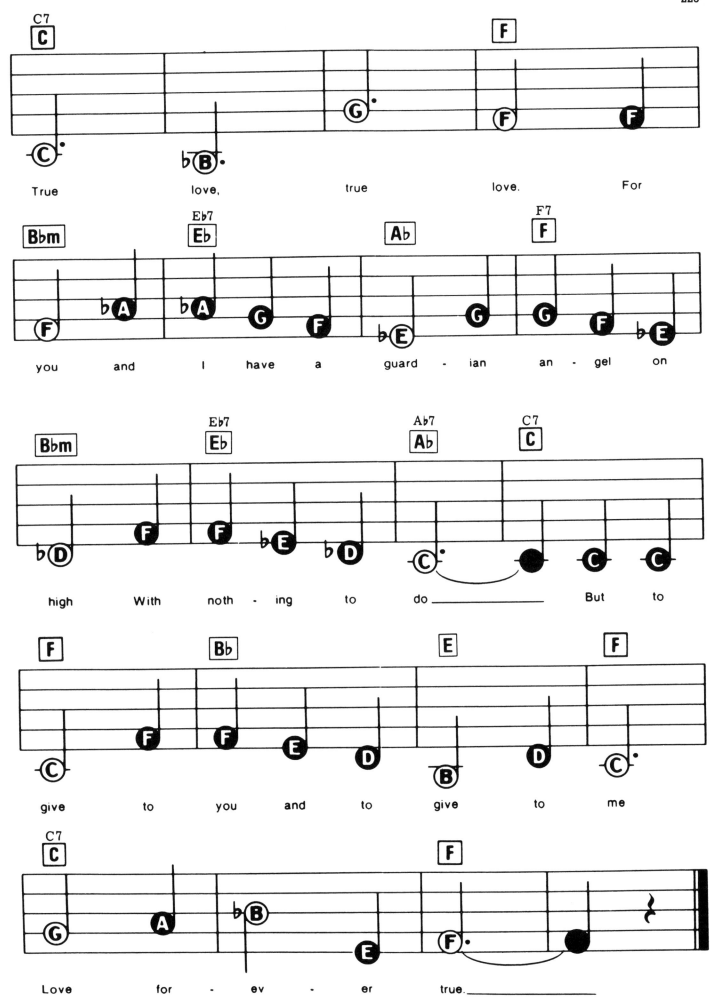

Unforgettable

Registration 3
Rhythm: Fox Trot or Swing

Words and Music by
Irving Gordon

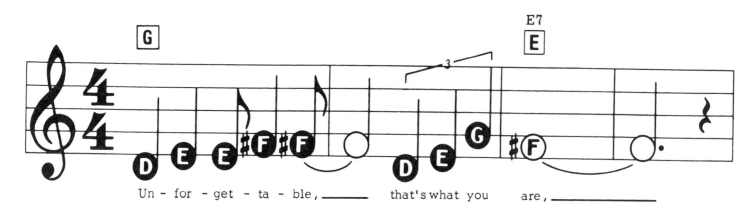

Un - for - get - ta - ble, _____ that's what you are, _____

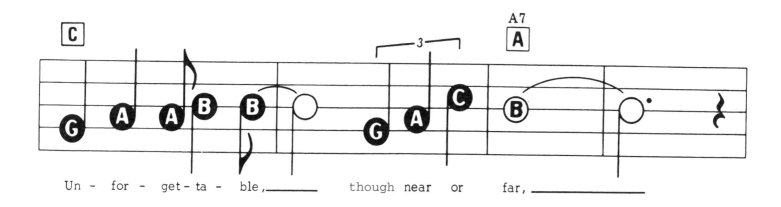

Un - for - get - ta - ble, _____ though near or far, _____

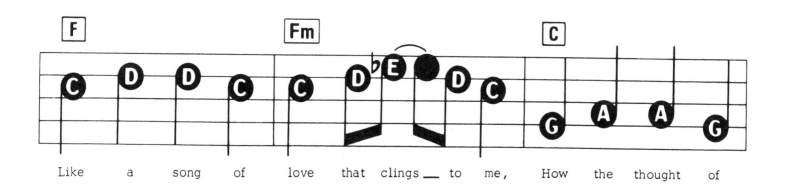

Like a song of love that clings __ to me, How the thought of

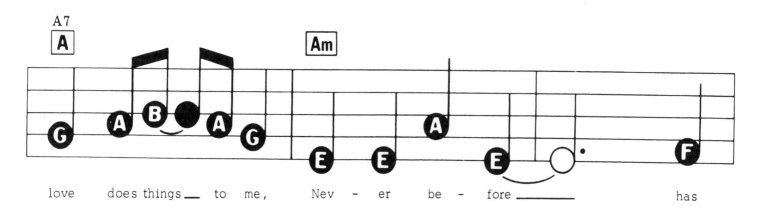

love does things __ to me, Nev - er be - fore _____ has

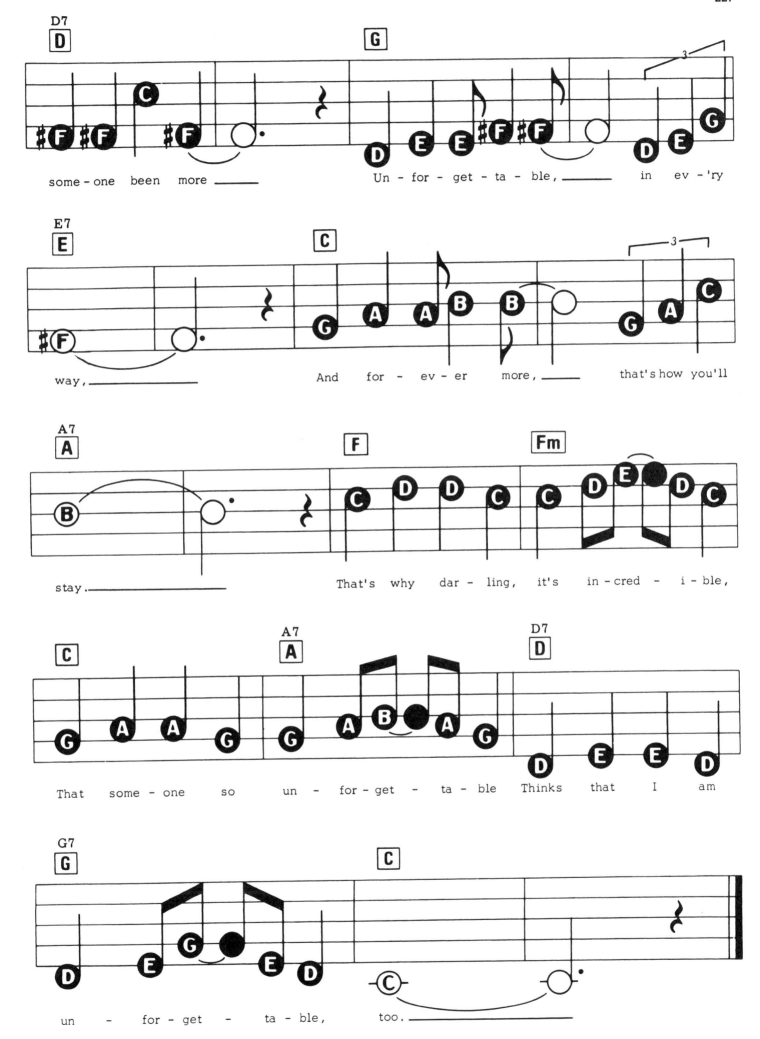

The Very Thought of You

Registration 8
Rhythm: Ballad or Fox Trot

Words and Music by
Ray Noble

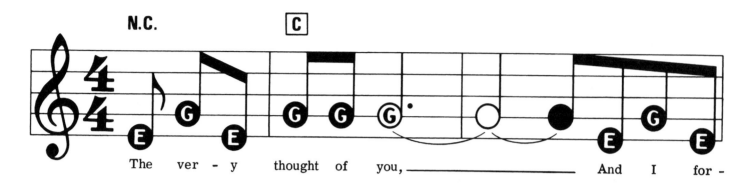

The ver-y thought of you, _____ And I for -

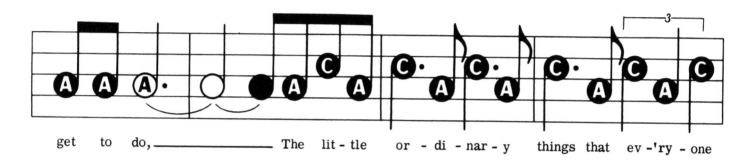

get to do, _____ The lit-tle or-di-nar-y things that ev-'ry-one

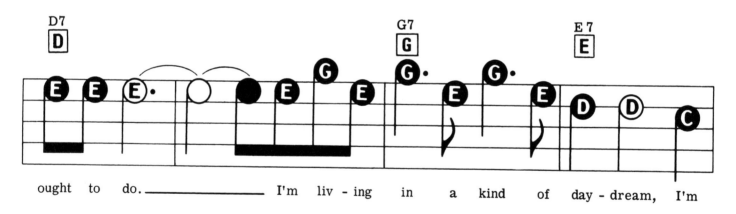

ought to do. _____ I'm liv-ing in a kind of day-dream, I'm

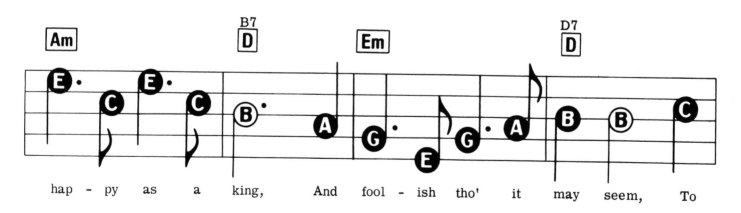

hap-py as a king, And fool-ish tho' it may seem, To

229

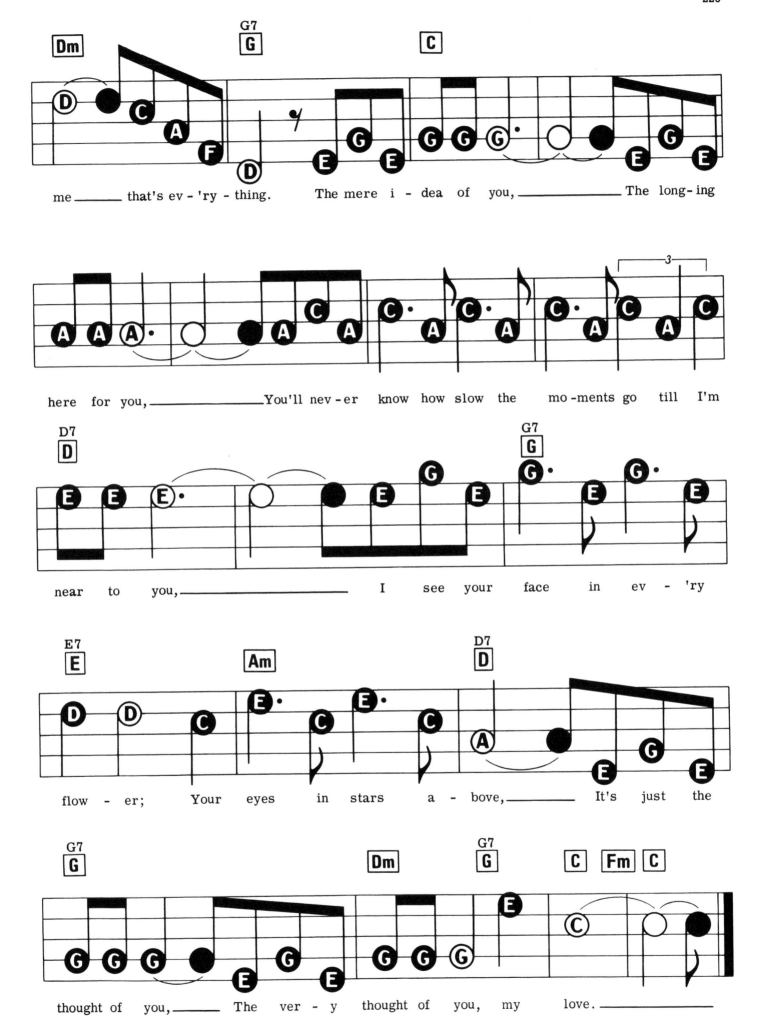

The Way You Look Tonight
from SWING TIME

Registration 1
Rhythm: Fox Trot or Ballad

Words by Dorothy Fields
Music by Jerome Kern

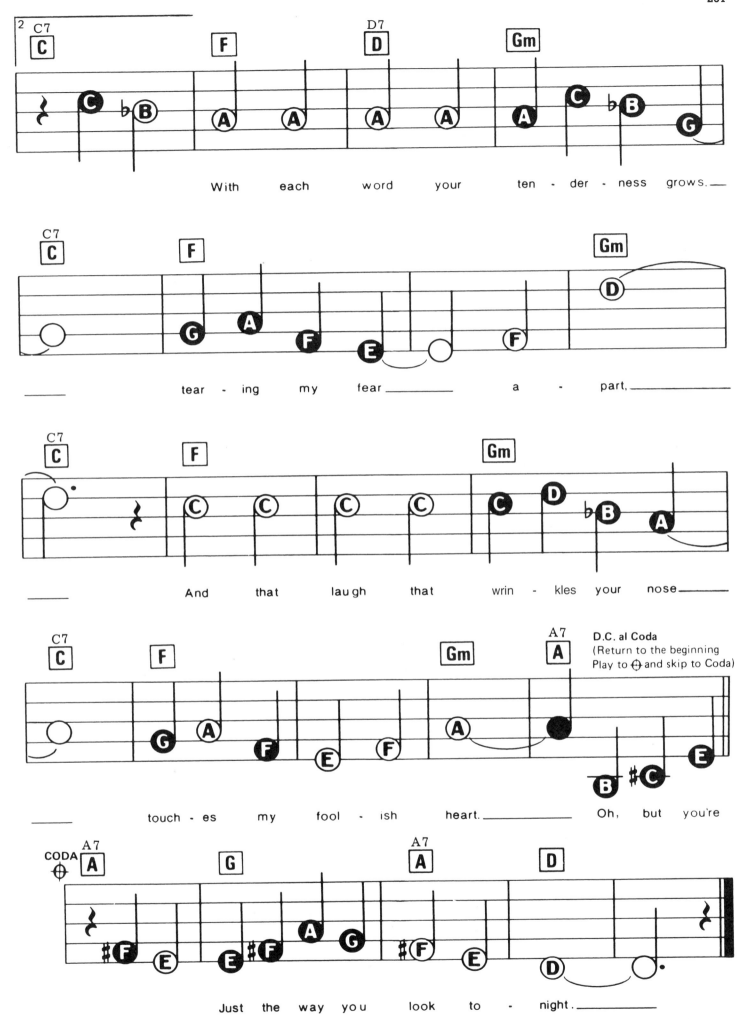

With each word your ten - der - ness grows.

tear - ing my fear a - part,

And that laugh that wrin - kles your nose

touch - es my fool - ish heart. Oh, but you're

Just the way you look to - night.

What a Diff'rence a Day Made

Registration 8
Rhythm: Latin or Rhumba

English Words by Stanley Adams
Music and Spanish Words by Maria Grever

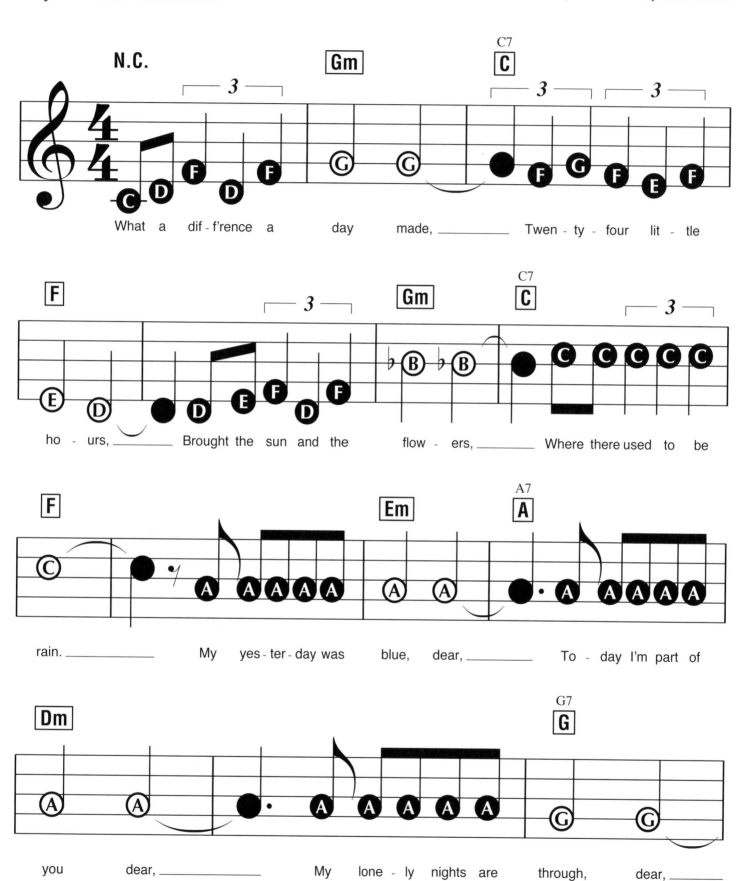

What a dif - f'rence a day made, _____ Twen - ty - four lit - tle

ho - urs, _____ Brought the sun and the flow - ers, _____ Where there used to be

rain. _____ My yes - ter - day was blue, dear, _____ To - day I'm part of

you dear, _____ My lone - ly nights are through, dear, _____

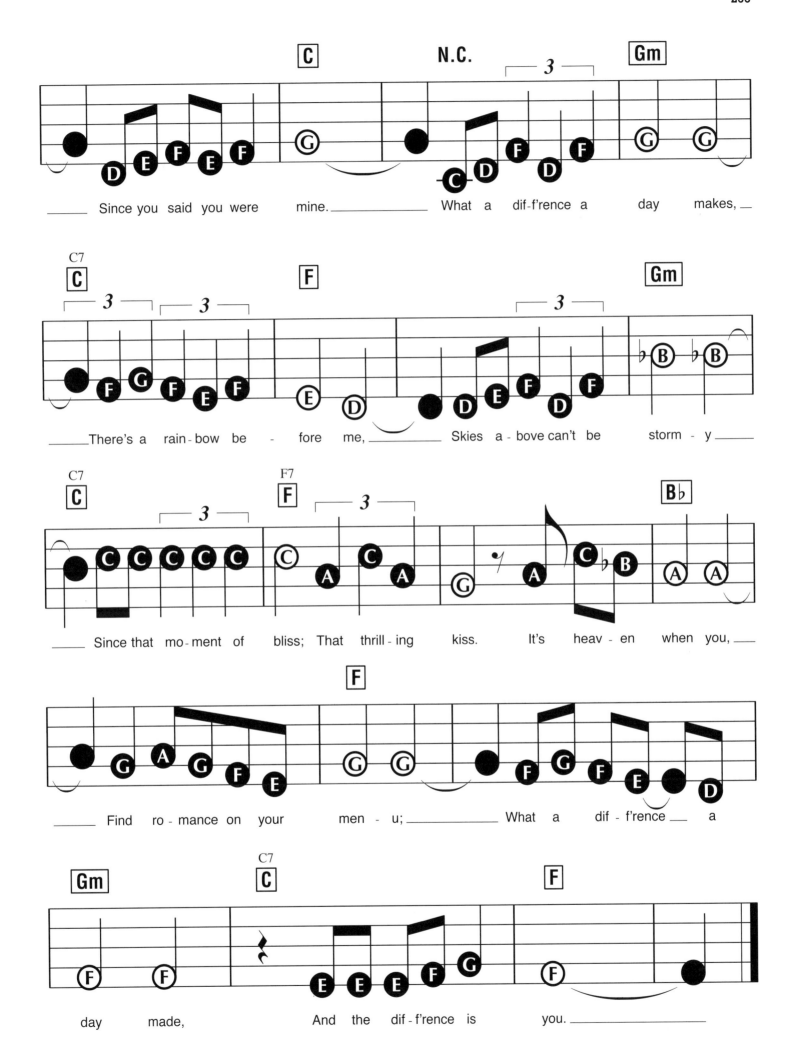

What a Wonderful World

Registration 2
Rhythm: Ballad

Words and Music by George David Weiss
and Bob Thiele

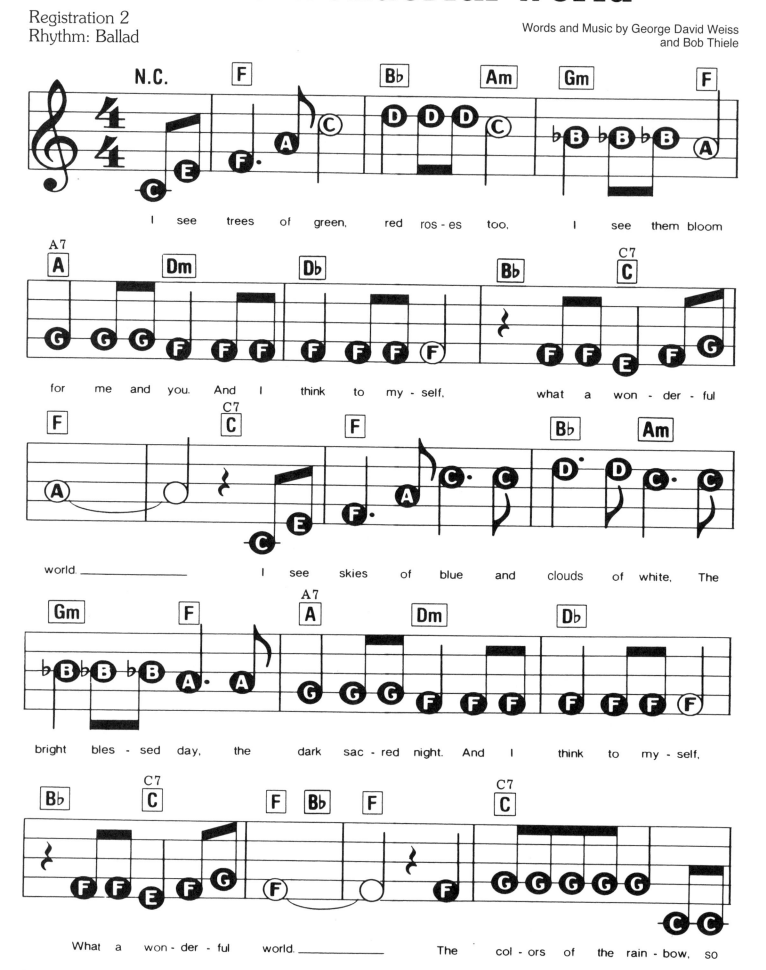

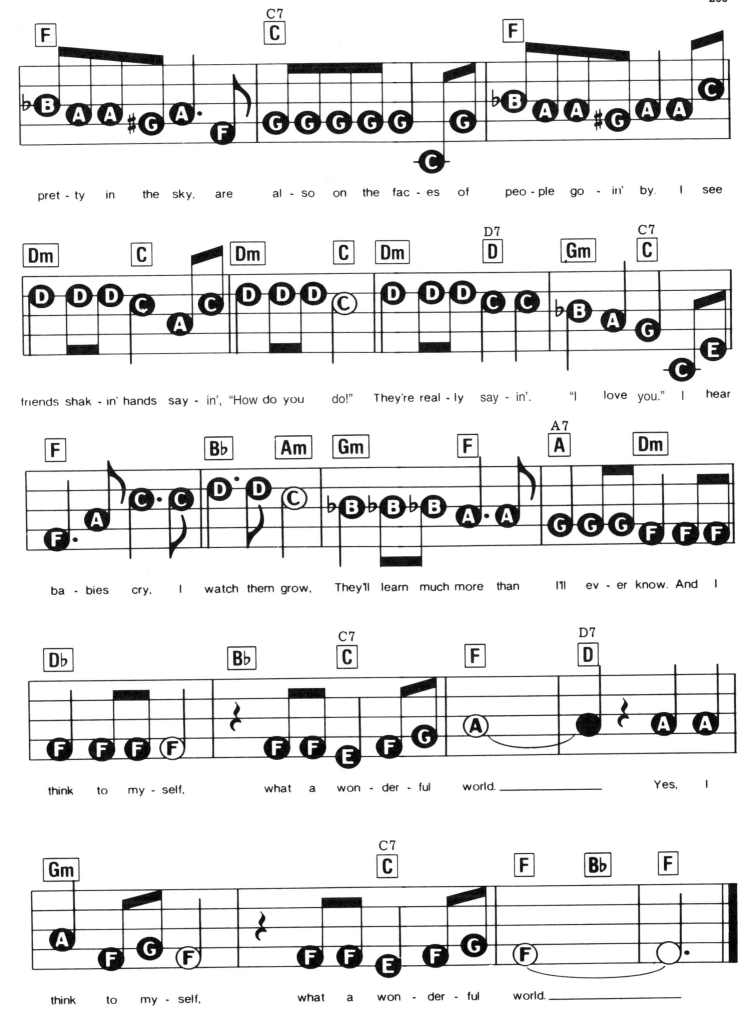

Where or When
from BABES IN ARMS

Registration 7
Rhythm: Fox Trot or Ballad

Words by Lorenz Hart
Music by Richard Rodgers

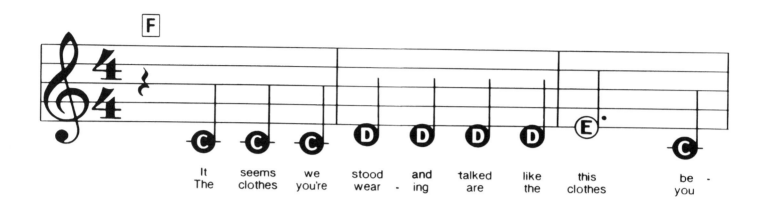

It seems we stood and talked like this be-
The clothes you're wear-ing are the clothes you

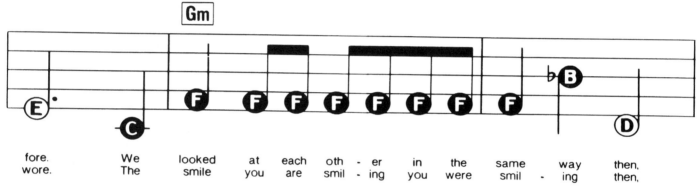

fore. We looked at each oth-er in the same way then,
wore. The smile you are smil-ing you were smil-ing then,

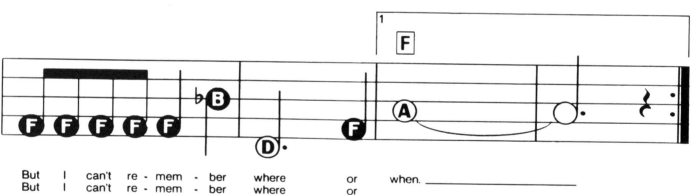

But I can't re-mem-ber where or when. _____
But I can't re-mem-ber where or

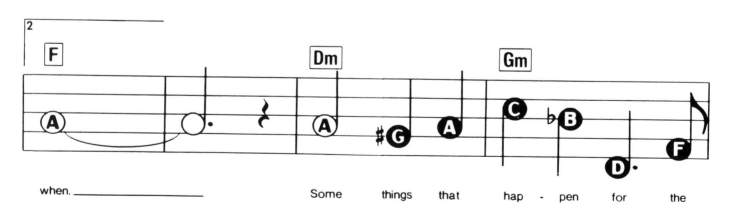

when. _____ Some things that hap-pen for the

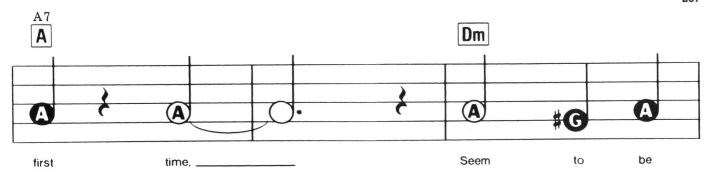

first time, _____ Seem to be

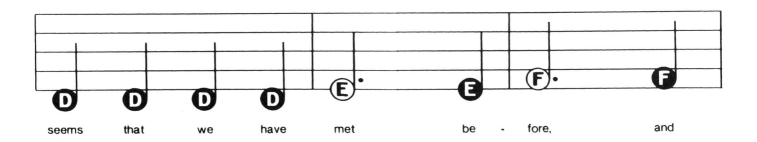

hap - pen - ing a - gain. _____ And so it

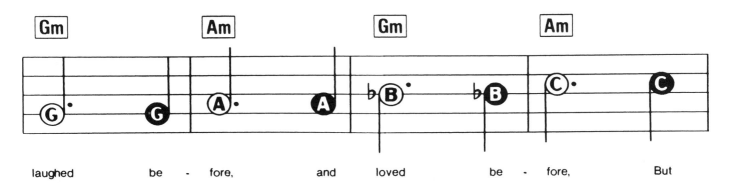

seems that we have met be - fore, and

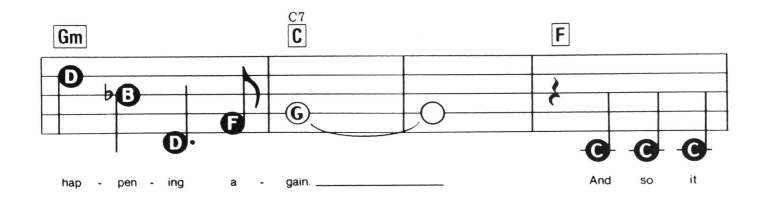

laughed be - fore, and loved be - fore, But

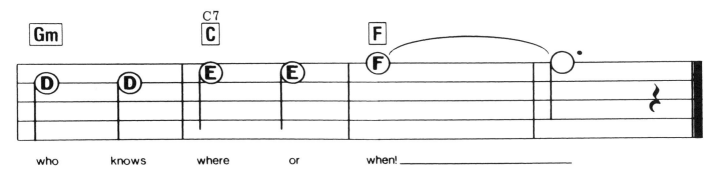

who knows where or when! _____

Where the Blue of the Night
(Meets the Gold of the Day)

Registration 1
Rhythm: Waltz

Lyric and Music by Fred E. Ahlert,
Bing Crosby and Roy Turk

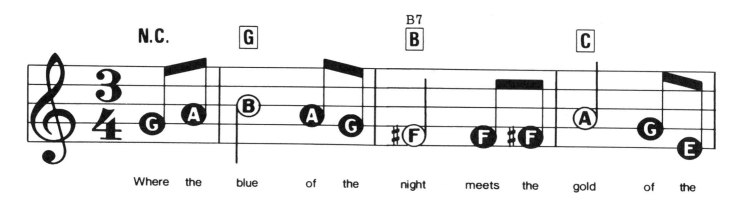

Where the blue of the night meets the gold of the

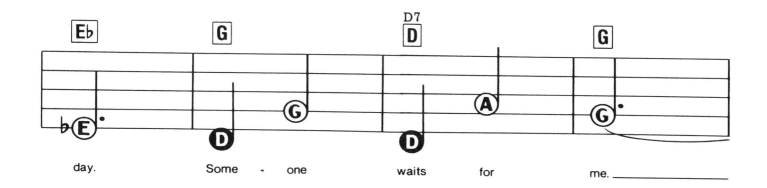

day. Some - one waits for me. _____

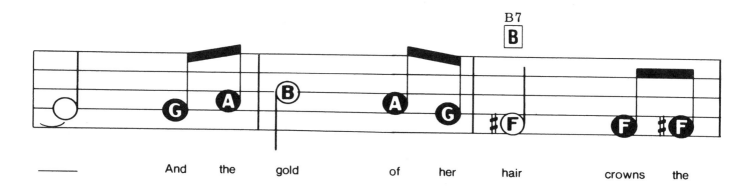

_____ And the gold of her hair crowns the

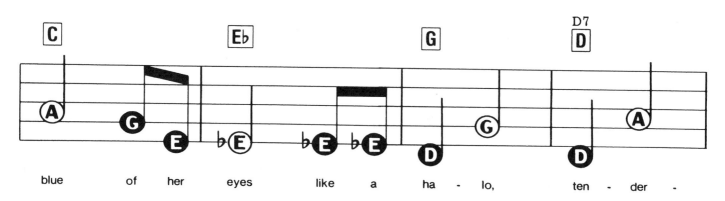

blue of her eyes like a ha - lo, ten - der -

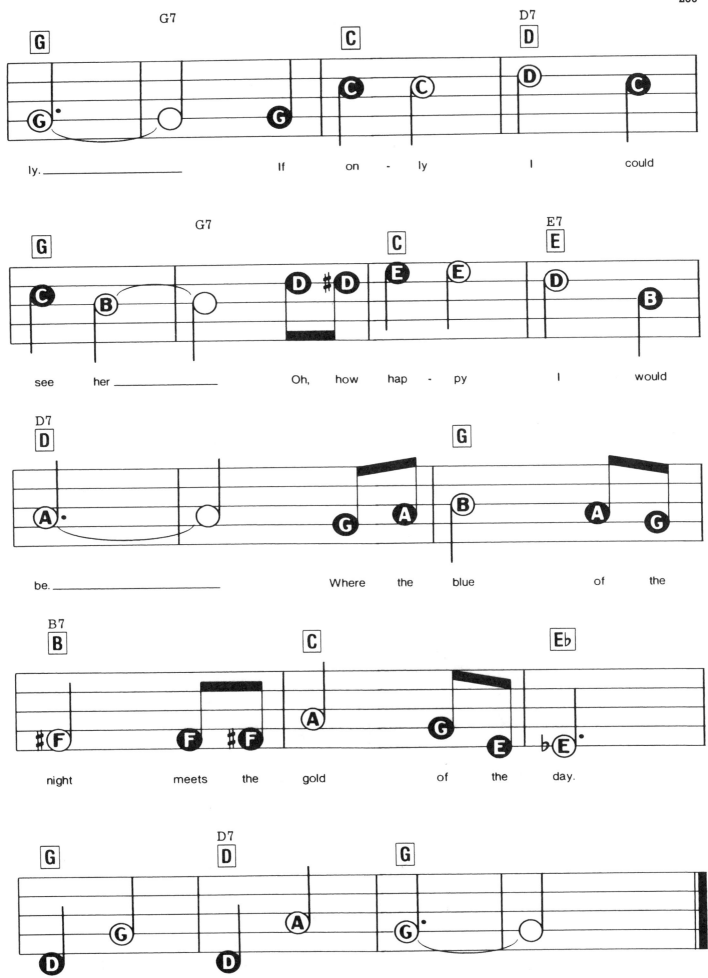

You Belong to Me

Registration 4
Rhythm: Ballad

Words and Music by Pee Wee King,
Redd Stewart and Chilton Price

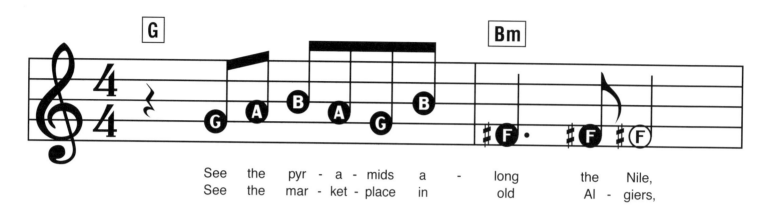

See the pyr - a - mids a - long the Nile,
See the mar - ket - place in old Al - giers,

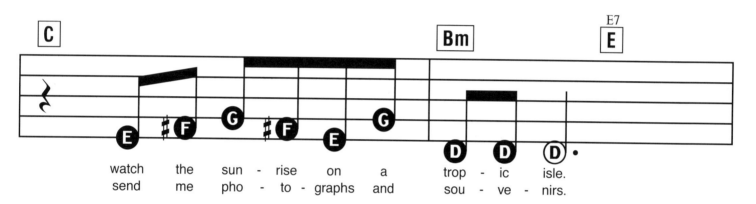

watch the sun - rise on a trop - ic isle.
send me pho - to - graphs and sou - ve - nirs.

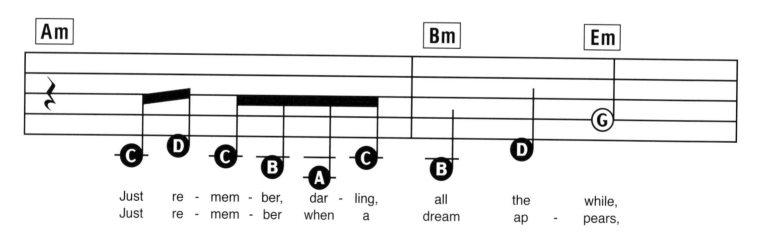

Just re - mem - ber, dar - ling, all the while,
Just re - mem - ber when a dream ap - pears,

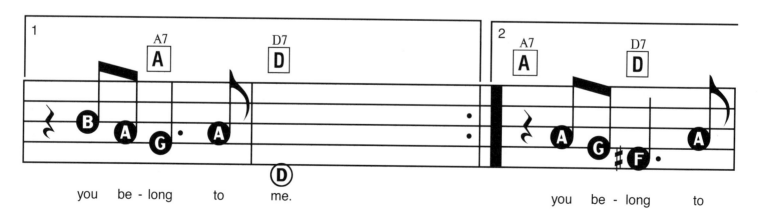

you be - long to me.

you be - long to

241

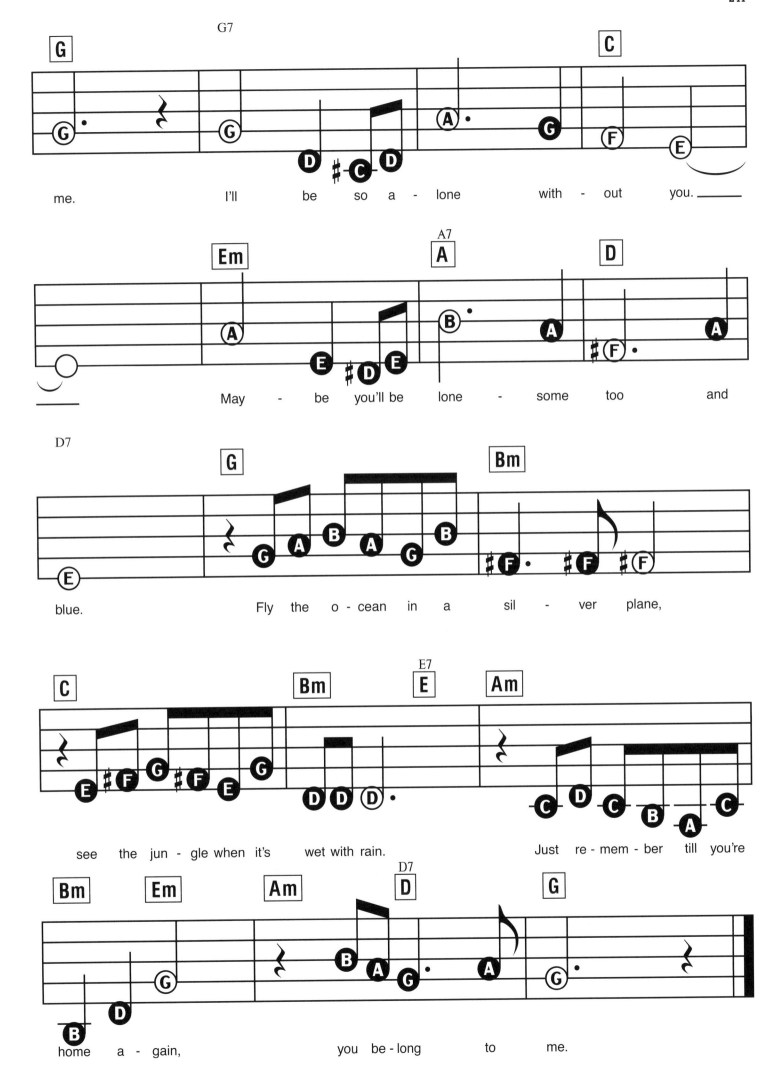

You're Breaking My Heart

Registration 5
Rhythm: Fox Trot

Words and Music by Pat Genaro
and Sunny Skylar

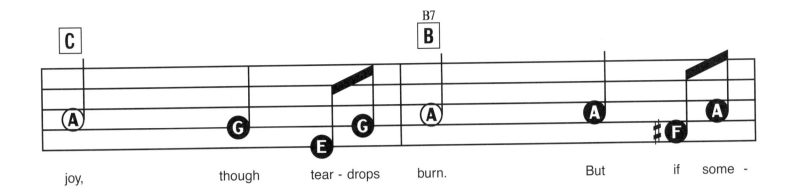

joy, though tear - drops burn. But if some -

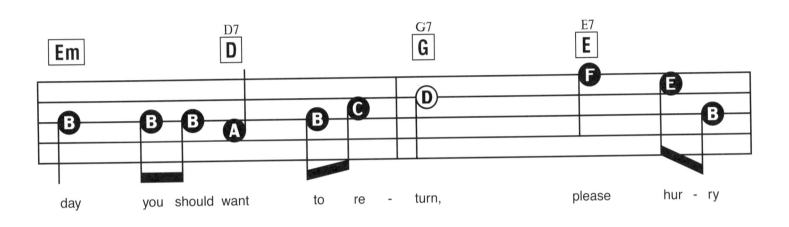

day you should want to re - turn, please hur - ry

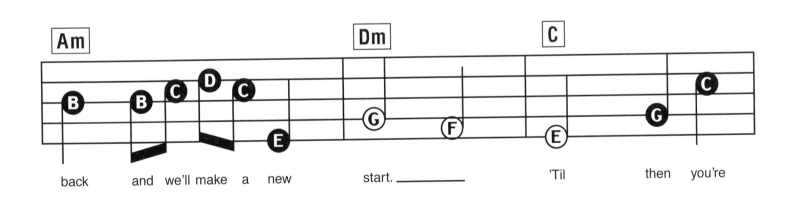

back and we'll make a new start. _____ 'Til then you're

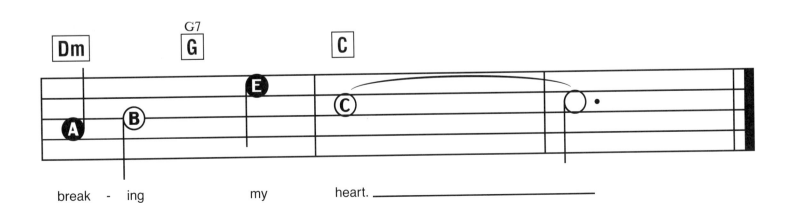

break - ing my heart. _____

Young at Heart
from YOUNG AT HEART

Registration 5
Rhythm: Swing

Words by Carolyn Leigh
Music by Johnny Richards

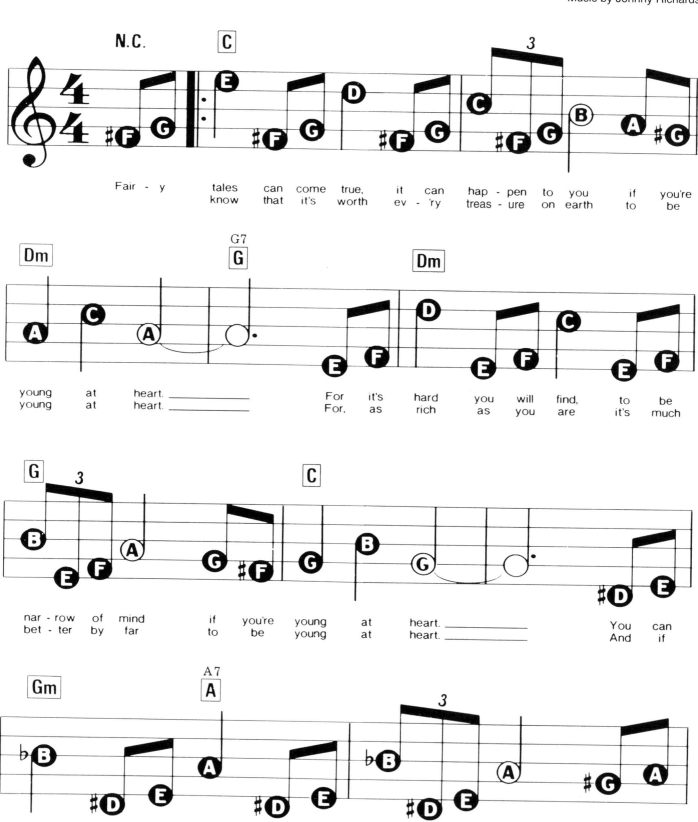

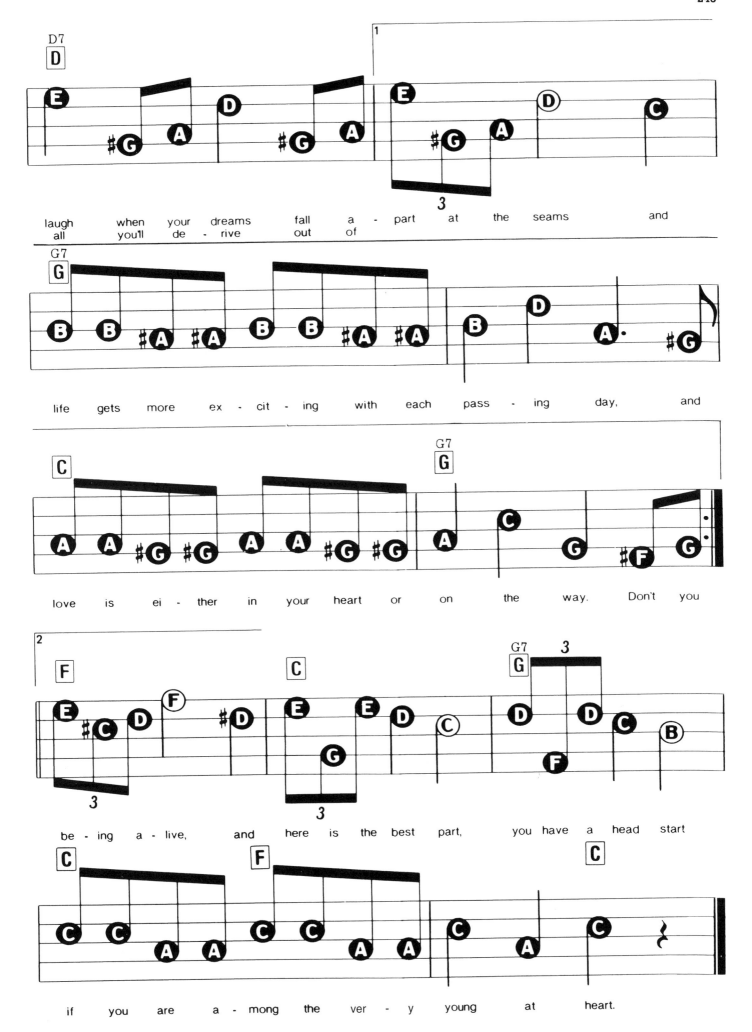

A Wonderful Guy
from SOUTH PACIFIC

Registration 4
Rhythm: Waltz

Lyrics by Oscar Hammerstein II
Music by Richard Rodgers

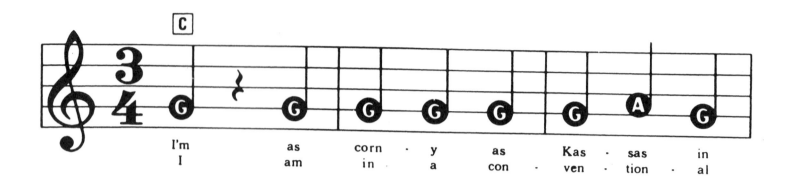

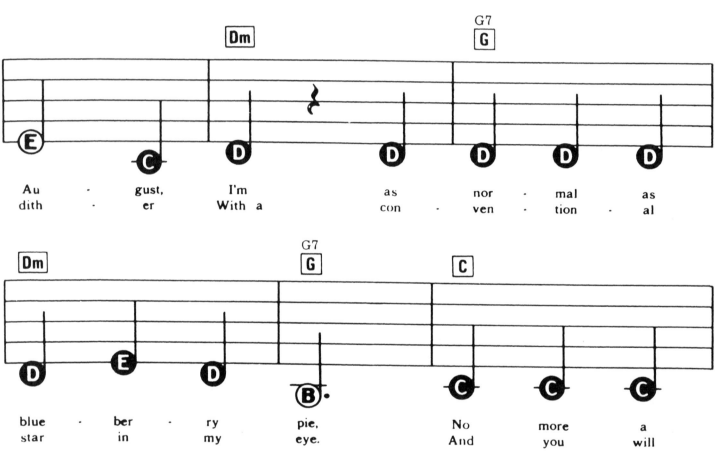

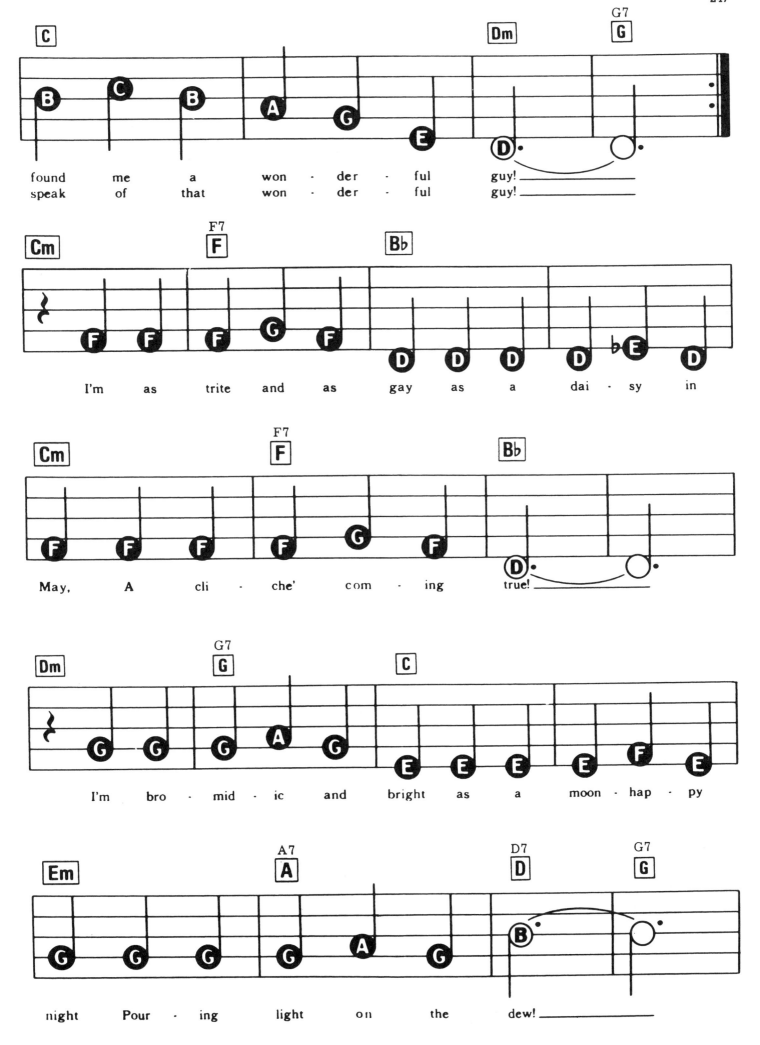

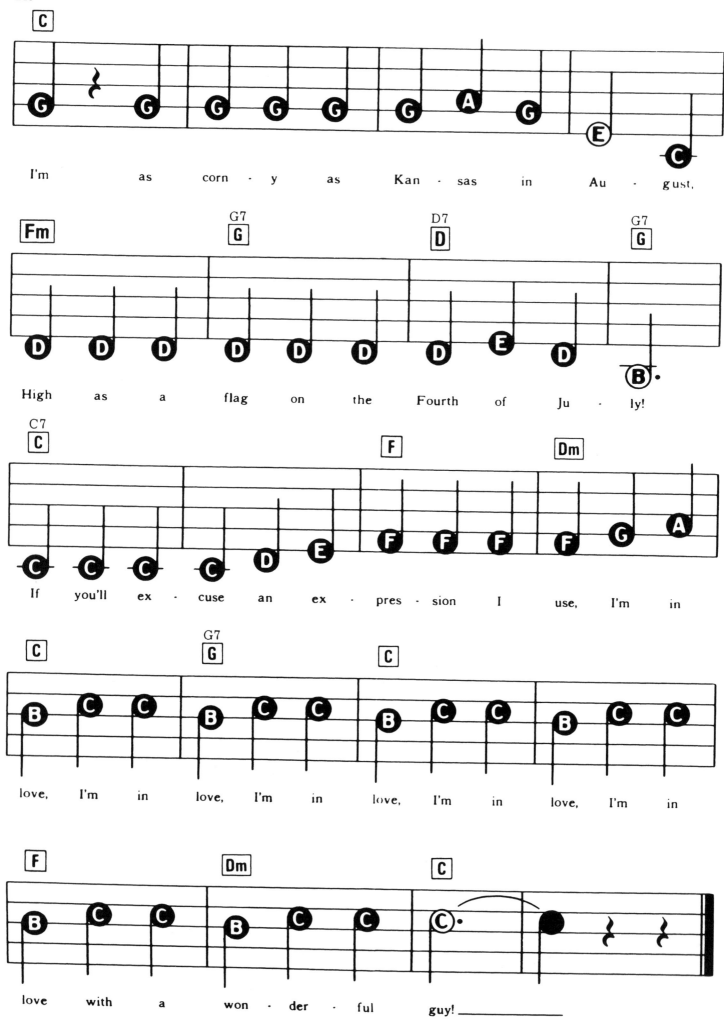